IRELAND 366

IRELAND
366

A Story *a* Day
from Ireland's Hidden History

FRANK HOPKINS

NEW ISLAND

IRELAND 366
First published 2013
by New Island
2 Brookside
Dundrum Road
Dublin 14

www.newisland.ie

PRINT ISBN: 978-1-84840-293-5
EPUB ISBN: 978-1-84840-294-2
MOBI ISBN: 978-1-84840-295-9

British Library Cataloguing Data. A CIP catalogue record for this
book is available from the British Library.

Typeset by JVR Creative India
Cover design by Sin E Design
Printed by ScandBook AB

10 9 8 7 6 5 4 3 2 1

For Sean MacConnell
January 2, 1947 to September 4, 2013.

Contents

Introduction

If you are looking for happy, positive or uplifting stories then this might not be the book for you. If on the other hand, tales of human tragedy, hanging, rioting, misery, mayhem, man-eating Kerry eagles, rat-eating Belfast gamblers and Ardee transvestites are the things that fascinate you, come right on in.

When I began, the idea was simply to randomly compile interesting or quirky stories of Irish historical trivia for every date on the calendar. Although the book contains a few pieces from as early as the thirteenth century and some from as late as the mid-twentieth, the vast majority of the stories are related to the eighteenth and nineteenth centuries and they were almost exclusively sourced in Irish newspapers published during that period.

While researching for the book, I deliberately tried to stay away from the marquee events of Irish history (although you will find the odd one) as I wanted to try and dig out tales of Ireland's lesser-known characters and events that don't normally see the light of day.

This wasn't initially intended to be a 'horrible history' of Ireland, but that's more or less how it has panned out. The ordinary citizens of this country were really only mentioned in the nation's newspapers if they had done something bad or if something untoward had happened to them.

Many of the tales relate to the punishment of poor people who found themselves on the wrong side of the law. Some ultimately faced the death penalty for quite barbaric crimes and many others underwent the most brutal and savage chastisements for relatively minor crimes. One man convicted of thievery in Armagh had his ears nailed to the pillory, while a pregnant woman found guilty of forgery was hanged, alongside her husband, in Dublin. Our ancestors were quite imaginative when it came to dreaming up punishments for transgressors of the law, and public hanging, burning, flogging and pillorying were all par for the course during those dark days.

Accordingly, the proprietors and editors of our newspapers were obsessed with crimes of every description and they are great sources for stories relating to highwaymen, pickpockets, gang warfare, grave-robbers, forgers, burglars, delinquency, infanticide, prostitution and every form of deviant behaviour known to man.

The years during and following the Great Famine in Ireland stand as some of the most harrowing times ever recorded in our newspapers. They range from a hungry little boy found dead in Clare after being forced to endure an eighteen mile march to women reduced to rioting for bread in a Tipperary workhouse.

Surprisingly, animal tales featured large in our newspapers of old and in the course of my research I encountered many stories relating to sea monsters, man-eating pigs, rabid dogs, mad cats, savage eagles, an ungrateful Westmeath ferret and any number of horrifying rat stories.

Just as it is today, the weather was a topical issue in Ireland, but it was generally only mentioned when an extreme event occurred. Consequently there are some weather stories that are related to the sinking of ships, property damage and, my own particular favourite, about a large number of barristers hiding under the tables in Dublin's law library after the glass roof was shattered by giant hailstones.

Our eighteenth century ancestors didn't really do sports reports in their newspapers, but there were a few mentions. One of these relates to a hurling match played for money between Galway and Clare during the late 1700s. And in 1896 an English women's football team played a match against an Irish men's team who dressed in skirts for the occasion and reportedly allowed the women to win!

Each tale recorded in these pages is but a brief glimpse into many aspects of our hidden history and I hope you will find them as interesting and entertaining to read as I found them to research.

Frank Hopkins
Rathfarnham, September 2013

JANUARY

1 January

Sliders and skaters do battle in Dublin

Although we've had some pretty cold winters to contend with in recent years, I can never remember it getting icy enough to go skating on the many ponds and waterways around Dublin. However, in times gone by, skating was a fairly common pastime during the winter months. The area now covered by Herbert Park in Ballsbridge was a particularly popular venue for this seasonal pursuit.

On New Year's Day in 1850, the Dublin skating fraternity was out in full force on Lord Herbert's property, which, according to a report in the *Dublin Evening Mail* on 2 January 1850, '... has been for the last two days, covered with skaters ... availing themselves of the transient visit of Father Frost'.

According to the *Evening Mail* correspondent, the skaters had been infiltrated by 'a strong muster of idle Dublin blackguards, ragamuffins and vagabonds', who were determined to ruin the fun for the law-abiding majority who had turned up at Ballsbridge.

For the greater part of the day, the rowdies kept to themselves, making a slide at one end of the ice while the proper skaters enjoyed themselves at the other end. However, at about three o'clock in the afternoon, the sliders made their way down to the skaters' end and caused mayhem by sliding into skaters.

Some of the skaters retaliated and attacked the sliders with sticks, and in no time at all a full-scale melee had broken out. 'The combatants were, however,' according to the correspondent from the *Evening Mail*, 'very closely packed together, and though there was a goodly display of sticks flourishing in the air, the best aimed blows did not, in all cases, alight on the heads for which they were intended.'

The row came to a sudden end when the ice broke and the protagonists were left floundering in the murky ice-cold pond. Some nearly drowned in the incident, but all were eventually rescued.

2 January

Sin city – Dundalk

I don't know what was going on in Dundalk in 1864, but judging by the amount of fairly racy adverts for 'marital aids', pills, potions and books on the front page of the *Dundalk Express* on 2 January 1864, the town must have been Ireland's answer to Sodom and Gomorrah. These adverts were particularly unusual for that period and were virtually never seen in any other newspaper at that time.

There were a number of marriage guides advertised in the *Express* that day. A 'New Medical Work' by a physician – who claimed to be an expert in the 'physiology and philosophy of the generative organs' – offered advice on increasing male practice of 'the most sacred duties necessary for the performance of married life'.

Other publications advertised a cure for 'spermatorrhoea' and offered help to those who were 'prevented from entering the married state by impediments' and those suffering from 'the dreadful results of early abuse, indiscriminate excesses', gonorrhoea, syphilis and all urogenital diseases. Dr Curtis's book, *Manhood*, offered a similar service.

Another book called *The Silent Friend on Marriage,* which was probably a forerunner of the pornographic magazine, featured prominently. The book, which featured fifty photographs, offered advice to 'those who have imperilled the power of manhood by youthful indiscretions' and included a recipe for a preventative lotion for all manner of sexually transmitted diseases.

3 January

Squib Molony's squalid death

The following letter was published in the Ennis-based *Clare Journal* on Monday, 3 January 1848:

'To the editor of the *Clare Journal*: Sir – In addition to my last letter, I hope you will give insertion to the following melancholy events which have taken place in the parish of Kilmurry, Barony of Ibrickane, Kilrush Union.

'A man named John Molony, commonly called *Squib*, being an old infirm man, but of a gigantic frame, and possessed of no means whatsoever, but living on unwholesome food such as seagrass, seaweed and turnips, until a short time before his death, which event took place about twelve days ago. For a short time previous he had received weekly a little meal as relief, but not half enough to support nature. This poor man's body remained stretched on his deathbed (if such I can call it), for eight days, as a coffin could not be procured for him. Application had been often made to the Relieving Officer for a coffin, but all in vain. This poor old starved man would have remained to this day without being interred, were it not that he had an old dresser which had been in his family for generations, and was so moth-eaten that it became almost impossible for the carpenter to work it. Of this old dresser a kind of coffin was made, into which his putrefied body was placed, the coffin being so slight and weak that it became exceedingly difficult to keep it together, so as not to let the body fall to the ground.

'Will the Executive Government of our country allow those creatures to be thus starved, and after death to remain unburied without coffins, until the bodies become so putrefied that it is sufficient to bring a plague amongst us? – I remain, Sir, with respect, your most humble and obedient servant, Patrick Fitzgibbon.'

4 January

Ringsend death by sewer fumes

Tragedy struck at the Pigeon House Main Drainage Scheme at Ringsend in Dublin on the morning of 4 January 1913 when a labourer at the plant, Christopher Leonard, was asphyxiated by poisonous sewer gas. Several of his workmates nearly lost their lives in a valiant, but ultimately futile, attempt to rescue him.

The dead man was overcome by fumes while clearing out a sewerage pipe at the plant. Bart O'Connor noticed that Leonard was missing and he descended into the pipe to try to find him, but he too succumbed to the deadly gas. Pat Saunders, Michael Roche and Sam Beamish then attempted a rescue, but were forced back to the surface by the poisonous fumes.

Hearing the mens' cries for help, the crew of the *Shamrock*, which was docked nearby, were alerted. Captain Patrick Archibald, First Mate John Tallant and Second Mate Henry O'Brien rushed to their aid. O'Brien tied a handkerchief around his mouth and Captain Archibald lowered him down through the manhole on a rope. However, O'Brien rapidly lost consciousness and he was quickly hauled up. Tallant bravely volunteered to go down the shaft and managed to tie a rope around O'Connor, who was quickly brought to the surface. Tallant descended a second time and attached the rope to Leonard, who was then hauled up.

The men were taken by ambulance to Sir Patrick Dun's Hospital, but it was too late for Leonard, who was already dead. It was touch and go for Henry O'Brien and Bart O'Connor for a time, but both men eventually recovered.

At an inquest on 6 January, the jury found that Leonard had died by the 'accidental inhalation of sulphureted hydrogen gas'. The men who had attempted to rescue Leonard were all commended for their bravery.

5 January

Visit for 'improper purpose' leads to prison riot

The City Marshalsea prison in Dublin was wrecked during a riot in early January 1787. One prisoner was killed in the incident and four others were so badly wounded that they were not expected to survive for very long.

The incident occurred when a Dublin police constable went to the prison to serve a warrant on two women prisoners who had been accused of assaulting another inmate. Some of the other prisoners resisted the constable, so he left and returned with more police, a party of soldiers and two magistrates. The prisoners again resisted and the police and soldiers opened fire on them, killing one inmate named Molloy.

Saunders' Newsletter on 5 January described the scene in the prison as being one of 'uproar, and the most horrid confusion; every part of the prison tearing down, and the police guard still obliged to keep close in their retreat'.

The true cause of the trouble later emerged when it was revealed that the women prisoners – two sisters named Jones – had been falsely accused of assault by a 'gentleman prisoner', identified only as 'Captain C'. The drunken captain had attempted to break into the women's room for what the *Hibernian Journal* described as 'an improper purpose'. He was caught and tried to save his own neck by claiming that the Jones sisters had in fact assaulted him.

The other prisoners who had heard the women's screams tried to go to their aid and broke down several doors in an attempt to rescue them. When the Marshalsea guards tried to stop them, the prisoners tore down walls and attacked them with bricks and stones.

The constable who had initially tried to serve the warrant on the women was subsequently made a scapegoat for the whole affair and was locked up in Newgate Prison for an unspecified period.

6 January

Galway pugilists

At 4.00 p.m. on 6 January 1860, Mr Blake of the *Galway Vindicator* newspaper and a Mr Mangan of Salthill went at each other with their fists in Eyre Square 'in an excellent battle for the championship of Galway'.

The fight only lasted five minutes but the encounter was so hot and heavy that there were literally 'wigs on the green'. Local magistrate Captain Forster, who was alarmed at the ferocity and intensity of the bout, called the police to disperse the growing throng of spectators, but by the time they arrived the action was all over.

7 January

Frozen ducks

There was a very cold start to the year 1768. In early January in Dublin, several people walked across the frozen River Liffey, and in Cork the snow was said to be six feet deep in places. Meanwhile, in Galway it was reported on 7 January that over two hundred ducks died on a lake near Ballquirk in west Connaught, where local people observed them frozen solid and stuck fast to the ice.

8 January

A man scorned

The *Munster Journal* of 8 January 1750 includes a definite case of a man scorned in the form of this advert taken out by Limerick man Michael Morony:

'Whereas Ellinor Morony, otherwise Grady, Wife of Michael Morony of Knocksantry, having falsely accused her said Husband of Impotency, to excuse herself for plundering and robbing his House and Goods, and having granted such Freedoms to a Pedlar and others as are improper here to be mentioned; therefore she is not to be credited on my Account.... Michael Morony.'

9 January

'A gang of unfortunate prostitutes'

An elderly woman was walking through Parliament Street, Dublin on the night of 9 January 1788 when she was attacked by a gang of young women. According to reports, there were at least eight and possibly ten young women involved in the attack. The gang, described in the *Hibernian Journal* as 'a gang of unfortunate prostitutes', beat and abused the elderly woman in a 'most barbarous manner' and stole her cloak. Sometime later, the same gang attacked a maid near Essex Gate, assaulting her 'in a very cruel manner' and stealing her apron and cap.

10 January

Sent to jail for her own safety

On 10 January 1759, *Pue's Occurrences* carried a report on two Donovan brothers who created uproar at St Patrick's Church in Waterford a fortnight earlier when they attempted to prevent their sister marrying an English soldier. The Donovans entered the church at the head of a mob and tried to remove their sister by force. The bishop, Dr Fell, had the doors closed and sent for the picket guard. The mob left in a hurry because they were afraid of being trapped in the church and arrested. One of the Donovans attacked his sister with a whip, but the bishop intervened and had her sent to Waterford Jail for her own safety.

Matters were let rest until another attempt was made to hold the wedding ceremony at the same place a week later. The mob returned in even greater numbers, smashed all the windows in the church and damaged the bell rope. The bishop sent for the picket guard again and four rioters were arrested. The as yet unmarried woman was taken to the safety of the prison once more.

The ceremony eventually went ahead a few days later, but only after the bride was escorted to the church by a strong force of soldiery and police.

11 January

Bread riots

Monday morning, 11 January 1847: the *Limerick and Clare Examiner* reported that the city of Limerick 'was thrown into the greatest state of confusion and excitement' by 'attacks' on bakeries in Broad Street. In fact, only a few loaves of bread were taken by a handful of starving people, but the response by the authorities in Limerick was disproportionate to the crime and only served to cause great alarm in the city.

At mid-day an entire company of soldiers was seen marching through George's Street in the city, followed by a large body of policemen and a 'troop of dragoons', effectively placing the city under military law. The *Examiner* writer was of the opinion that it would have taken no more than half a dozen policemen to handle the disturbance.

Meanwhile, in Dublin on the same day there were many bread riots all over the city. Shops and bakeries were attacked on Bridgefoot Street, Church Street, Pill Lane and in the Liberties. One of the more serious incidents took place in Dorset Street, where a mob of over two hundred hungry people attacked and robbed a bread cart.

12 January

122 years old

A seemingly farfetched report in the *Cork Evening Post* on 12 January 1758 concerned an Antrim woman who had died at the age of 122.

The woman was named as Catherine Gillis of Glenwhorry or Glenwherry in County Antrim. Her longevity was attributed to the fact that she worked hard, ate a simple diet of potatoes, kale and buttermilk, and didn't drink alcohol or tea. It was said that she had been able to walk three miles to church every Sunday until two months before her death.

13 January

Fury at Kingstown board meeting

Tempers flared at the January meeting of the Rathdown Workhouse Board of Guardians in Loughlinstown, County Dublin on 13 January 1909. Two journalists covering the meeting were threatened with violence, while two members of the board became embroiled in a fist fight after one threw a handful of gruel at the other.

The meeting began in stormy form when Mr O'Donnell, a Kingstown (now Dún Laoghaire) representative of the board complained vociferously that a local journalist had misrepresented remarks that he had made at an earlier meeting. If it happened again, he said he would 'throw the press representative out the window'.

Chairman Thomas Clarke, speaking for the board, complained that the paper in question had given space to a 'man of bad character' to criticise the nuns who ran the Rathdown Workhouse by referring to them as 'a band of proselytisers'. That set the tone for the rest of the meeting. The Chairman became embroiled in a row with Isaac Jones, who accused him of insulting other board members during meetings. Mr O'Donnell then accused Jones of insulting him at a previous meeting and told him that he would 'throw him through the door' if he ever did it again. Jones replied that he would pull out Mr O'Donnell's 'long tooth' for him.

O'Donnell, who was by that stage 'very much excited', first threw a punch at Jones's head and followed up by hitting him in the face with a handful of gruel and calling him a leprechaun and a 'puckaun'. A general melee followed and O'Donnell was eventually subdued.

Once order was restored, Mr Rocheford, another board member, wryly observed that, after his behaviour, it would be very difficult for O'Donnell to ever complain again about what the press might chose to write about him.

14 January

Turnpike tragedy

A young boy who collected tolls at the turnpike between Doneraile and Mitchelstown in Cork was killed on 14 January 1772. The boy, who was supporting his bed-ridden father, had set off in pursuit of a carriage that had driven through the turnpike without paying the toll. He chased the carriage, which contained two 'gentlemen' and their servant, for about four hundred yards. When he eventually caught up with it, the servant hit him over the head with the handle of the whip, killing him instantly.

15 January

Snow joke

The weather was extremely cold on the east coast of Ireland in January 1789. Huge amounts of snow fell on Dublin and it was reported on 15 January that the village of Crumlin was covered to a depth of fifteen feet. The cold snap led to a number of deaths and injuries and there were scores of snow and ice-related incidents recorded all over the city.

Two young men who had been skating on a lake in the Phoenix Park were drowned when they fell through the ice. A man passing through Kevin Street shot a boy dead because the boy had thrown a snowball at him. Another young man was blinded by a snowball in Hanover Street. There were numerous instances of limb breakages and other injuries.

One boatman had to be rescued after his boat became jammed between two large lumps of ice on the Liffey. A considerable crowd looked on as some men at Coal Quay undertook a hazardous operation to rescue him. The crowd cheered and held an impromptu collection to reward the men for their bravery as they brought the boatman ashore.

16 January

Run over by a sleigh

During the month of January 1881 Ireland shivered under some extremely cold weather conditions. The north of the country was particularly badly affected. As you might expect, there were a number of snow- and ice-related accidents and fatalities caused by the cold snap, such as deaths from hypothermia and falling through the ice on frozen ponds.

There was one unusual case recorded in Strabane, County Tyrone, where a man died after being run over by a sleigh. George Bailey, a resident of the Strabane Workhouse, was found lying injured in the snow in a ditch in Strabane on 16 January 1881. A man named Madden went to his assistance and Bailey told him that he was unable to walk because he had been run over by a sleigh. Madden helped him to the workhouse where he was given some food and put to bed, but he died a few hours later. The inquest into his death found that Bailey had died from exposure to the cold weather.

17 January

Death of Watty Cox after unusual times

Watty Cox, gunsmith, journalist and wannabe United Irishman, was probably born near Summerhill in County Meath sometime around 1770, the son of a prosperous tradesman.

As a youngster, Cox trained as a gunsmith in Dublin and, on completing his apprenticeship, went into business for himself at a premises in Bedford Row. He married his first wife soon afterwards, but Cox, described by R.R. Madden as being 'a man of violent and ungovernable passions', was said to have treated her badly. She died during childbirth.

Then, in 1797, Cox married the widow of Benjamin Powell, his former master. He soon squandered all of his new wife's fortune. While he continued to live in her fine Abbey Street residence, she was forced to live – in an almost penniless state – in what was described as 'a miserable lodging' on Clarence Street in North Strand.

Although it's not clear if Cox was ever officially a member of the United Irishmen, he was involved with several radical organisations in Dublin such as the Huguenot New Penny Club. In 1797, he began production of the *Union Star*, a pro-United Irishmen news-sheet, in a cellar in Little Ship Street. However, the *Union Star* – which advocated the assassination of leading Dublin loyalists – was too radical even for the leadership of the United Irishmen, who quickly distanced themselves from Cox and his ranting.

Cox's role in the rebellion of 1798 is unclear, although he would claim in later years that he 'enjoyed the confidence of' several leading members of the United Irishmen, including Lord Edward Fitzgerald and Thomas Addis Emmet, brother of Robert Emmet.

Following the debacle of Robert Emmet's insurrection 1803, Cox went to the US but returned to Dublin three years later to establish his *Irish Magazine and Monthly Asylum for Neglected Biography*, which was similar in tone to the *Union Star*. His new venture didn't win Cox any new friends in Dublin Castle and he was publicly pilloried (punishment by public humiliation) and jailed on a number of occasions. Cox continued to run the magazine from his cell in Newgate Prison until 1815, when the government offered him a pension of £100 per annum and a once-off payment of £400 on condition that he left the country for good.

Cox took the money and ran, but returned to Dublin during the 1820s. He died in poverty on 17 January 1837 after spending his final years living in no. 12 Clarence Street, North Strand, where his second wife had died many years earlier. For a long time afterwards the house was known locally as 'Cox's Cot'.

18 January

Ireland's Eye murderer released

William Burke Kirwan was released from Spike Island prison in Cork Harbour on 18 January 1879 after serving twenty-seven years for the murder of his wife Maria Louisa on Ireland's Eye, an island in Dublin Bay.

Kirwan was found guilty in 1852. The trial was one of the most sensational ever seen in Ireland. The prosecution believed that Maria Louisa had been stabbed to death with a sword cane. Kirwan had originally been given the death sentence, but his wealthy friends mounted a vigorous campaign to save him from the noose and the sentence was commuted to penal servitude for life.

Kirwan was released on compassionate grounds on 18 January 1879 on the condition that he left Ireland forever. He was taken under escort to Cobh (then Queenstown), where he was placed on board a ship bound for the US. He was never heard from again.

19 January

Birth of the letter box

Could Dublin possibly have been the birthplace of the humble letter box that we now all take for granted? This extract from the *Hibernian Journal* of 19 January1774 certainly suggests that a Dublin carpenter might have come up with this very simple and effective feature that no self-respecting front door should be without.

'A carpenter recommends it to all house-keepers in lonely streets, and of [sic.] small families, to have a square hole, with a slide to cover it inside, in the same manner that they have at the Bagnios, to receive all messages or letters, without opening the door, as it would by the means of preventing many robbers from getting into houses under colour of being messengers or servants. It is hoped this scheme will take place, as it will prevent many robberies from being committed.'

20 January

Overloaded ship sinks – thirty-five lives lost

On the night of 20 January 1838, the SS *Killarney* sank off the Cork coast, sending thirty-five of its passengers and crew to their deaths. The *Killarney*, a cargo ship, had left Cork the previous day, and was bound for Liverpool with a cargo of 600 live pigs and 48 passengers and crew.

The ship – clearly overloaded – ran into a blizzard soon after leaving the harbour, and Captain George Bailey decided to put in at Cobh to wait out the storm. However, by 8.00 p.m. that evening, with the blizzard still raging, Bailey made the fatal decision to put to sea again.

The *Killarney* had no sooner left the safety of Cobh when it ran into trouble again. The wind had increased and the vessel was soon rolling helplessly in the heavy seas. To make matters worse, the pigs in the ship's hold caused the vessel to list alarmingly. The captain ordered the crew to throw the pigs overboard, but in the appalling conditions this proved to be an impossible task.

The men worked at the ship's pumps throughout the night in an attempt to clear the hold of water, but at daybreak the pumps failed and the water levels rose rapidly. At midday on Saturday the ship's steward ordered all passengers and crew to go on deck, warning them that the vessel was in imminent danger of sinking. To make matters worse, a dense fog had fallen and no one – including Captain Bailey – had any idea of the ship's position.

When the mist cleared a few hours later, it became clear that the vessel was drifting towards the rocks in Robert's Cove near Kinsale. By this time the wind was, as one survivor later put it, 'blowing a complete hurricane', and passengers and crew realised that it was only a matter of time before the ship would be thrown onto the rocks.

Just then, a tremendous wave struck the *Killarney*, clearing the deck of its cargo of pigs and some of the steerage passengers. A second wave struck the doomed vessel soon afterwards and drove it onto the rocks some fifty metres away from the mainland.

The passengers and crew tried to make their way onto the rocks as best they could, but many fell to their deaths in the attempt. The survivors were forced to spend the remainder of Saturday night and all of Sunday in freezing conditions on the rock.

Several more died during the night from hypothermia, while a man and a woman were washed off the rock early on Sunday morning. The alarm wasn't raised until midday on Sunday, when the survivors were spotted from the shore, but even then the possibility of rescue seemed remote. The storm was still blowing and it was not viable to attempt a rescue by sea.

Those on shore did manage to pass a rope to the marooned survivors, and two survivors attempted to use it to climb up the cliff to safety. But the rope snapped, throwing them to their doom in the churning sea below.

The remaining survivors, who were by then starving and in an advanced state of hypothermia, were forced to spend another night on the rock. On Monday morning, they managed to gather a small amount of seaweed which helped to keep them from starving to death.

Several more rescue attempts were made on the Monday morning, all to no avail, and four more of the shipwrecked survivors died. Then, on Monday afternoon, a rescue team from Cork managed to get a line to the island by firing a two pound shot from a cannon with a rope attached, and the remaining thirteen survivors – including one woman – were safely brought ashore.

21 January

Noble shoemaker

Cases of domestic violence were regularly reported in newspapers in nineteenth-century Ireland, but some newspaper reporters were prone to treat these in an offhand and flippant way. Some were even inclined to see these cases as a source of hilarity and amusement. This case, heard at the Trim Petty Sessions Court on 21 January 1859 and reported in the *Meath Herald*, is a good example:

'Constable Mills charged an unfortunate besotted-looking shoemaker, named Noble Carroll, late of the Royal Meath, with beating his better-half in the streets of Trim on the 9th inst. The defendant in his defence said she was "hard of hearing" and for the purpose of making her feel, when she could not hear, he gave her a thump. Moreover, she had sup in, which probably in conjunction with the "thump" caused her to lose her equilibrium. He had been locked up all night for the offence. The defendant acknowledged he got drunk "by times" and it also appeared that his wife attempted to stab him once or twice, so that the home of the worthy Crispin does not appear to be a pattern of domestic bliss.

The Chairman said that as the defendant's wife had not appeared to complain, he supposed she had forgiven him, but if she had come forward, he would be compelled to fine him 10s. Fined 6d. and costs.'

22 January

Poured boiling water on her children

'The *Freeman's Journal* of 22 January 1840 recorded the details of an appalling court case held at Henry Street Police

Office on the preceding day. Patrick Owens of 28 Denmark Street was accused of boring a hole in the floorboards of his apartment with a hot poker and pouring boiling water down on the children of the McSweeney family, who lived on the floor below, scalding some of them.

It was reported in the newspaper that Owens had admitted his guilt to a policeman, complaining that the McSweeney children were disturbing his wife, who was seriously ill at the time. Owens also issued a counter-summons against Patrick McSweeney and his brother, claiming that they had threatened to assault him.

The counter-summons was dismissed and Owens was found guilty of a breach of the peace and was bound over to keep the peace. The judge expressed his regret that he had not been able to try Owens on a charge of assault and described his conduct as 'most cruel, inhuman, and utterly unjustifiable'.

23 January

'The celebrated Owen Christie'

Belfast Police Court, 23 January 1858: 'The celebrated Owen Christie', who had previously served separate prison terms amounting to seven years, six months and fourteen days, was jailed for the 136th time. He had been arrested by Constable Haslett, who told the court that Christie had been trying to kick down the door of a brothel in Belfast's Talbot Street at 1.00 a.m. previous Sunday.

Christie told the judge that he had only been knocking at the door in order to get payment for some chickens that he had sold when he was rudely interrupted by the constable. 'An honest man can't live in Belfast,' he said. He was fined five shillings plus costs.

24 January

A savage custom

Munster News, 24 January 1751: 'A few days ago an honest Farmer, who was carrying home his Bride from a Priest's House at Ballyna in the County of Kildare, where he was married, was, agreeable to a savage Custom, so pelted with Cabbage Stalks etc. as to occasion a Fracture in his Skull, of which he died the next Day.'

25 January

Attempted suicide

An old soldier named James Monaghan appeared before the Northern Court in Dublin on 25 January 1893, charged with attempting to commit suicide by stabbing himself in the stomach with a penknife. Monaghan had been arrested at his home in Benburb Street, Dublin on 17 January. He admitted the charge, but didn't say why he had wanted to kill himself. The judge remanded Monaghan and directed the prison doctor to evaluate his mental condition.

26 January

Municipal sheep roasting

On 26 January 1740, the year of the 'Great Frost', the *Dublin Evening Post* reported that a feast was held on the frozen River Boyne at Navan, County Meath. It was reported that a 'municipal sheep roasting' took place there, while the local gentry and their wives had 'several dances on the ice, being attended by a large band of music'.

27 January

Meath murder

On 27 January 1308, Hugh Le Rede stood before the Court of Common Pleas in Dublin on the charge of murdering Richard Saundre in Painestown, County Meath.

On the day of the murder, which occurred at the end of June 1307, the two men met in the main street of Painestown – then known as Paynestown Dullard – and harsh words were exchanged in relation to an earlier grievance between them. The row quickly escalated and Hugh threw a rock at Richard, hitting him in the face. Richard retaliated and a number of blows were struck before Hugh, believing his life to be in danger, drew his knife and stabbed Richard in the belly, killing him instantly.

Hugh then fled to the church in Painestown where he claimed sanctuary from the law and, the record states, 'abjured the land of Ireland and chose … to pass to Dublin'. Under the medieval laws of sanctuary, Hugh was permitted to claim immunity for his crime, but only on the basis that he renounced his right to live in Ireland.

The court found that, while he had indeed killed Richard, Hugh had been acting in self-defence. He was pardoned and permitted to go to England.

28 January

Pelted with cabbage stalks on her wedding day

New Ross, County Wexford, 28 January 1824: a large mob assembled outside the Catholic church in New Ross, County Wexford, in which a young local woman was being married to an English sailor. Father Doyle, the parish priest, dispersed the crowd and the newly married couple decided that it would be best to return to her lodgings on the quay separately.

As the bride was making her way home, she was accosted by the mob – reported to be at least five hundred strong– and pelted with cabbage stalks and other missiles. She was forced to run the gauntlet for the length of two streets and no one tried to help her. When the local magistrate heard about the incident he had two of the perpetrators arrested and issued warrants for the arrest of the others involved. The only excuse given for the attack on the young woman was that it was an old tradition in New Ross.

29 January

Burke and Hare

William Burke and William Hare were two Irish navvies who progressed from working as labourers on the Union Canal in Scotland to becoming two of the most infamous serial killers of the nineteenth century. William Burke is believed to have been born in Tyrone in 1792, while Hare's origins are unclear.

Burke and Hare first teamed up in 1826 in the West Port district of Edinburgh, where Hare was running a beggar's hotel. They embarked on their nefarious career in 1827 when an old lodger named Donald died, owing Hare four pounds in unpaid rent. Hare reckoned that he could make up the arrears by selling old Donald's corpse to one of the many anatomists then practising in the city. Burke and Hare took the old man's body to Professor Robert Knox, who paid them the princely sum of seven pounds, ten shillings, leaving them with a handsome profit for their efforts.

The two partners in crime agreed to supply the surgeon with more corpses, but they were of the opinion that grave robbing was too much like hard work. They decided that it would be much easier to supply the medical schools with bodies by murdering some of Hare's aged and infirm lodgers.

The men's first victim was a sickly lodger named Joe the Miller. The two 'entrepreneurs' plied Joe with enough Scotch whisky to render him unconscious and they finished him off by suffocating him with a pillowcase. In fact, this method of dispatching their victims was to become Burke and Hare's grisly trademark. Their deeds would later give a new phrase to the English language – to 'burke', meaning to suffocate.

During the following year, Burke and Hare were alleged to have killed at least sixteen people. While Burke was eventually charged with sixteen murders, it has been estimated that the two men could have been responsible for the deaths of up to thirty people.

Burke and Hare's grotesque money-making scheme finally came unstuck after they murdered their sixteenth known victim, a widow named Mary Docherty. They hid her body under a bed, but another lodger found her and called the police.

Burke and Hare were arrested. There wasn't enough evidence to convict them both, and Hare was offered his freedom in return for giving evidence against his friend. At the trial, which began on Christmas Eve 1828, Hare's evidence was enough to guarantee his former sidekick an early date with the grim reaper.

Burke was sentenced to death, and the execution was carried out on 29 January 1829. He made a full confession of his crimes before he went to face the hangman. After his execution, his body was handed over to the College of Surgeons for dissection.

30 January

Cromwell dug up and buried again

On 30 January 1661, just over two years after his first funeral at Westminster Abbey, London, the body of 'Cursed' Oliver Cromwell – Ireland's public enemy number one – was exhumed from his tomb, publicly hanged, beheaded and thrown into a pit at Tyburn, Middlesex.

Following Charles II's restoration to the English throne in 1660, the royalists had the bodies of Cromwell, Henry Ireton and John Bradshaw exhumed and subjected to a symbolic execution at the gallows at Tyburn. The three badly decomposed bodies were dragged through the thronged streets of London in their coffins and publicly hanged. It was a grisly sight, very well described by a man named Samuel Sainthill: '...they were hanged by the neck, from morning till four in the afternoon. Cromwell ... very fresh, embalmed; Ireton ...hung like a dried rat, yet corrupted about the fundament. Bradshaw in his winding sheet, the fingers of his right hand and his nose perished...'.

As dusk fell, the three bodies were taken down from the gallows and beheaded to the loud approval of the cheering mob. Cromwell lost several teeth and an ear in the process, and Bradshaw's toes were lopped off and distributed to the crowd. The three corpses were thrown into a pit at the foot of the gallows, and their heads were mounted on poles on top of Westminster Hall.

(For Cromwell's first funeral, see the entry for 23 November.)

31 January

Thirteen-year-old jailed for rape

Finn's Leinster Journal, 31 January 1767: A thirteen-year-old boy was convicted of the attempted rape of a seven-year-old girl and committed to Carlow Jail.

FEBRUARY

1 February

Animal cruelty

Three horses were mutilated in an appalling case of animal cruelty at Tallaght, County Dublin on the night of 1 February 1824 and the incident was reported in the *Freeman's Journal*. The three horses – which belonged to Ballinascorney man Bryan O'Hara – each had an ear hacked off. One horse had its jaw split, while another had its lips cut off. An ass belonging to Hugh Dolan, who lived nearby, was also attacked and had part of its head cut off.

The perpetrators of these savage acts left the following note pinned to one of the horse's tails:

'O'Hara, we expect this is sufficient warning for you to give up the poor people's land immediately, and if it is a thing you persevere in holding, you may depend a small piece of land will serve you before you are much older. O'Hara, advance this letter to your intended neighbour, Dolan, as soon as you read it; and Dolan, take this as a warning for you, or if not [sic.], you shall share the same fate.'

In the same report it was stated that two brothers, Francis and Garret McDermott, had recently been evicted from lands in the neighbourhood for non-payment of rent. It didn't explicitly state that the brothers had been responsible for the attack, but anyone reading the report would have been in no doubt that the finger was being pointed in their direction.

2 February

'Neck-yoked'

Extreme measures to hold prisoners were not unusual in eighteenth-century Ireland. The following report appeared in the *Hibernian Journal* on 2–4 February 1774:

'Dawson Whiteacre, who was lately committed to Carlow Gaol for robbing the shop of Miss Archdekin of this city, was very near effecting his escape a few nights ago, having his bolts almost filed off, when the gaoler luckily discovered him; but he is now double-bolted and neck-yoked, to prevent any further attempts of that kind.'

3 February

Death of Robert Layfield

On 3 February 1761, *Faulkner's Dublin Journal* announced that 'Layfield junior, one of the State Trumpets' had passed away some days earlier. The Layfield in question was Robert Layfield, son of the famous Lewis Layfield, an actor and musician who featured prominently on the Dublin theatrical and musical scene between the years 1719 and 1751.

Like his father, Robert was also a musician and an actor of note on the Dublin theatre scene between 1729 and 1750. He made many appearances at Smock Alley, Aungier Street, Crow Street, Rainsford Steet and Capel Street theatres, and was manager of Capel Street Theatre from 1749 to 1750. He was also 'State Trumpeter' for several years, right up to the time of his death.

His father Lewis Layfield became a city musician in 1720 when he petitioned the Dublin Assembly for a place. Three years later, in April 1723, he was appointed as overseer of the Dublin City Musicians. He also held the title of 'State Kettledrummer to the Lord Lieutenant of Ireland' for a time.

Lewis Layfield had a reputation for being moody and violent. On one occasion he became embroiled in a public slanging match at the theatre with a monied member of the audience who had indecently assaulted a theatre manager's wife. Layfield told the young gentleman that if he had done that to Layfield's own wife, he would have strangled him.

Knowing Layfield's fiery reputation, the young nob didn't try any rough stuff with him, but instead hired a dozen Dublin sedan chair carriers to give him a horse whipping. The gentleman lured Layfield to the Rose and Crown Tavern in Dame Street and sat back to watch the show.

However, the chef at the Rose and Crown had warned Layfield about the plan and Layfield had borrowed a carving knife from him. Layfield entered the Rose and Crown and just as the sedan chair carriers were about to surround him, he grabbed the gentleman who had set him up and threatened to cut off his head. The men duly backed off and Layfield dragged the gentleman out into Dame Street where 'he kicked and rolled him in the kennel [sewerage channel], until his life was endangered by the severe castigation.'

Lewis Layfield died insane in Dublin in 1751.

4 February

Westport riot

The history of the theatre and stage in Ireland is littered with instances of mayhem and violence. For the most part, these took place in Dublin. An exception to this was an incident that took place in Westport, County Mayo on the night of 4 February 1913, when George A. Birmingham's play *General John Regan* was abandoned during the second act because the stage was wrecked by protesters.

During the trouble the rioters – who were angry at the play's portrayal of a Catholic priest and a young girl in the play – tore down props, destroyed the scenic backdrop and threw missiles at the stage. The actor playing the role of the priest was physically attacked. His collar was torn off and later burned in Westport town.

At the height of the trouble, an estimated crowd of six to seven hundred had gathered outside, and a policeman was badly injured during one of many scuffles with the protesters. Twenty men were arrested.

George A. Birmingham was the pseudonym of Canon James Hannay who had been rector of the Church of Ireland in Westport until 1913. Hannay, a native of Belfast, was a prolific writer of satires and comic novels. He was a fluent Irish speaker and a member of the Gaelic League, but he was expelled after the fallout from his play in 1913.

Hannay seems to have had a degree of popularity outside of Mayo, but his Westport neighbours weren't too fond of his satires. Hannay wrote a story about an alcoholic priest, and a Catholic priest in Westport was convinced that Hannay had written it about him. The priest attacked Hannay in the local newspapers, and the playwright was a marked man from that time on. Locals burnt an effigy of him, and he was subjected to verbal attacks by other members of the clergy.

The twenty young men who were charged with public disorder were tried in Castlebar in July 1914 and were subsequently acquitted. Hannay left Westport after the controversy and became a British army chaplain in France during World War I. He died in 1950.

5 February

John Delahunt

In early March 1841 Irish newspapers reported on 'one of the most horrible and cold-blooded murders perpetrated in this country for the last century'.

They were referring to the murder of an Italian organ grinder named Domenico Garlibardo, whose lifeless body was found on the banks of the River Dodder near Rathfarnham, Dublin, on 28 February 1841.

Garlibardo was found early that Sunday morning with his throat slashed in several places. Suspicion initially fell on three of Garlibardo's room-mates, who were taken into custody at Rathfarnham Police Station.

However, the three Italians were released when new information came to light implicating a Roundtown (Terenure) man Richard Cooney and his wife Mary in the murder. The two were committed to stand trial for the crime, but the case subsequently collapsed.

The trail went cold after that, and nothing more was heard until 20 December of that year when an eight-year-old boy, Thomas Maguire, was found dead with his throat cut in Pembroke Lane. Before the child's body was cold, a seventeen-year-old Dubliner, John Delahunt, walked into a city police station giving details of the murder and implicating a man named Doyle and a prostitute in the crime.

However, there was something strange about Delahunt's demeanour and he was promptly arrested. It then emerged that Delahunt had also given information to the police in relation to the Garlibardo murder ten months earlier, and he immediately became the number one suspect in both murders.

Delahunt was subsequently charged with the murder of the boy, who lived on Cherry Lane off Great Britain

Street (now Parnell Street), and he eventually confessed to having killed Maguire. Delahunt said that he had planned the crime for two months, and his statement made for harrowing reading: 'At that moment,' said Delahunt, 'with his head drawn back, I cut his throat and threw him from me. He fell on his face. He uttered no cry...'. After a brief trial, Delahunt was found guilty and sentenced to death.

Delahunt was never actually tried for the Italian organ grinder's murder, but he was suspected of it. He admitted that he had sworn false evidence against the Cooneys in the hope that the police would pay him, but he made a sworn statement on his deathbed that he was not responsible for the Italian's death.

Delahunt's death sentence was carried out at Kilmainham Jail on 5 February 1842. His was the first hanging to take place in the city for over seven years and it attracted enormous public interest.

He was said to have been quite calm right up to the time of execution, but as he approached the gallows and the masked hangman, his courage failed him. Delahunt collapsed on the trapdoor in a dead faint and the executioner struggled to get him to stand up.

The hangman eventually gave up and placed the rope around his neck where the prisoner lay. He pulled the lever and Delahunt dropped through the trapdoor to meet his fate without ever regaining consciousness.

6 February

Fishamble Street disaster

The new Music Hall in Dublin's Fishamble Street was the scene of a horrific accident on 6 February 1782. The Guild of St Luke, also known as the corporation of cutlers, painters, paper strainers and stationers, had gathered there for an election. The election was held in the Grove Room beside the Music Hall and an estimated three to four hundred people had crammed in for the meeting. About ten minutes into the proceedings the floor collapsed, hurling the whole assembly twenty feet into the room below.

Reports of the tragedy were confused, but many people were badly hurt in the accident and at least two to three people died afterwards. Three days later, *Faulkner's Dublin Journal* reported that 'thirty-five people, mainly lawyers and tradesmen' had broken limbs, while 'a few died from their injuries'. The *Freeman's Journal* reported that two or three had died and that several others were not expected to live.

7 February

Irishmen's execution in Britain

Cinemas were closed, sporting events were cancelled and flags flew at half mast all over Ireland in protest at the execution of two Irishmen, Peter Barnes and William McCormick, at Winson Green Prison in Birmingham on 7 February 1940.

Barnes (32), from Banagher in County Offaly, and McCormick (29), a Mullingar man, both members of the Irish Republican Army, had been convicted of causing an explosion in Coventry on 25 August 1939, in which five people – including a fifteen-year-old boy – were killed.

Sporting events all over the country were also cancelled, including a rugby match between Old Belvedere and Queen's University, a coursing meeting in Kilkenny and a Leinster Chess Championship match. Mill workers in Belfast wore black ribbons in solidarity with the men, and several county councils adjourned business for the day.

In New York, a support group managed to infiltrate the World's Fair exhibition and flew the tricolour at half mast in protest at the execution of the two men.

On the same day, at Liverpool Assizes, a sixteen-year-old Brendan Behan was sentenced to three years imprisonment for being in possession of explosives. The young Behan told the judge that the potassium chlorate powder found in his suitcase was for his ears and he produced a doctor's note to prove it. This didn't wash with the judge, however, and he sentenced Behan to three years in a borstal, telling him that he would have given him fourteen years' penal servitude if he had been any older. Behan gave a very eloquent speech from the dock for one so young. As he was taken below, he shouted 'God save Ireland'.

8 February

'Several dead bodies'

Bully's Acre Cemetery at Kilmainham in Dublin provided a ready supply of fresh corpses for the city's bodysnatchers as well as the anatomists of Trinity College and the College of Surgeons.

Almost as soon as the grieving family had buried their loved ones in the ground at Bully's Acre, the 'sack 'em up' men went straight to work, digging them up again. And it wasn't just the odd corpse that was involved, if this report of 8 February 1827 from the *Freeman's Journal* is anything to go by:

'Between two and three o'clock yesterday morning, the guard of the 26th Foot on duty at Kilmainham, from some suspicious appearances, were led to examine a gentleman's gig, which was stopping on the road opposite the Hospital-fields, better-known by the name of Bully's

Acre. Their suspicions turned out to be well-founded, for in the gig were several dead bodies, closely packed, which [had] just been disinterred. The gig, and two men who were in charge of it, were sent to Arran-quay Police-office by the guard. Mr. Cooper, Chief-Constable, caused the bodies to be re-intered [sic.]; the gig and the men, who gave their names as James Fitzgallon and John Byrne, have been detained, until the circumstances can be fully investigated.'

9 February

Shanks' nightmare

A Dublin widow suffered a frightening ordeal at the hands of one of her employees when she believed his tale that her dead husband had come back to haunt her. An extract from *The People*, Dublin, 9 February 1833 reveals the story.

'Dublin Police College Street. Mrs. Anne Shanks appeared at this office on Tuesday and complained of the conduct of Peter Reilly, her journeyman cord-wainer. She said – "I live at Sir John Rogerson's Quay, No.78. I lost my husband, as good a workman as ever took up an awl, by the cholera, leaving four children. All last week I was not left worth a ha'penny, in truth, disturbed from midnight to morn by what they said was my poor husband's ghost. Truth it made noise enough, ricketting, clattering, battering, trampity tramp, clumpity clump, thump went the chairs, jump went the candlesticks, and then there'd be a noise. I was shrunk up abed, covered with curtains, and the ghost would be for raking the fire. I saw him says Reilly, so did I says the watchman –'twas poor Ned Shanks (not his mare) himself, and he looked dry and hungry. Well, I gave Reilly and the watchman tea and sugar, whiskey and chops, to keep the life in me, for a whole week. The landlord sent his son to aid in this vigil and sure enough, says Peter, says he. I seed him, and a great, big, black, cholera-hospital tarpaulin all over him; but he'll not appear to you, says he to my landlord's son, for you're a Protestant, says he. So, with that, matters passed on in this way; the groanings and the moanings went on every night ... when I found out that the roguish thief himself was the ghost. I caught him stealing a pair of my boots, and I followed him, so I did; and my boots were worth twelve shillings, and more than that." This extraordinary tale being ended, the poor woman's informations were taken against Peter Reilly, and a warrant issued for his apprehension.'

10 February

The hair-dresser's boy

A boy, 'belonging to Mulhern the hair-dresser', was making his way along the Blind Quay in Dublin at 10.00 p.m. on the night of 10 February 1776 when he was accosted outside the watch house at Michael's Lane by three men armed with knives. No watchman came to the boy's aid, and he was robbed of twenty-three silver shillings and a case of razors. The thieves even took the buckles off his shoes.

11 February

Base ingratitude

A woman calling herself Jane Tolan arrived at the house of a poor weaver named Robert Hunter in the village of Maralin, County Down on the night of 11 February 1833.

Tolan told Hunter and his wife that she was ill and asked them for a bed for the night.

The Hunters were only too happy to oblige, and they took her in and gave her all the care and hospitality at their disposal. The couple allowed Tolan to stay a second night, but when they awoke the following morning they found, to their dismay, that their guest had done a runner, taking with her all of the yarn that the weaver had been working on, as well as a wide variety of other materials. She even stole some of the children's clothes along with a pair of Mrs Hunter's shoes.

Tolan was described in the *Newry Examiner* as being about '50 years of age; stout made; black hair; slightly pitted with the small-pox; nose very large at the end; appeared to have the Munster brogue in perfection; wore a worsted stuff gown striped, and blue cloak'.

12 February

The pickled herring cure

What did our ancestors do when they were ill in eighteenth-century Ireland? Well, in the days before doctors' surgeries and accident and emergency departments, many were forced to rely on quack remedies and dubious potions to cure their everyday ills. The *Hibernian Journal* on 12 February 1772 advertised a number of these.

Dr Solomon's Powders were popular kill-all cures in their time, and the good doctor promised that his remedies could cure persons 'afflicted with scurvies, cancers and evils'. Doctor Solomon, who had an office in Fleet Street in Dublin, published a range of testimonials from grateful patients who had benefitted from his treatments. One of these was from 'Lady L', who claimed that the potion had cured her servant boy of 'an inveterate evil', while Major Holt-Warren testified that one of his troopers had been cured of nose cancer after taking Doctor Solomon's medicine.

Another favourite was 'Maredant's Antiscorbutic Drops' which, it was claimed, had cured cases of 'Leprosy, scurvy, ulcers, the evil, fistulas, piles, inflammation of the eyes ... and every other disorder arising from foulness in the blood'.

The one that I like best is the 'absolute cure for rheumatism' outlined in the newspaper: 'Take the pickle of barrelled herrings and rub all along the parts afflicted before a good fire and wrap up in flannel. Five or six applications effect a cure in the worse cases.'

13 February

They wore scarlet ribbons

On Monday night, 13 February 1832, Dundalk man James Carragher was shot dead during an altercation with police outside Lennon's pub in the town. The reports relating to this incident are quite confusing, but it appears that there had been some fighting outside Lennon's which led to an arrest. A crowd gathered, and some of them got involved in a scuffle with the police. At the inquest into Carragher's death on the day after the incident, evidence was heard that one of the policemen drew his pistol and shot Carragher dead in the street. The policemen then fled for the safety of Dundalk Barracks, pursued by an angry crowd.

The perpetrator of the killing was identified at the inquest as Sub-constable William McMenomy, and the jury ruled that he had shot Carragher in the groin, 'which caused instant death'.

There was a huge crowd at Carragher's funeral on 15 February. Many of them wore scarlet ribbons in their hats, which the *Newry Examiner* of 18 February described as being 'emblematic of the revenge that the enraged population are nursing'.

McMemony was tried for Carragher's murder at Louth Crown Court at the end of February. Having heard all of the evidence, the jury retired for twelve minutes before returning a not-guilty verdict.

14 February

Stocking thief

Punishment was brutal in eighteenth-century Ireland. On 14 February 1763, the *Cork Evening Post* reported that Thomas Mannin, a former soldier, was whipped from the North Gate in Cork to the weigh house on Bandon Road – for stealing a pair of stockings belonging to John Barry.

15 February

Balloon Man

Belfast balloonist John Dunville set out from Dublin on 15 February 1910 in an attempt to cross the Irish Sea in a balloon. His voyage began at the Dublin Gas Company works on Barrow Street. Dunville and his travelling companion set off at 10.08 a.m. and their ascent was witnessed by a small crowd who cheered the men on their way. The wind was so strong at the time that it took forty men to hold the inflated balloon down.

Dunville's wife Violet had intended to make the cross-channel trip with her husband, but at the last moment it was decided that the trip was too dangerous for three people to undertake in the heavy winds. Violet was an experienced balloonist in her own right and had already flown across the English Channel to Belgium with her husband a year earlier.

When the right moment came, the balloon – the St Louis – was untied and ascended rapidly, heading towards Howth at a rate of forty miles per hour, where it disappeared from sight in the sea mists enveloping the east coast. The balloon was spotted later on, flying high over Holyhead in Wales, and it finally came to land in Macclesfield in England at 2.55 p.m.

16 February

Sheemore duel

In the late 1780s the courts decided to crack down on the practice of duelling, which was rampant amongst the upper classes in Ireland at that time. Leitrim land agent Robert Keon, who killed his neighbour George Reynolds in a duel, bore the brunt of this new severity. His high-profile case was heard in 1786.

There had been bad blood between Keon and Reynolds for some time. The resentment boiled over when Keon publicly horsewhipped Reynolds at the Leitrim Assizes in Carrick-on-Shannon following a family dispute. Reynolds challenged Keon to a duel, and Keon quickly agreed to the proposal. Both concurred that the pistols would only be loaded with gunpowder, which would allow the quarrel to be settled with honour and without either party getting hurt. The duel was fixed for the morning of 15 October 1786 at Sheemore.

Things didn't go to plan, however. Reynolds arrived on the morning of the duel for what he expected would be a brief exchange of powder, before heading home for breakfast with his honour intact. But Keon had other ideas. He shot Reynolds – who was unarmed – in the head, killing him instantly.

Keon was arrested and charged with murder. The Attorney General decided that the case should be heard in Dublin because it was felt that he would not get a fair trial in Leitrim. The trial began on 27 November 1787, and Keon was quickly found guilty. He was remanded in custody.

Chief Justice Lord Earlsfort was determined to stamp out the practice of duelling once and for all, and he was keen to make an example of Keon. On 31 January 1788 he imposed a savage sentence on Keon that was usually reserved for those convicted of treason. The judge ordered for Keon to be taken to the gallows at Newgate Prison in Dublin, where he was to be hanged by the neck. '…[B]ut not until you are dead,' said the judge, 'for whilst you are still alive you are to be cut down, your bowels are to be taken out and burned, and, you being yet still alive, your head is to be severed from your body … your head and your body is to be divided into four quarters, and your head and quarters are to be at his Majesty's disposal.'

The gruesome sentence was duly carried out on 16 February 1788.

17 February

La Grande Horizontale

Lola Montez, once described in Britain as 'the biggest whore in Christendom' or more politely by the French as 'La Grande Horizontale', was a famous actress and dancer, courtesan to the king of Bavaria and general hellraiser extraordinaire.

Irishwoman Montez, to paraphrase a TV ad for a certain chocolate bar, couldn't dance and couldn't sing, but she most certainly went a long way. Lola first saw the light of day as plain old Dolores Eliza Gilbert. There have been some question marks over her place of birth. Some claim Lola was born in Grange in County Sligo on 17 February 1821, while other biographers have claimed that she was born in Limerick.

Lola was the daughter of a British army officer and she was educated in Scotland and England. She eloped to Dublin in 1837, where she married a young British lieutenant named Thomas James. The marriage didn't last for very long, and Dolores set off for London where she launched her career as a Flamenco dancer, using the name Lola Montez for the first time. She had a disastrous debut performance and was booed off the stage.

Lola then moved to mainland Europe, where she developed her renowned 'tarantula dance', which apparently went down very well with continental male audiences. She also had a fearsome temper, and any man that dared to cross her path or annoy her was liable to have his face rearranged by Lola's whip.

What made Lola a household name, however, was her string of affairs in Europe and the US. Her lovers included Franz Liszt, the German composer, and Alexander Dumas, the novelist. In 1846 she met King Ludwig of Bavaria, who gave her a generous allowance from the public purse and built her a palace.

When Ludwig was deposed during the revolution of 1848, Lola fled to the east coast of the US where she tried to resurrect her dancing career. She embarked on a tour of the gold fields of California and Australia, but the miners didn't appreciate her tarantula dance.

Lola returned to New York where she died from the after effects of a stroke on 17 January 1861.

18 February

Cockfighting at the Sod and Jockey

Would you go to see an All-Ireland cock match organised by the Sod and Jockey club? Well, if you were into your sport in the late eighteenth century, you just might have found yourself attending such an event.

Cockfighting was a very popular sport in Ireland in the eighteenth and nineteenth centuries. Its popularity was spread across all classes of society, and it had the advantage that matches could be held in all kinds of weather.

Participants sometimes travelled long distances to take on other clubs and, during the week beginning 18 February 1805, several Dublin newspapers announced the holding of a week-long cock match between the gentlemen of Fermanagh and the gentlemen of King's County (Offaly).

The contest took place at the New Pit, Farmer's Repository on St Stephen's Green, and prize money was twenty guineas per battle, with five hundred guineas going to the winner of the grand final at the end of the tournament.

It was also announced in the *Freeman's Journal* that, for the duration of the contest, the noblemen and gentlemen of the Sod and Jockey Club intended to hold daily dinners at Falkner's Tavern in Dawson Street. The dinners were open to 'all gentlemen and sportsmen who wish to join in the amusement', providing they were introduced by a member.

19 February

Whipped

From the *Cork Evening Post*, 19 February 1759: 'Last Saturday was whip'd through the City, James Forrest, for stealing a parcel of Twigs, the property of Boyle Travers, Esq.'

20 February

Killed rats with his teeth

This entry comes with a health warning so don't read it if you're squeamish or just about to have your dinner. The *Northern Whig* of 20 February 1858 reported on what it called a new low for Belfast: 'a human beast' had killed rats with his teeth for a bet at a house in the city.

The man in question apparently wagered that he could kill two rats with his teeth quicker than a dog could kill three on the ground. Two live rats were duly tied to a couple of nails that had been hammered into a table and three other rats were let loose on the floor. The dog won the bet, and the man was severely bitten on the face for his trouble.

21 February

Dead centre of Dublin

Glasnevin Cemetery, sometimes called the 'dead centre' of Dublin, was officially opened on 21 February 1832. It was originally named Prospect Cemetery and the first burial – that of eleven-year-old Michael Carey from Francis Street – took place there on 22 February. To date, over 1.5 million people have been buried in Glasnevin.

22 February

Comedian's death blamed on newspaper review

The famous Dublin actor Jack Edwin was only in his mid-thirties when he died suddenly on 22 February 1805. His passing kicked off a minor storm in the pages of the Dublin newspapers. The *Freeman's Journal* lamented the death 'of this excellent comedian', describing his demise as 'not only a loss to the stage but to society at large, of which he was a pleasant and most worthy member'.

During the days and weeks following the comedian's passing, many blamed an article written by theatre critic John Wilson Croker as being the main cause of his death, citing that the article was 'an illiberal and unjust attack on his professional character'. However, it seems likely that Edwin's seemingly uncontrollable drinking habits and wayward lifestyle were the real cause of his tragic demise.

Croker's 'attack' – if it can be described as such – seems innocuous enough by today's standards, but in a society where even the slightest insult could have you up in the Phoenix Park at dawn with pistols drawn, face and honour were everything.

On reading the offending article, Edwin is supposed to have written the following words to a close friend: 'Come and help me destroy myself with some of the most splendid cognac that I have ever exported to cheer a broken heart.'

Edwin was described in the article as the 'lubbard spouse' of Mrs Edwin and was compared unfavourably with John 'the elder' Edwin, whom Croker described as being 'high on the rolls of comic fame'.

Edwin's wife Elizabeth also blamed Croker for her husband's death, and in 1810 it was reported that she had a tombstone erected over his last resting place at St Werburgh's Church in Dublin. The tombstone contained an inscription that ran like a short story rather than an epitaph to the dead man.

The inscription, too long to reprint here in its entirety, read: 'Here lies the remains of Mr. John Edwin of the Theatre-Royal who died Feb. 22, 1805 aged 33 years. His death was occasioned by the acuteness of his sensibility. ... [H]e experienced an illiberal and cruel attack on his professional reputation from an anonymous assassin. This circumstance preyed upon his mind to the extinction of his life...'.

23 February

Kyleclare

On 23 February 1943, the *Kyleclare*, a ship owned by the Limerick Steamship Company with a crew of eighteen Irishmen, was destroyed by a German U-Boat. All eighteen on board, all crew, perished. The *Kyleclare*, under the command of Captain Alan Hamilton from Galway, had left Lisbon two days earlier and was steaming northwards across the Atlantic to Ireland when it was spotted by a German submarine. The U-456 was skippered by battle-hardened wolfpack commander Captain Lieutenant Max-Martin Teichert.

Teichert fired a fan of three torpedoes at the unarmed *Kyleclare* at precisely 2.38 p.m., and the ship was blown asunder. Teichert said that he went to the scene of the explosion but there were no survivors, only wreckage. He also claimed that he had not seen *Kyleclare's* brightly painted markings, which indicated that the ship was neutral.

24 February

Tipperary nicknames

There were a few mundane cases of petty crime in Clonmel, County Tipperary, reported in the *Hibernian Journal* on 24 February 1773. What made this particular report stand out from others was the fact that the defendant's nicknames were given.

Up for stealing sheep was William Kennedy, better known in Tipperary as Billy the Barrel-man and *Fear na Caoire* (the Sheep Man). John Clevane, a.k.a. Shane the Pig and *Fear na Muc* (the Pig Man), was charged with stealing 'four fat hogs' at Ardfinnan in Limerick.

Jemmy the Mumper, a.k.a. Leem the Creeper, was charged with robbing James Dennison of Tipperary Town, while Mary Leahy, a.k.a. Varow the Sitter and Rump and Raggs, was charged with stealing linen and other items from the home of James Laler in Clonmackoge.

25 February

Cahir killing

The killing of an Englishman in County Tipperary was recorded in detail in the *Freeman's Journal* on 25 February 1800:

'Wednesday night, in the evening, between five and six o'clock, Alexander Mollison, steward to Lord Cahir, was barbarously murdered on his way from Kilcommon to the town of Cahir by two desperadoes, who came out from the lands of Suir-bank on the high road, and after passing him, one of the ruffians fired a pistol, the ball from which entered the back of Mollison, and came out under his right breast; the unfortunate man died shortly after. A poor old man that was going the road at the time made some little observation against the barbarity of the act – upon which one of the assassins said, *hold your tongue, you old rogue, or you will be served in the same manner.* Mollison was a Yorkshire man, and we suppose, his being a faithful servant, averse to United Irishism and treason, was the reason the cruel wretches put him to death...'.

26 February

Hurricane causes havoc

On the night of 26 February 1903 one of the worst hurricanes in living memory hit the east coast of Ireland, with Dublin City and its environs being particularly badly affected. The storm caused a huge amount of destruction in the city and led to many houses and public buildings being damaged beyond repair.

Several newspapers compared the storm with 'The night of the big wind', which caused untold destruction throughout the country in January 1839, and described it as a 'night of terror'. Many houses and crumbling tenement buildings all over the city collapsed. Thousands of windows and chimney pots were smashed, entire roofs were blown away and thousands of trees were snapped in half or pulled up by the roots.

The telegraph link between Ireland and Britain was severed. The only lines that remained intact were the Dublin–Belfast and Dublin–Cork links, while links between Dublin and all of the smaller towns were down.

The high winds created a state of panic in the tenements of the city, and many women and children were seen running through the streets screaming with terror. In the houses surrounding Green Street, many families abandoned their homes and sought refuge in Green Street Police Station. It was reported that, by 3.00 a.m. the following morning, there were 200 women and children sheltering in the station.

Several people were trapped in a tenement at 29 Arran Quay when several floors collapsed. The fire brigade, who were stretched to breaking point, managed to rescue at least eight people from the house, including an 84-year-old man named Richard Lacy.

The severe weather also caused problems on the River Liffey. Several boats were smashed to pieces and high seas delayed the funeral of Charles Gavan Duffy, whose remains were due to arrive at the North Wall on the morning after the storm. Some of the mourners waiting at the North Wall observed that the gale had been as fierce as the storm that raged when the remains of Charles Stewart Parnell were brought across the Irish Sea in 1891.

The villages and suburbs of Dublin's exposed south-east coast sustained a tremendous pounding, with Ringsend, Irishtown and Sandymount suffering the most. The roofs of the Star of the Sea Church and St Matthew's Church in Irishtown were blown away, as were the roofs of the two glass bottle factories in Ringsend.

On the north side of the city, many roads in Santry and Finglas became impassable due to flooding and fallen trees. Over one thousand trees were destroyed in the Phoenix Park, including an entire avenue of elm trees leading to the Viceregal Lodge. The nearby Botanic Gardens also sustained damage to many of its exotic trees, while at Glasnevin Cemetery many monuments and gravestones suffered damage.

27 February

Lured to his death in Copper Alley

This report of the murder of a man at a Dublin brothel does not conceal the writer's opinion. It was published in the *Dublin Courier* on Wednesday, 27 February 1760:

'[On] Wednesday night a man intoxicated with liquor was seduced into one of the infamous brothels in Copper-alley [Dublin], where he was barbarously murdered. It is greatly wished that some method was found to remove so dreadful a nuisance, as examples of this most shocking nature are frequent in this infernal den.'

28 February

'...this Provender-prickt Son of Insolence'

Dublin, 28 February 1784: 'A servant was wandering through Dame Street, amusing himself by indiscriminately scorching innocent passers-by with a flambeau [flaming torch].' One of his victims failed to see the funny side, however, and he 'thought proper to bestow a severe, but wholesome discipline on this Provender-prickt Son of Insolence, to the very great Satisfaction of the Spectators.'

What a lovely way our ancestors had with words! You wouldn't get away with simply saying someone got a good hiding in the columns of the *Hibernian Journal*.

29 February

Sticks and stones

There was an unusual case reported in the Dublin newspapers on 29 February 1832. Mrs E. Nicholson, described as 'a highly respectable lady', was summonsed to appear at the Dublin Magistrate's Court for committing trespass in St Peter's churchyard by depositing a coffin filled with sticks and stones there. The coffin had been dug up and left exposed by Dublin's bodysnatching fraternity.

Mrs Nicholson denied the charge, saying that she had paid for the plot where the coffin was found and was therefore entitled to do what she liked with it. She told the court that her son had died and that she had come up with the scheme to protect her son's remains from the predations of the bodysnatchers, who were extremely active at that time. Mrs Nicholson then produced a letter from a clergyman from another part of Ireland which stated the real location of her son's body. The case was dismissed.

MARCH

1 March

'The English Pale spoiled daily'

This is an extract from a letter written by Lord Deputy of Ireland Henry Sidney to the Earl of Leicester, dated 1 March 1566 and recorded in the *Calendar of State Papers* for Ireland. Sidney, who had only begun his stint as lord deputy six weeks earlier, is pessimistic in his assessment of the condition of Ireland, and he asks Lord Leicester to communicate his views to Queen Elizabeth I, particularly in relation to Shane O'Neill or 'Shane the Proud', as he was commonly known:

'Arrived January 13. The English Pale spoiled daily, and in utter poverty. The soldiers so beggar-like and insolent and allied with the Irish, that nothing can correct them. Kilkenny and Munster all spoiled. The Earls cannot attend the Queen's service, as formerly. One may ride 30 miles and not see one house left standing, where Sidney has known it as well inhabited as many counties in England. Thomond worse still. In Connaught the Earl of Clanrycard is greatly distressed.... Shane O'Neill the only strong and rich man in Ireland.... He never made peace with the Queen, but by her own seeking.... He can bring 1,000 horse and 4,000 foot into the field.... He is able to burn and spoil to Dublin gates and go away unfought...'.

In the eyes of the English administration in Ireland, O'Neill was clearly public enemy number one. Sidney turned the heat up on him, harassing him in Tyrone and turning his neighbours against him.

O'Neill was defeated by the O'Donnells at the Battle of Farsetmore in 1567. He then tried to form an alliance with the MacDonnells of Antrim, but he was killed by Alexander Oge MacDonnell in June of that year. O'Neill's head was taken to Dublin where it was put on public display at Dublin Castle.

2 March

Smock Alley wrecked

There was rioting on a grand scale in Dublin's Smock Alley Theatre on 2 March 1754 when the audience perceived that theatre manager and proprietor Thomas Sheridan changed some of the words of Voltaire's play *Mahomet* for his own political ends. Angry punters called Sheridan out to explain himself, but he had fled in a sedan chair for the safety of his home in Dorset Street. The angry mob proceeded to vent their anger by hurling missiles at the actors. The curtains and scenic backdrop were slashed to ribbons with swords, and the stage was set on fire. The theatre was totally wrecked in the incident, and it spelled the end of Sheridan's reign as manager of Smock Alley.

3 March

Hawk, Rook and Wren

You couldn't make it up. I had to re-check the date of this report in the *Daily Express* on 3 March 1851 to make sure that it wasn't actually April Fool's day.

The report refers to a young man named John Rooke. Some days earlier, Rooke was arrested by a policeman named Hawk and charged at the Dublin Police Court with stealing a brush from the property of John Wren at

59 Patrick Street in Dublin. The reporter, who couldn't resist having his fun, tells us that Wren 'saw Rooke endeavouring to fly away with the article in question, and being determined that he should not make game of him, he immediately clipped his wings, and gave him into custody of a policeman named Hawk, who, it appeared, provided the aforesaid Rooke with a suitable aviary in the station-house'.

Despite the light-hearted nature of the report, his brush with the law didn't end well for Rooke. Judge Frank Porter found him guilty as charged and he was given four dozen lashes as a punishment.

4 March

Dirty dancing

The *Irish Independent* of 4 March 1935 seems to have given the bishops of Ireland free rein to ram home their holy message to churchgoers at the beginning of the Lenten campaign for that year.

No section of Irish society was immune to a lash of the crozier as the bishops turned the full heat of their wrath on communists, socialists, 'scandal givers', 'accomplices of Satan', professional agitators, the IRA, the Republican Congress, dancing during Lent, 'immodest dress and dances, company-keeping, evil films and literature', and best of all to my mind, 'comfort-loving, pleasure-seeking, infidel excesses'.

Most of the leading lights of the hierarchy were given an opportunity to instruct the faithful in how their lives should be conducted. The Archbishop of Tuam Dr Gilmartin led the charge with an attack on the heinous crime of dancing when he called for the closure of all dance halls in his diocese during Lent and asked young people to choose the 'sweet air of the church' as opposed to the 'fetid atmosphere' of the dance hall.

The Reverend Dr Foley of Killaloe railed against the craze for dancing, cinema and general pursuit of pleasure. He launched an attack on the women of Ireland who, he claimed, sometimes appeared in dance halls, 'dressed to leave the body nearly nude'.

The bishop, however, had great faith that the young men of his diocese would resist this 'indecency' by refusing to dance with any hussy 'who presented herself in a costume more fit for the privacies of life than for a gathering of decent people'.

Continuing the attack on the dance halls of Ireland, Bishop Browne of Cloyne described dancing as a kind of mania and a 'great danger to modesty and decency' and described the dance halls in his diocese as 'promiscuous, ill-assorted dancing assemblies'.

Bishop McNamee of Ardagh and Clonmacnoise joined his clerical colleagues in the attack on what he referred to as the practice of 'devilish dancing' and jazz, calling them 'negroid importations' and 'incitements to sensuality and sinful passion'.

5 March

Murderous assault

Martin Doyle, an Irish labourer, , appeared before York Magistrate's Court in England in 1865, charged with assaulting fellow Irishman Michael Cannon with a hatchet. The two men, who lived beside each other on Black Bull Lane, Walmgate exchanged insults before Doyle went into his house and emerged with a 'murderous looking weapon, answering the double purpose of a hammer and a hatchet'.

He made a savage attack on Cannon with the weapon, leaving him with seven severe head wounds. Doyle was remanded in custody.

6 March

Little Phil

US Army General Philip Henry Sheridan (1831–1888), also known as 'Little Phil', was born on 6 March 1831, but the place of his birth is still a mystery. Some say he was born in County Cavan in Ireland, while Ohio and New York in the US have also been mentioned as possible places of birth. Others claim that he was born on board a ship during a voyage from Ireland to New York. Whatever the truth of the matter, Sheridan said in his memoirs that his parents, John and Mary Sheridan, were born and reared in Cavan where his father worked on the Cherrymount estate. Sheridan is today claimed by Cavan people as one of their own.

Sheridan grew up in the village of Somerset, Ohio and he received his early education in the village school, where he was taught by an Irish schoolteacher named McNanly.

He entered West Point Military Academy in 1848 and, on graduating in 1853, he received his first posting as a 2nd lieutenant with an infantry regiment in Texas, where he remained for the next eight years. Sheridan became known as 'Little Phil' by his men because he was only five feet, five inches tall and was of slight build.

When the American Civil War began in 1861, Sheridan was still a lieutenant, but in 1862 he was given command of the 2nd Michigan Cavalry of the Union Army. Over the following months, he distinguished himself in many engagements and at the Battle of Chattanooga in Tennessee.

This latter victory brought Sheridan to the attention of Major General Ulysses S. Grant, and in 1864 Grant appointed him to command the cavalry division of the Army of the Potomac, the main Union Army in the eastern theatre during the American Civil War.

Sheridan repaid Grant's faith in him when he orchestrated his brilliant campaign at the decisive Battle of Shenandoah Valley. Following Sheridan's major victory at the Battle of Five Forks, he cut off General Lee's retreating armies at Appomattox in an action that effectively ended the Civil War.

After the war, Sheridan became military governor of Texas and Louisiana for a time. He was also heavily involved in the campaigns against the Native American Indians during the 1868 war with the Cheyenne and Comanche tribes. He was responsible for coining the derogatory and racist slogan, 'The only good Indian is a dead Indian'. When Tosawi, the Comanche chief, went to Sheridan to offer his unconditional surrender, Tosawi is alleged to have said, 'Tosawi, good Indian'. Sheridan's actual reply was: 'The only good Indians I ever saw were dead.'

Sheridan became general-in-chief of the US Army in 1884 and he held this post until his death in 1888. He was buried in Arlington National Cemetery in Washington.

7 March

Police brutality

Policing in eighteenth-century Dublin was a haphazard affair. In the 1780s, the municipal authorities made several attempts to reform the police in the city. Newspapers often expressed concern in relation to the inhuman and abusive treatment inflicted by the police on the citizens of Dublin.

An extreme example of this abusive behaviour was reported in the *Hibernian Journal* on 7 March 1788. Thomas Linn, a hosier from Bow Street, was on his way home a few nights earlier, when he approached 'one of those insolent guardians of liberty and property' (i.e. the police) and asked him for the time. The policeman responded by drawing his cutlass and lopping off the poor man's ear. Linn was taken to the Charitable Infirmary in Jervis Street, where he was said to be recovering from his ordeal.

8 March

The boys — and girls — of Fair Hill

The entry for 8 March 1772 in Francis Tuckey's *Cork Remembrancer* provides some interesting detail about a battle fought between 'the warlike sons and daughters of Fair Lane and Blackpool' in a field near Fair Hill in Cork.

During the fight, which lasted until nightfall, the women fought each other with stones, while the men laid into each other with newly designed tomahawks (axes), described as being four feet long with a hook and a spear on the end.

9 March

Cure for the cholera

Ballyshannon Herald, 8 March 1832: An Irishman and his wife appeared in a London court charged with the illegal possession of four gallons of poitín. The woman told the judge that she only had the illicit liquor because a health officer had told her that it was the only cure in the world for cholera. She told the court that for as long as she and her husband had been drinking poitín, neither had contracted cholera, 'English or Indian'.

10 March

Cornelius McGrath

The Irish giant Cornelius McGrath, who was born near Silvermines in County Tipperary on 10 March 1736, was at least seven feet tall by the time he turned sixteen. McGrath was sent to Youghal, County Cork, for a salt-water treatment for his growing pains.

His phenomenal stature began to attract crowds of curious onlookers. He was persuaded to go to London in 1753, where he was exhibited as a boy giant at Charing Cross. He also toured many of Europe's major cities, but he became ill in Belgium and was forced to return to Ireland.

He became friendly with some medical students from Trinity College. However, when he died, on 17 May 1760, his new-found friends are believed to have stolen his body and dissected it. His skeleton is still on display today at the Anatomy Museum in Trinity College.

11 March

Female gang boss jailed

The *Evening Freeman*, 11 March 1831:

'Thames Police. An old Irishwoman, named Mary Lannon, was placed at the bar, with twelve girls of … ages … ten to sixteen years, whom she was charged with sending out to procure money by stealing and singing ballads. All the girls appeared half-starved; some were afflicted with disease, and others had scarce any clothing.

When the officers entered the woman's residence in Marmaduke-court, St George's, they found it in a most filthy state. The woman was in bed drinking gin, and two boys, who exhibit slight[sic.]-of-hand tricks in the streets, were lying by her side. The girls were huddled round a fire, eating potatoes, and, not withstanding their tender age, made use of the most obscene language. The effluvia arising from the place was so great, that the officers could scarcely endure it. A cooper said that one of the children, a girl, twelve years of age, who had neither shoes nor stockings on, and no other clothing other than an old frock, was his daughter. She left his house on Monday, well clad, and was decoyed into the woman's hovel, where her clothing was taken from her. The girl was given to her father, and others were sent – some to the hospital, and some to the parishes to which they belonged. The woman was sent to prison.'

12 March

Blinkers for women

'Blinkers for women', featured in the fashion section of the *Belfast Telegraph* on 12 March 1921, have got to be a candidate for the world's worst-ever fashion innovation.

The newspaper announced them thus:

'Blinkers have been introduced as one of the latest vogues and are already assured of wide popularity. These blinkers, which take the form of highly-decorative little curtains, are arranged on the brim of the hat, and are especially suited to the needs of modest or nervous jurywomen. Flat little panels of lace, tulle or chiffon are placed on either side of the wearer's headgear, and by the use of a simple draw-string, can be brought forward and pulled right across the face at the wearer's will.'

13 March

Domestic violence

In the vast majority of domestic assault cases reported in eighteenth-century newspapers, women were the victims. However, this wasn't always the case, as we can see from this unusual advert placed in *Saunders' Newsletter* on 13 March 1798:

'Whereas, Mary Norton, otherwise Beatty, my wife, has behaved herself in the most improper manner, by cruelly and otherwise assaulting me at several times heretofore, and behaved herself in a violent manner towards me by drunkenness and otherwise. I therefore caution the public from giving her any manner of credit on my account, as I am determined not to honour any debt or debts she may contract, Dated this 8th day of March, 1798. THOMAS BEATTY.'

14 March

'Dead as a mackerel'

On 19 March 1851, The *Ballina Chronicle* reported the following statement from an unnamed prisoner who was tried at Limerick Assizes for burglary on 14 March 1851:

If I committed all the murders and robberies in the county my lord, 'I am as innocent of this charge as the child unborn and I only wish I had half an hour's liberty and I would shoot Malone as dead as a mackerel, the bloody perjured villain. I hope the Lord will take me out of this world soon and I pray to God that my ghost may be an evil spirit and haunt for life everyone who had anything to do in my prosecution. You have all done your best and I don't care a damn for it all, for I could live in a bastable oven if I had only a smoke of a pipe.'

15 March

First maternity hospital

The Dublin Lying-in Hospital, the forerunner of the present-day Rotunda Hospital, opened for business on 15 March 1745 in a house on George's Lane (South Great George's Street) to alleviate the atrocious conditions then experienced by expectant mothers giving birth in the poorer sections of Dublin. Bartholomew Mosse, a native of Maryborough (now Portlaoise), opened his little hospital with only ten beds, and the first baby – a boy – was delivered there five days later. The hospital moved to its present location in December 1757.

16 March

'To make a salutary impression on the spectators'

On St Patrick's Day in 1798, the Dublin newspapers reported on the violent death of Daniel Carroll at Charles Farren's house at the top of Rathmines Road. Carroll was a carter and worked in the service of Farren, who was deputy clerk of the pleas in the Court of the Exchequer.

During the early hours of 16 March, a number of armed men entered the gate lodge of Farren's house and shot Carroll through the head and chest. Suspicion immediately fell on Farren's gardener, a man named Kelly. These suspicions grew stronger when it emerged that Carroll had earlier complained to his master that Kelly had threatened to kill him.

Alderman James, who was investigating the murder, also found that the shotgun that Farren had given to Kelly for his protection had disappeared. Kelly said that it had been stolen by the gang who had murdered Carroll.

The gun was found a few days later in a ditch close to the murder scene, along with a pair of blood-spattered boots belonging to Kelly. A few days after the murder, it was reported in the *Freeman's Journal* that Carroll had been killed because he had refused to join a local branch of the United Irishmen.

Kelly was tried for the murder of Carroll. He was found guilty and sentenced to death, but his execution was postponed 'at the request of the people of Rathgar', who wanted to wait until the trial of the four others accused of aiding and abetting Kelly in the murder was completed.

On Monday, 29 October 1798 three men and a woman – Laurence Rooney, Dennis O'Donnell, Thomas Beahan and Peggy McKeon – went on trial for the crime. Beahan and McKeon were acquitted but Rooney and O'Donnell were found guilty as charged and were sentenced to be publicly hanged along with Kelly in Rathgar.

Two days later, the three men were brought from Kilmainham Jail in a cart to place of execution in Rathgar. At the front of the cart hung the blood-stained shirt of the murdered man which, according to one newspaper report, was placed there 'in order to make a salutary impression on the minds of the uninformed spectators', who had gathered to witness the execution.

Before the noose was placed around his neck, Kelly claimed that the killing of Carroll had been politically motivated and requested that he and his companions be allowed to wear green cockades and ribbons 'to show that they died in the good cause'. The request was turned down.

The three men were duly executed and their bodies were brought back to Dublin for dissection by surgeons in accordance with the terms of the death sentence.

17 March

Bare-knuckles in Ballybough

Jack Langan, the famous bare-knuckle boxer from Ballybough in Dublin, died on St Patrick's Day in 1846. Langan's formative years were spent on Mud Island at Ballybough, infamous as a refuge for highwaymen and thieves, where his family had a small business.

From a very young age Langan had developed a taste for boxing. He is said to have had his first proper bare-knuckle bout – which he won – on the banks of the Royal Canal when he was just thirteen. His opponent on that occasion was five years older and much bigger than him.

Langan gained a formidable reputation as a scrapper in Ballybough. One of these fights is recorded in Pierce Egan's book *Boxiana* published in 1824. According to Egan, Langan once hit an opponent named Savage so hard that he was feared dead. The unfortunate Savage was carried home and his body was prepared for a wake. However, proceedings came to a swift end when Savage sat up abruptly and demanded to know what had happened.

The highlight of Langan's boxing career came when he twice fought Tom Spring, 'Champion of England and all the civilised world', in 1824. The first fight, which lasted for an incredible seventy-seven rounds, took place in front of a huge crowd at Worcester Race Course in England on 7 January 1824. Spring was declared the winner after Langan failed to emerge for the seventy-eighth round. A re-match took place at Birdham Bridge near Chichester in June that year but, after standing toe-to-toe with Spring for seventy-six rounds, Langan lost out again to the English champion.

Although Langan was only twenty-six years old, he retired from the ring after the fights with Spring. He built a pub at Clarence Dock in Liverpool, making enough money from this venture to retire to Neston in Cheshire, where he died at the young age of forty-eight.

18 March

William Crotty

The famous Waterford outlaw and rapparee William Crotty was one of a number of highwaymen who plied their trade in eighteenth-century Ireland. Crotty was born near Russellstown in Waterford sometime around 1712 and is believed to have been the son of an impoverished tenant farmer who had been evicted from his small farm for non-payment of rent.

Some biographers describe Crotty as a 'Robin Hood' character who only robbed the rich for the sole purpose of helping his poorer neighbours, while others note his enthusiasm for hurling, handball and dancing. On the negative side he has been accused of inflicting unnecessary cruelty on his victims. One source goes so far as to claim that he was a cannibal who ate the flesh of his enemies.

By the time Crotty was seventeen he had already earned a notorious reputation for robbery with violence, and for several years he and his gang of rapparees operated with impunity from his stronghold in the Comeragh Mountains.

Crotty was eventually apprehended when he was betrayed by his right-hand man David Norris. On the night of 16 February 1742, while Crotty was staying at Norris's house in the Comeragh Mountains, Norris and his wife drugged him and poured water in his pistols and gunpowder while he was asleep. Norris then alerted the Sub-sheriff of Waterford, who was lying in wait nearby with a detachment of militia. Crotty was subdued and taken to Waterford city in chains.

At his trial on St Patrick's Day in 1742, Crotty and his companions, John Cunningham, William Cunningham and Patrick Hickey, were found guilty of being 'tories, robbers and rapparees and out in arms and on their keeping and not amenable to law'.

Crotty was sentenced to death and was hanged and beheaded at Waterford Jail on 18 March 1742. His head was displayed on a spike over the front gate. His skull continued to be an item of morbid fascination for visitors to Waterford Jail, and local legend has it that hair continued to grow on the skull long after the flesh had rotted.

19 March

Road rage

Road rage is not a new phenomenon in Dublin's fair city and it seems that some Dubliners were intimately acquainted with the concept even before the invention of the motorised vehicle.

One such incident took place on the afternoon of 18 March 1830, while Standish Stamer O'Grady was making his way on horseback through Nassau Street on his way to Merrion Square. At the same time, Captain John Smith of the 32nd Regiment of the British Army and a companion were approaching Nassau Street in a horse and trap from Dawson Street.

Smith drove too close to O'Grady's horse for comfort, and, fearing a collision, O'Grady grabbed Smith's horse by the reins in order to keep him away. Smith took great exception to this interference. He ran after O'Grady and beat him severely across the back and shoulders and once over the head with his whip.

O'Grady didn't return the blows but, as was reported in several newspapers, 'he demanded Smith's card' – meaning he challenged him to a duel. Smith told O'Grady where he could find him, and later that evening O'Grady sent him a message challenging him to a duel with pistols on Kilmainham Commons at dawn the following morning.

The meeting duly took place on 19 March, as arranged. O'Grady, no match for a man of the military prowess of Smith, was fatally wounded in the stomach.

Smith left the scene immediately and O'Grady was carried to a nearby house by four workmen who witnessed the duel. He was taken to Portobello Barracks to the lodgings of his cousin Captain McNamara, where he subsequently died from his injuries. Before he died, O'Grady claimed that Smith had fired at him before he was ready.

It later emerged that the police had gotten wind of the proposed duel on the night before it took place, and they decided to take O'Grady into protective custody. A police officer was despatched to a house on St Stephen's Green, where he mistakenly arrested William O'Grady, Standish's brother. William was detained overnight and the police only realised their mistake later the next day when news of the killing at Kilmainham emerged.

Smith and his second, Captain Markham, were later found guilty of manslaughter and sentenced to two years' imprisonment.

20 March

Arming the postmen

Down through the years there have periodic calls to provide gardaí on the beat with guns, but most people would probably baulk at the idea of arming postal workers with weapons. However, the editorial writer in *Saunders' Newsletter* on 20 March 1786 was led to ask: 'Why could not our mail carts be so contrived, as conveniently to carry a man armed with a blunderbuss? Besides which the post boy could also have pistols in a belt about his waist.'

This proposal was made against the backdrop of increasing mail-coach robberies in Dublin. The writer also recommended the development of what we'd see now as the forerunner to the armour car: '[T]he mail should be confined in the cart, within a strong iron kind of cage, the key of which to be kept only by the respective Postmasters on the road.'

In the same edition of the *Newsletter* it was reported that Alexander McLivery, a young post boy, had been executed at Newgate Prison in Dublin two days earlier for the theft of a number of letters.

21 March

Triple execution in Roscommon

Sixty-year-old Michael Scally and his wife were executed at Roscommon Jail on 21 March 1849 for the murder of Isabella Brennan a year earlier. They had apparently strangled her and dumped her in the River Shannon near Roosky. James Commons, who had been sentenced to death for the murder of Major Mahon, was hanged at the same time.

On 24 March the *Roscommon and Leitrim Gazette* observed that, while all three had confessed their guilt just before they were hanged, they had all declared 'most solemnly' in court 'that they were innocent as the child unborn'.

22 March

Caught her by the ears

Anne Ford of Newmarket in Dublin appeared before Judge O'Donnell on 22 March 1893 on a charge of assaulting another woman. Ford had attacked Mabbot Street woman Kate Williamson the previous day by knocking her to the ground, grabbing her by the ears and beating her head off the pavement. Ford was found guilty of the assault and sentenced to two months in prison with hard labour.

23 March

Sent to prison for twenty-four hours

The following extract appeared in the *Munster News* on 23 March 1874:

'Limerick City Petty Sessions – A little girl was charged by Constable Curran with the larceny of a pair of boots from Mr Herbert's establishment in William Street. Mr Herbert deposed that he saw the prisoner steal the boots. She had been buying another pair of boots from him, and on following her out into the street he found a pair of boots under her arm. Mr Herbert said he did not wish to press the case, as the little girl had got a passage ticket from her mother who was in America, and was about to go away. Mr M. O'Halloran having deposed to this fact, their Worships sent the little girl to prison for twenty-four hours.'

24 March

Mad dog stoned to death

Dublin newspapers reported on the death of a mad dog in Dublin on 24 March 1760. The dog was first spotted on Cork Hill beside Dublin Castle. He was pursued by a mob into Copper Alley, where they stoned him to death 'before he could do any mischief'.

There were many cases concerning rabies and rabid dogs reported in Irish newspapers during this period in history. Once you were bitten by an animal carrying the disease, the results were usually fatal. There was no cure for rabies at that time, but it was reported in the *Dublin Courier* a few weeks after the above incident that a famous French surgeon, Monsieur Petit, had come up with a rather dubious method of ascertaining if a dog had rabies. First you had to kill the rabid dog, then rub its throat, teeth and gums with a piece of meat and offer it to a non-rabid dog. 'If he refuses it, with crying and howling,' said Monsieur Petit, 'the dead dog was certainly mad; but if the victuals have been well received and taken, there is nothing to fear.'

25 March

The miracle of the cross

Under the heading 'Crowds Watch For Cross', the *Irish Press* edition of 25 March 1932 reported that a large crowd had gathered outside the home of Lord Iveagh at 78–81 St Stephen's Green on the previous day, 'waiting and watching for a cross to appear on one of the windows of the house'.

Some of the onlookers told the *Irish Press* that this apparently miraculous occurrence happened every Easter during Holy Week. One man, who claimed he had seen the cross, stated that it 'was of Celtic design and had a purplish outline with a rainbow effect'.

Several onlookers gave a variety of explanations for the phenomenon and one told the *Press* that it had first occurred some years earlier after a young Catholic maid had tried to leave the room to go to mass. Finding the door stuck, she attempted to leave the building via the window, but fell to her death.

A caretaker at the house gave a more plausible explanation for the appearance of the cross. According to him, the house had been unoccupied for a considerable period of time, during which several posters had been pasted on the windows. The posters had been stuck on the windows for so long that after they were taken down they left impressions on the glass. 'In point of fact,' said the caretaker, 'the cross can be seen in any of them on any day of the week, provided that you gaze on them when the sun strikes them at a particular angle.'

26 March

Sweet Vitriol

An article written in the *Christian Herald* on 26 March 1891 made the extraordinary claim that there were 46,000 ether drinkers in the north of Ireland, consuming 18,000 gallons of ether on an annual basis. The claims were dismissed as a gross exaggeration.

During the 1890s there was serious concern expressed in the columns of the press in relation to the practice of ether drinking in some parts of Ireland. Ether drinking was particularly prevalent in the north of the country, mainly in parts of south Derry, Tyrone and Fermanagh.

Ether – discovered in 1275 and originally known as 'sweet vitriol' – was mainly used for medicinal purposes and as an anaesthetic, but during the second half of the nineteenth century it became popular as a cheap alternative to alcohol. The type of ether consumed in Ireland was generally methylated ether, which was exempt from government taxes.

Ether dealers sold the drug at a penny per draught and three draughts were considered to be sufficient to have the desired effect on your average tippler. The attraction of ether was that it allowed drinkers to get drunk much quicker than whiskey, and its effects wore off fairly rapidly, thereby allowing them to get drunk several times in the one day. It was also much cheaper than whiskey.

Another advantage of drinking ether over drinking whiskey or poitín was the lack of a hangover the following morning. However, ether was known to cause depression. Several instances of extreme hysteria and some cases of blindness were attributed to ether abuse. Chronic abusers of ether sometimes reported hearing heavenly music while under the influence and others even claimed to have been visited by angels.

The practice of ether drinking eventually died out after it was reclassified as a poison and its sale was restricted to chemists. This measure led to an immediate 90 per cent fall in consumption, and the drinking of ether was outlawed by the British government in 1923.

27 March

Knocker nickers

It was reported in the Dublin newspapers on 27 March 1827 that three Dublin 'gentlemen' had been caught stealing door knockers in Merrion Square a few nights previously. The men pleaded not guilty to the charge, but the police found a wide variety of brass, bronze and iron knockers in their possession. Treating the incident as a prank, the magistrate fined the men five pounds and ordered them to pay to have all the knockers replaced.

28 March

A drink leads to death

On 28 March 1882, at 1.00 p.m., three young Dublin men – Joe McMahon, Thomas Martin and Edward Brennan – were sitting in the snug of Mrs Dunlap's public house in Dorset Street. Suddenly, there was a loud bang, and customers looked on in amazement as Brennan burst through the snug door and ran from the pub. Behind him on the floor lay two revolvers and the slumped and blood-stained form of his friend Joe McMahon.

Policemen patrolling nearby heard the gun going off and were on the scene in seconds. There they found the dying McMahon lying in the snug with a bullet wound in his chest along with the two revolvers and a dazed-looking Thomas Martin. McMahon was rushed to the nearby Mater Hospital, but he died soon afterwards.

Meanwhile, Edward Brennan was chased along Dorset Street by members of the public, and he was eventually captured in Dominic Street and taken back to Dunlap's. He told police that he had run off to look for a doctor as he had mistakenly shot his friend while inspecting the gun.

The police, however, were not prepared to accept McMahon's death as an accident and believed that all three men were Fenian activists. Their suspicions deepened when they uncovered rifles and ammunition during a search of Martin's house. They also found 144 rounds of ammunition and two bayonets at the dead man's house. The police believed that Brennan and Martin had shot McMahon during a dispute, and both were charged with willful murder and remanded in custody until their trial in June.

While the two men were awaiting trial at Green Street Courthouse, Chief Secretary of Ireland Lord Frederick Cavendish and Undersecretary Thomas Burke were stabbed to death in the Phoenix Park by the Invincibles, a radical republican group. The authorities at Dublin Castle were convinced that Martin and Brennan were part of a greater plot to undermine British rule in Ireland.

When their trials opened on 7 June 1882, Crown prosecutors wanted to know 'what secret obligations these young men were bound to or what they may have been plotting to do' on the day in question. The men were ably defended by Edward Carson, who was a junior barrister at that time. Carson argued that the killing of McMahon had been accidental and without a motive.

The jury was unable to agree on a verdict and the men were sent forward for retrial during the next court session. This time, both men were found guilty of the lesser charge of manslaughter. Thus, they avoided the death penalty, but were sentenced to serve short terms of imprisonment.

29 March

'There's a County Limerick touch for you'

John Deane and Patrick Seymour were charged at Tipperary Assizes on 29 March 1830 with violently assaulting a farmer named John Vaughan during a land dispute.

The incident occurred on 28 June 1829 when a number of men — believed to be Whiteboys — dragged Vaughan out of his home at Combe and cut off his ears. The men took him back into the house where Deane shot him in the leg, saying: 'There's a County Limerick touch for you.'

The Whiteboys were a secret agrarian-based organisation formed to protect the rights of poor tenant farmers and labourers in the 1760s. The organisation — so called because they wore white shirts at night — was particularly active in the counties of Cork, Limerick and Waterford during the 1820s.

Deane and Seymour were found guilty and both were hanged in Clonmel on 15 April. Seymour — a next door neighbour of Vaughan — was believed to have been seventy years old at the time of his execution.

30 March

Medical mix-up

The following is an extract from *Saunders' Newsletter*, 30
March 1878:

'Galway, Friday. – A rather important subject turned
up at the Board of Guardians here today, and one which is
likely to lead to awkward consequences. It appears that last
week two persons died in the Galway Union, one of whom
was claimed by the relatives and the other was unclaimed.
This latter was about being conveyed by night as a subject
for the Anatomical School of the Queen's College, but the
procurator in mistake removed the wrong body. Next day
the funeral took place, and the coffin being light when
they reached the churchyard, as the clergyman was about
reading the service, they removed the lid from the coffin
and the horrible spectacle presented itself of the intestines
of the deceased, and the scene that ensued was lamentable.
The daughter of the deceased madly rushed forward, and
taking all into her apron ran with them to the union, and
threw them at the gate, and the clergyman with difficulty
pacified the people.'

31 March

Cork crime

There were a few harsh sentences handed out by Judge
Torrens at the City Criminal Court in Cork on 31 March
1826. Mr Justice Torrens sat in judgment over a number
of cases, which were mainly of the petty theft variety. First
up was Miles Carland, alias Kearney, who was found guilty
of stealing a considerable amount of silver from his master
Daniel Connor, who lived at the South Mall in Cork. The

defendant was found guilty as charged and sentenced to seven years' transportation.

John Swiney received the same sentence for stealing goods from a shop in Drawbridge Street. Swiney had claimed that he found the goods in a field near Cork, but the jury didn't believe him. Another woman to suffer the sentence of transportation that day was Mary Connor, a habitual offender, who was caught red-handed stealing a cloak from the hall of William Osbourne's house in Castle Street.

APRIL

1 April

'...the eyes were picked out of the head'

In 1767 a Kerry man suffered a horrific fate when he tried to raid the nest of an eagle at the Lakes of Killarney. The *Leinster Journal* of 1 April that year records what happened:

'From Killarney in the county of Kerry, we are told that one Laughlin Brady lately attempted to rob an eagle's nest over the famous lake in that place, when the parent bird was in sight. The eagle flew at him with great fierceness, upon which he tried to make a prudent retreat, but being too precipitate, he slipped from the rock and fell into the lake.

This circumstance would not have been attended with any fatal consequence, as he was an excellent swimmer, had not the eagle pursued him into the water, and striking with unceasing fury at his head, reduced him to the necessity of diving every moment, so that he became quite exhausted at length, and was actually drowned.... [It is] remarkable, that when the body was taken out of the water, the eyes were picked out of the head, and the whole face so dreadfully mangled that a more shocking spectacle could not be raised up to imagination.'

2 April

Three hundred arrests at a cockfight

Three hundred cockfighting fans were arrested in a field near Ballyclare in County Antrim on Monday, 2 April

1923. The cockfight had apparently been in progress for about six hours when it was discovered by a lone member of the Royal Ulster Constabulary (RUC). The crowd attempted to flee, but the RUC man fired his pistol in the air and held them in the field until reinforcements arrived. All three hundred were taken to a nearby farm where they had their names taken.

3 April

Voluntary Starvation

On 3 April 1850 at Birkenhead in Liverpool, an inquest was held into the bizarre death of James Dwyer, a Dublin barrister, who arrived in Liverpool determined to starve himself to death.

Dwyer first appeared in Birkenhead in early March, where he rented a room at a lodging house in Chapel Street. He told the landlady that he was over in Liverpool on business and informed her he wouldn't be taking any meals while he was there. The landlady Mrs Holden told the inquest that Dwyer had eaten nothing for a fortnight. He did drink some ale and water a few nights later, but still refused to eat.

Dwyer went to visit a local surgeon named Edgar and told him that he was suffering from an unspecified disease. He told Edgar that he didn't want any treatment, but said that he wanted to pay the surgeon to do a post-mortem on him as he would be dead in a few weeks. Edgar thought he was joking, but Dwyer persisted and promised the surgeon a guinea to perform the procedure.

The two men met a number of times after that and, although Edgar urged the Irishman to eat, he steadfastly refused to take any food. The surgeon contacted Dwyer's relatives and some of them travelled to Liverpool to try and persuade him to give up his fast. However, Dwyer refused to listen to them and he died soon afterwards.

Edgar told the inquest that he believed the dead man has been suffering from monomania (partial insanity) and the jury returned a verdict that Dwyer had 'died by the visitation of God'.

4 April

Child trampled to death in Limerick

A young boy named Thomas Kent was killed when a party of armed insurgents broke into his father's house at Ballinaholee near Pallaskenry in Limerick on the night of 4 April 1825. The men – believed to be Rockites, a militant agrarian movement – entered the house and attacked John Kent, flogging him severely. It's not certain if the child was deliberately attacked, but it was reported that he was trampled on after his cradle was overturned during the assault of his father. He died the following day.

Another man, Michael Meade, who lived nearby, was attacked in the same fashion and seriously injured. There was a great deal of Rockite activity in that area at the time and a few weeks later the following notice was posted in Ballinaholee:

'Take notice – I do hereby caution any person sending a man or horse to work on the lands of Ballinaholee to James Hill that I will cut off their ears from the roof of their scull, and I caution the said James Hill not to go to any further trouble on these lands as he shall never enjoy the benefit of them, if he was guarded by all the Peelers and Soldiers in the County of Limerick. JOHN ROCK.'

5 April

Michael Collins hanged

Michael Collins made an extraordinary last confession at the foot of the gallows in Waterford, admitting to two murders and three robberies – crimes that five other men had already been executed for. Collins, who was twenty-three, was hanged on 5 April 1759.

An extract from *Pue's Occurences* on 7 April, referring to the hanging of Collins, states:

'Last Saturday Michael Collins, aged 23, was executed at Waterford for a rape on Margaret Bryen. He confessed at the Gallows to be the Person that murdered Mr. Butler and his Wife; John Leary, near Feathard-Hill, and robbing three other Persons; for all which Crimes, Thomas Gibbons, Thomas Cooney, Daniel Dwyer, and Patrick and James Drishloe, were tried, found guilty and executed, on the evidence of said Collins; he declared that they were all innocent, and that he only was the Person concerned in those horrid Crimes.'

6 April

'Choked by the hangman'

A family quarrel in County Meath in 1889 led to the deaths of two men – one by gun and the other by hangman's noose.

The *Freeman's Journal* on 6 April 1889 recorded the events:

'Unless a respite arrives tomorrow Peter Stafford will be executed at Kilmainham Jail on Monday for the murder of Peter Crawley. The condemned man was convicted at the last Maryborough Assizes and was sentenced to death on the 8th March by Judge Holmes.

The condemned man was a labourer, and lived at a place called Ballyhoe in the county of Meath. The evidence at the trial showed that the deceased was shot by Stafford three times in the body on the 28th January last, and that he expired from the wounds on the 1st February. It appeared that there had been a family quarrel between the men .... If the execution takes place, the gallows will be that upon which some of the Invincibles were hanged.'

The execution did take place, and Peter Stafford was hanged at Kilmainham two days later. The black flag was hoisted over the prison at 8.03p.m. to indicate to the large crowd gathered outside that the sentence of execution had been carried out.

Among the crowd were Stafford's wife and brother. When she saw the flag, Stafford's distraught wife asked the question, 'Have they choked him yet?' The execution was carried out by Britain's travelling hangman James Berry.

7 April

Dublin woman shoots Mussolini

On Wednesday, 7 April 1926, newspapers all over the world reported on the attempted assassination of Italian dictator and fascist leader Benito Mussolini. He had just emerged from a conference in Rome when a middle-aged woman brandishing a pistol fired a single shot at the dictator, hitting him in the nose. The woman was immediately set upon by the angry crowd, which tried to lynch her, but she was rescued – on the orders of the injured Mussolini – and taken to a nearby prison.

It later emerged that the assailant was fifty-year-old Dalkey woman Violet Albina Gibson, a sister of Lord

Ashbourne, a prominent member of the Gaelic League in Dublin. When questioned by the Carabinieri about her motive for the attack, Gibson – who suffered from violent delusions and 'religious mania' – told her captors that 'supernatural forces entrusted me with the lofty mission of attempting to kill Mussolini.'

Gibson's sister Constance said that Gibson had become unstable following the death of her brother some years earlier and had spent some time living in a mental institution. It also emerged that Gibson had threatened to kill the Pope on a number of occasions.

In the days following the attack, Mussolini reportedly received thousands of telegrams congratulating him on his survival, including one from the President of the Irish Free State William T. Cosgrave, who congratulated Il Duce on his escape from 'this odious attempt' on his life.

Violet Gibson remained in custody in Rome for the next year while she underwent a rigorous psychological examination by the Italian authorities. She was found to be suffering from delusions, declared insane and deported to England, where she remained in a mental hospital until her death in 1956.

8 April

'Cowardly hirelings of Britain'

Irish and British newspapers published an account of an altercation on the streets of Limerick on 8 April 1877 between members of the public and soldiers of the 90th Regiment of the British Army, which was then stationed in the city. It was reported in some newspapers that there were ructions in the city when British soldiers attacked an elderly woman without provocation.

The *Connaught Telegraph* of 14 April published the following report on the incident:

'Bravo Limerick! The *Daily Express* headline read with an account of a collision, which occurred on Sunday night between the soldiers of the 90th Regiment and a number of inoffensive civilians. According to our Tory contemporary the redcoats began the onslaught by maltreating a poor old woman. This dastardly conduct aroused the indignation of the lookers-on, who soon taught the cowardly soldiers a lesson they will not soon forget.

A handful of boys and women chased the gallant 90th through the streets of the City of Sarsfield, and showed themselves more than a match for the vaunted hirelings of Britain. The uniformed heroes, after one feeble effort, sought refuge in flight, and were pursued to the very gates of the barrack by the indignant crowd. One soldier sought to escape dressed in female attire – a garb which admirably suited his craven temperament. Every true Irishman must feel glad that military insolence has at last received an effective check ....As it is, there is, we believe little cause to fear that the gallant 90th will attack any more old women during their stay in Limerick...'.

9 April

Unfriendly welcome for Duke

On the morning of 9 April 1885, during a royal visit to Ireland, the prince of Wales, accompanied by his son the Duke of Clarence, two military officers and Dr Charles Cameron, president of the College of Surgeons and chief medical officer of Dublin, left Dublin Castle in a private coach to inspect the slums at Golden Lane, which were described by the *Times* in London as 'both physically and morally one of the worst purlieus of the city'.

As the royal party descended from their carriage in Golden Lane, a woman emerged from one of the tenements and emptied a bucket of 'foul water' into the gutter beside the carriage. The Duke of Clarence duly slipped and fell into the gutter. The young duke's clothes were ruined in the incident, and he was forced to spend the rest of the morning traipsing around the streets of Dublin in a borrowed coat that was several sizes too big for him.

The prince didn't fare much better on his trip to Cork a week later. The royal party received a warm reception at Cork train station, but some Corkonians were less than thrilled with the visit and, when the prince was crossing Parnell Bridge in his open carriage, someone in the crowd threw an onion at him, narrowly missing him and striking his footman.

A man was later arrested for stoning the royal party, and a riot ensued when his friends tried to rescue him. Later that evening, large numbers of Parnellites, who were opposed to the royal visit, burned loyalist memorabilia, including decorations and newspapers commemorating the royal visit. Many demonstrators were hurt in what were described as 'savage' clashes with the police.

10 April

Crime watch

There were some interesting court cases and crimes listed in the *Newry Examiner* on 10 April 1833. One of the main reports was from the Newry Quarter Sessions court concerning a major sectarian riot in Newry on 18 March of that year. Twenty-seven men – thirteen Catholic and fourteen Protestant – were indicted for riot and affray in High Street. Seventeen were given lengthy prison sentences and a variety of lesser punishments were handed down.

Meanwhile, in Derry, a young boy named William Hegarty was transported for life for stealing a cow, while Bernard McCloskey received the same sentence for stealing a horse. Bernard Callaghan was sentenced to death for uttering a forged note and escaping from the Magherafelt Bridewell with his wife Jane two years earlier. Jane was acquitted. Owen McCloskey was bound over to keep the peace, having been convicted of the 'blowing of horns and playing of fifes, exciting alarm in his Majesty's peaceable subjects'.

The *Examiner* also reported on the jovial demeanour of three men who had been hanged at Maryborough (now Portlaoise) Prison for murder a few weeks earlier. The three men, John and James Holmes and Charles Thompson, were executed for the murder of a man named William Brown. Far from being subdued by their impending fate, the condemned men laughed and joked as they were being led to the gallows. While waiting to be hanged, James Holmes called out to the executioner, 'Billy, come here and fix the rope around my neck. It is too loose!'

11 April

Get thee out of the nunnery

Nuns at a newly built convent in Ardee, County Louth were alarmed when a gang of desperadoes forced their way into the nunnery late on Monday, 11 April 1859. The nuns heard the gang breaking in and they immediately bolted themselves into their sleeping quarters. The gang escaped with five pounds in cash and a few other items.

12 April

Harvey Duff

Tommy Fitton, aged seven, and Dan Hanrahan, aged nine, two schoolchildren — from Newcastle West in County Limerick, were arrested on 12 April 1881 on a charge of seditious whistling. The two children were arrested after whistling the tune of 'Harvey Duff' at police as they passed by. Harvey Duff was a villainous character and police informer from Dion Boucicault's play *The Shaughran*. To call someone Harvey Duff or whistle the tune in their presence was akin to calling them a traitor.

The police took the two boys and lodged them in the black hole at the barracks in Newcastle West, where they were held overnight. Dan Hanrahan was beaten by one of the policemen. The next day, the police, who completely overreacted in this case, marched the two little boys to the courthouse under an armed guard. There they were given a telling off by the magistrate and released without charge.

Later that year, in August, another man whistling the tune in Newcastle was arrested and charged with abusive language. The following year, a policeman named Bassett struck a little girl at Cappamore in County Limerick and killed her after she and her friends had whistled the Harvey Duff tune in his presence.

There were numerous other incidents in relation to the Harvey Duff tune. The police attacked a fife and drum band in Dublin for playing it in 1882 and it was said that a Derry donkey became famous because of its ability to bray the tune.

13 April

Quaker school of the banned

The Religious Society of Friends, more commonly known as the Quakers, has been active in Dublin since the middle of the seventeenth century. The term 'Quaker' is said to originate from the fits of trembling experienced by church members at their services.

In 1839 some of Dublin's wealthier Quakers, including members of the Bewley and Pim families, joined forces to open a boarding school at no. 29 Upper Camden Street. The school was called The Friends' Boarding School and it opened with four pupils on 17 February 1840. There was a heavy emphasis on the teaching of languages at the school. Other subjects taught were mental arithmetic, mnemonics, book-keeping and woodwork.

During leisure time, traditional children's games such as leapfrog and skipping were encouraged, as was the reading of 'suitable' material such as biographies and travelogues. The reading of fiction was banned as it was deemed to have 'an injurious effect on young minds', and the reading of newspapers was also discouraged.

Playing marbles and chess was also banned at the Camden Street school. The Quakers objected to marbles as they saw it as the first step on the slippery slope to gambling. Chess was forbidden because it was too exciting and promoted 'undesirable habits of mind', and led to mental and physical exhaustion.

Other items on the banned list were singing, playing musical instruments and cricket. It seems that the game of cricket in itself was approved of; the problem lay in the cricket clubs which were deemed to be places where one's 'moral and religious interest might be greatly endangered'.

The Friends' Boarding School ran into financial difficulties not long after opening. For whatever the reason, the school failed to attract enough pupils to allow it to be financially viable and it was closed on 13 April 1844.

14 April

Patrick Street tragedy

It was a black day for Dublin on 14 April 1861, when ten people died in a blaze at a tenement house in Patrick Street, one of the poorest areas of the city. On the night of the fire, no fewer than thirty-two people were crammed into the crumbling tenement building at no. 9 Patrick Street.

The blaze was first noticed at 1.30 a.m. when the alarm was raised. The majority of the residents escaped from the building with their lives, but when the flames died down later that day, ten charred bodies were removed from the ashes. Most of the dead were children. A Mrs Reilly and her five children – aged between seven and eighteen years – accounted for six of the dead. The others were John and Rose McGarry, aged three and five, and William and James Forsythe, aged two and four years. Another child who was seriously injured in the blaze died later.

15 April

The prince's apprentice

It was reported on 15 April 1790 that a man named Redmond, an accomplice of the notorious 'Prince of pickpockets' George Barrington, had escaped from Newgate Prison in Dublin. Redmond, who had been convicted in Dublin's Tholsel Court and sentenced to transportation, had escaped on 12 April and had frustrated all efforts to recapture him. It was suspected that a young prison hatch boy named Nulty had colluded with Redmond in the escape, and he himself was lodged in the prison.

16 April

Sentenced to be burnt

The *Cork Evening Post* of 16 April 1781 reported on the execution in Cork of John Daly and Julia Geran for the murder of Geran's husband James. At their trial, which took place at the county court three days earlier, Daly was sentenced to death by hanging and quartering, while Geran and another woman Catherine Donoghue were sentenced to death by burning. The sentence of burning was almost exclusively reserved for women and took place after they had been hanged. Donoghue was reprieved just before the execution was to be carried out.

The sentences were duly carried out at Gallows Green in Cork. It is interesting to note that two others were sentenced to death in the same court on the same day for seemingly lesser crimes than the one committed by Daly and Geran. Michael Scannell was sentenced to death for burglary, while Patrick Connelly was capitally convicted for cattle theft.

17 April

A frequenter of the pushing school

James Hamilton of Kilmore in County Down was 'turned off', a contemporary term for hanged, at the scaffold in Downpatrick on 17 April 1714 for the murder of a pedlar named William Lammon on 5 March of that year. Before he was hanged, Hamilton lamented the fact that he had become 'saucy' and vain and had spent his time dancing and visiting 'pushing schools' or brothels. He asked for forgiveness for his crime and dissolute lifestyle, which he said included, 'sotting and drinking, horrid swearing and gaming…' (from *The Last Speech and Dying Words of James Hamilton*, printed by Hugh Broun, Glasgow, 1714).

18 April

Rabid dog pole-axed in Sackville Street

There was consternation on the streets of Dublin on Sunday, 18 April 1880 when a large rabid dog – described as a water spaniel – ran amok in Sackville Street, now O'Connell Street, barking furiously and attacking several pedestrians, seriously injuring two people. The dog was pursued by Constable 164c of the Dublin Metropolitan Police and a large crowd, who chased him into Henry Street and then into Moore Street. The rabid animal took refuge in a house in Sampson's Lane, where he was cornered and killed with a pole-axe.

19 April

Teacher hanged for high treason

On the morning of 19 April 1700, Antrim schoolteacher John Larkin, alias Robert Young, was taken from his cell in Newgate Prison in London and dragged on a sledge to the gallows at Tyburn, where he was hanged. Larkin had been charged with high treason and was condemned to death for counterfeiting money.

Larkin had studied Philosophy at Glasgow University in Scotland as a young man and he returned to Antrim where he became a teacher. Growing restless, he became a minister and travelled around Ireland for a time. Eventually he ended up as a minister at a school in Lancashire in England.

However, Larkin had expensive tastes and he soon found that his meagre salary was not enough to support his extravagant lifestyle. He became involved in a variety of scams and established himself as an expert forger and counterfeiter. He was eventually caught, pilloried and sent to prison. While he was in prison, Larkin became involved in a coining enterprise that led to his ultimate downfall.

20 April

Hangman attacked by Cork mob

Jeremiah Twomey was hanged at Gallows Green in Cork on 20 April 1767 for the murder of publican Robert Norton at Crosses Green. Twomey and his accomplices had attacked Norton with swords while robbing his house, and Mrs Norton was badly beaten during the raid.

Twomey continued to protest his innocence right to the very end. After the hangman had finished with him, Twomey's friends and relatives cut down his lifeless body and carried it to Mrs Norton's house, where they proceeded to smash all the windows. The widow managed to fend the mob off with a pistol until the sheriff arrived with a party of soldiers to disperse them. The night passed without further incident.

But the drama didn't end there. On the day after Twomey's execution, the hangman was spotted near the North Gate in Cork and he was chased out of the city. The mob caught up with him near Glasheen and pelted him with sticks and stones, leaving him for dead. He was eventually rescued by the Sheriff and taken to the charitable infirmary in Cork.

It seems that the mob was particularly upset with the executioner because he had taken Twomey's shoes from him as his body was hanging from the scaffold.

21 April

Disorder and disgrace

'Disunion, disorder, disgrace' was one disgusted report-er's judgment of this Gaelic Athletic Association football match played in Balla, County Mayo on 21 April 1889. In his article in the *Mayo Examiner*, the reporter states that the season was going swimmingly until this county championship game between Balla Granuailes and Castlebar Mitchels descended into violence. The writer blamed the Balla team for 'having brought about a state of affairs than which nothing more reprehensible has yet been witnessed in connection with Gaelic contests'.

The Castlebar Mitchels team had already been threatened on their way to the game and, straight from the throw-in, 'play of unusual roughness' resulted in a number of severe injuries to the Mitchels players. One of them was head-butted in the stomach, even though the ball was at the other end of the pitch at the time.

The reporter complained that there were no markings on the pitch, the Balla umpire overruled the referee at every possible opportunity and Balla supporters made numerous 'hostile' incursions on to the field of play and refused to leave when asked by the referee. Balla Granuailes won the game by a controversial goal, scored in the dying seconds of the game, by which time several Mitchels players were off the pitch due to injury.

22 April

Johanna Lovett

The biggest crowd in living memory turned up in front of Tralee Jail on 22 April 1822 for the hanging of Johanna

Lovett as, according to *Chute's Western Herald* on that day, 'there had been no execution of a female in this county, since that of Nancy Cody, for the murder of Patrick Hands the Gaoler, near 40 years since.'

Lovett was being executed for the murder of her former husband Thomas Creane. Just before she was hanged, Lovett – who had delivered a baby just three weeks earlier – blamed her lover, and current husband, Thomas Lovett, for the murder. She said that she had played no part in the killing, but she acknowledged that she hadn't done anything to prevent it either. She also repented for having co-habited with Lovett and vehemently denied that she 'had misconducted herself with other men'.

Thomas Lovett had been hanged a few weeks earlier for Creane's murder, but Johanna's execution was delayed because of her pregnancy.

23 April

St George's Day in Dublin

South Great George's Street in Dublin, known as George's Lane until the middle of the eighteenth century, was named after St George's Church, built in honour of St George, patron saint of England, dragon slayer, protector of women and all-round philanthropist. The church was built outside the city walls during the early part of the thirteenth century.

During medieval times, the religious guild of St George was attached to this church, and every St George's Day, 23 April, it was the guild's duty to drape the church with black cloth and to provide a dragon for the parade.

Richard Stanihurst, in his description of Dublin in 1577, had some interesting things to say in relation to

George's Lane, 'where in old times were builded diverse old and ancient monuments'.

Stanihurst said that this could have been one of the better areas of Dublin if it had not been for the fact that its inhabitants were 'being daily and hourly molested and preyed [upon] by their prowling mountain neighbours', forcing them to abandon their homes and retreat inside the relative safety of the city walls.

Stanihurst also mentioned St George's Church, which he supposed was built by 'some worthy knight of the garter', and tells us that the mayor and corporation of Dublin went there annually on St George's Day to pay homage to the saint.

He also had some choice words to say in relation to the City Assembly which had recently demolished the church and used the stones to build a common oven, thereby, as he acidly observed, 'converting the ancient monument of a doughty, adventurous and holy knight, to the coal-rake sweeping of a puff loaf baker'.

24 April

Tragedy at chimney sweep's whipping

In April 1815, a tragedy occurred when a stone balcony collapsed at the Royal Exchange in Dublin's Dame Street, killing nine people. Thousands had gathered there to witness the public whipping of chimney sweep John Young, for cruelty to his apprentice, a six-year-old boy named William Cullen.

Young had been found guilty on 11 April of inflicting wounds on the child's back, stomach and sides with a whip, and for lighting fires under him while he was cleaning chimneys.

One witness, a Mr A. Murphy of South Anne Street, said that he had employed Young to clean his chimney. Young had refused to go up the chimney himself because it was too narrow, so he tied a rope around the boy's leg and forced him to climb up instead. When the job was finished, Young pulled the boy back down the chimney. Murphy noticed that little boy was covered in sores, and he immediately took him to the Lord Mayor, who had the sweep arrested.

Young was found guilty of cruelty, and he was sentenced to be whipped from Green Street to the Royal Exchange. The sentence was to be repeated two months later and followed by two years in prison.

The first part of the sweep's punishment was carried out on 24 April 1815, and thousands gathered to witness the event. However, too many people had gathered on the balcony of the Royal Exchange and it gave way, killing nine people and injuring many more.

Despite the catastrophe, the authorities went ahead with the punishment of the chimney sweep and he was given 421 lashes and committed to Newgate Prison to serve out his sentence.

25 April

Bullock battle

Down through the ages, Bullock Harbour was a popular rendezvous point for smugglers and pirates, and there have been many tales recorded in relation to conflict with the forces of law and order.

The *Dublin Weekly Journal* of 25 April 1735 reported that two smugglers had been killed during a major clash with the customs men:

'Last week some of the King's officers made a seizure of a large quantity of tea and brandy at Bullock, and next morning several persons attempted to rescue it from the officers, which occasioned a great battle, in which several were wounded on both sides; one Mr. Brown, an officer, was shot through the thigh, and 'Tis thought two of the smugglers were killed.'

26 April

Eaten by rats

An inquest was held in Dublin on 26 April 1910 into the gruesome death of an elderly woman named Anne Isabella Robertson, who had been found in her home in Herbert Road, Ballsbridge. She had apparently been dead for about a week and her body had been partially eaten by rats.

Miss Robertson, who lived alone, was found by her gardener John White after neighbours became concerned that they hadn't seen her for a few days. White enlisted the help of Dublin Metropolitan Police Sergeant J.R. Gray, who broke into the house and found the deceased woman in a bedroom at the back of the house. Miss Robertson was almost naked, and her feet and ankles had been eaten by rodents.

The coroner heard evidence that the house had been in a filthy condition. A large sum of money had been found in the house and it was reported that Miss Robertson – who was considered to have been a bit of an eccentric – refused to have anyone into the house to help her.

27 April

Boy hangs himself in Belfast prison

A particularly shocking event occurred in Crumlin Road Jail in Belfast on 27 April 1858. Thirteen-year-old orphan

Patrick Magee, who had been convicted of stealing earlier that month and sentenced to three months' hard labour, was found hanged in his cell. The terrified child had fashioned a noose from his hammock and tied it to the bars of his cell.

Magee wasn't the youngest boy to be locked up in the 'Crum'. In 1826, six-year-old John Cullen was sentenced to a year's imprisonment for stealing shawls from a shop in Belfast. Cullen was said to have been so small that the judge couldn't see him in the dock at his trial.

28 April

Match of the Lord's Day

'A great match at football' was played between the bakers and the brewers at Dublin's Royal Hospital in Kilmainham on Sunday, 28 April 1765. There was no match report in the papers at the time, but thousands were reported to have watched the game 'to the great detriment of the improvements thereabouts and to the scandalous Breach of the Lord's Day' (*Freeman's Journal*, 30 April 1765).

29 April

Abandoned in a pig-sty

A new-born baby, abandoned by his mother near Newry, County Down in 1813, survived a night in a pigsty thanks to the protection of a farmer's dog.

Saunders' Newsletter, published on 29 April 1813, recorded the following:

'Some time ago an inhuman wretch had by night placed a new-born babe close to a farmer's pig-sty, in the townland of Benagh, about six miles from Newry. In the morning the poor infant was found surrounded by the swine. Providence, however, had not left the helpless innocent unprotected. A large mastiff dog, belonging to the farmer, stood over, and, like a faithful guardian, kept all the voracious animals at a distance. The baby was found alive in this extraordinary situation. It has since been baptized by the name of John Benagh, and sent to the Foundling Hospital in this city.'

30 April

Kilmallock martyr

Maurice MacKenraghty, a Limerick-born priest, was hanged in Clonmel on 30 April 1585. He was executed during a turbulent period in Irish history when many Catholics were being persecuted for practising their faith. MacKenraghty had served as a chaplain to the Earl of Desmond during the Second Desmond Rebellion, which ended in 1583. He was captured in September of that year and incarcerated in Clonmel Jail in Tipperary, where he was held in chains for long periods.

At Easter in 1585, Clonmel man Victor White bribed the jailer to release MacKenraghty to say mass. However, the jailer double-crossed White and told the authorities that the priest would be serving mass at a house in Clonmel the following day. The house was surrounded, but MacKenraghty managed to escape. However, he gave himself up when he heard that White was going to be executed in his place.

McKenraghty was dragged at the back of a horse to the the market square in Clonmel on 30 April and hanged. His remains were exhibited in the square for a few days before being handed over to local supporters who buried him.

Maurice MacKenraghty was beatified in 1992 by Pope John Paul II.

MAY

1 May

The May bush

Many years ago in Dublin, one of the most eagerly antici-
pated days in the social calendar was the annual May Day
celebration. It wasn't universally welcomed, but in some
parts of the city, especially in the Liberties, the day was
celebrated with great vigour and enthusiasm by the working classes.

One of the main features of the day was the decorating
of the May bush, and the various Dublin gangs vied with
each other in their efforts to have the biggest and best
decorated tree. This quest often led to conflict with the
municipal authorities as the gangs travelled far and wide in
their search for a suitable tree. The gardens of the wealthy
were considered fair game to the gangs, and every year, as
May Day approached, the city's newspapers were full of
'tree outrage' stories.

May Day in 1774 was no different and there were a
number of incidents in the city during the days leading
up to the festival. It was reported in the *Hibernian Journal*
on 27 April that many of the 'gentry, nobility and farmers'
of Dublin were arming themselves in order to protect
themselves from the nocturnal tree thieves.

The Lord Mayor of Dublin issued instructions that
anyone caught felling a tree during the hours of darkness
was to be treated as a felon, and ordered a complete ban on
May bushes being brought into the city.

Eight men were arrested in Dorset Street and lodged
in Kilmainham Jail for cutting down four huge trees in

Santry, 'which they brought on cars in great triumph to Dublin'. It was reported that another large tree had been felled in Harold's Cross on the same day and a tall elm tree was erected in New Street. The tree was later cut down by a detachment of the Poddle Guard in front of 'a prodigious number of desperate vagabonds'.

Meanwhile, a man named James Leeson had his skull fractured during a row over a maypole in Dolphin's Barn.

2 May

Stoned in Gloucester Street

A little boy named Michael Riordan of no. 6 Beaver Street in Dublin's north inner city was hauled before the courts in Dublin on 2 May 1892 on a charge of throwing stones at the Salvation Army. The Salvation Army were parading through Gloucester Street followed by a hostile crowd. The constable who arrested Riordan saw the boy throw a number of stones at the procession. He was fined ten shillings. If he defaulted, he would be imprisoned for seven days.

3 May

Repentant Ribbonman

On Wednesday, 3 May 1820, a young Sligo man, Thomas Collery, who had been convicted of burglary, Ribbonism[*] and the larceny of firearms was hanged in front of Sligo Jail. As was usual on these occasions, a huge crowd turned up to witness the spectacle. It was reported that Collery

---

[*] The Ribbon Society was a secret Catholic tenant farmers' organisation, formed in opposition to the activities of landlords and their agents.

seemed resigned to his fate and was at peace with himself during his final hours.

He climbed the scaffold and addressed the crowd. Speaking in Irish, Collery confessed that he had stolen firearms on a number of occasions and he urged those present not to follow the path that he had chosen. He attributed his fall from grace to the evil practices of 'night-walking, dissipation and attending wakes', along with a few other bad habits.

He ended what was described as a long and eloquent speech by urging his friends and neighbours to attend to their religious duties and, strangely enough for a man who had been convicted of Ribbonism, by admonishing them to obey the law and the government.

Having said his piece, the rope was placed around his neck, and Collery was hanged at precisely 2.00 p.m.

4 May

Butterly and Ennis

Two young women, Bridget Butterly, aged nineteen, and Bridget Ennis, aged twenty-one, were publicly hanged at Kilmainham Jail in Dublin on 4 May 1821 for the murder of a Miss Thompson at Captain Peck's house in Portland Place, Dublin. The nineteen-year-old Thompson was Captain Peck's mistress at the time of the murder.

Bridget Butterly – a former servant at Peck's house – had been a previous mistress of Captain Peck. Peck had sacked her after she had a miscarriage. Butterly and her friend Ennis had decided to rob Peck's house and go to England with the proceeds, but Butterly beat Thompson to death with a poker in the course of the robbery.

Thousands turned up to witness the double execution, which took place in front of Kilmainham Jail. It was reported that, while Butterly died instantly, her accomplice Bridget Ennis had a much harder death, 'convulsing' at the end of the rope.

Despite the fact that Ennis suffered an appalling death, there seemed to be more sympathy shown afterwards in the *Freeman's Journal* for a 'poor dog' who was hacked to pieces at the execution by the Horse Police. The dog found itself surrounded by the horsemen, who were keeping the crowd at bay at the front of Kilmainham Jail:

'The riders amused themselves by cutting at the animal until it was literally hewn to pieces!! We confess that we never witnessed a more brutal or a more wanton piece of barbarity. The time, the place, and circumstance, under which the poor animal was immolated, add ferocity to the act for which the perpetrators deserve the severest punishment; it was most scandalous and base!'

5 May

Extraordinary feat

A man, described as middle-aged, took on a novel challenge in Kells, County Meath on 5 May 1859 when he wagered that he could walk two miles around the town in sixteen minutes, carrying a fifty-six pound weight with his teeth for the last halfmile.

The man began his challenge at the high cross in Kells, walked on to the National Bank and then went back around the town at a good pace. For the last half mile, he carried the weight suspended from his teeth with a handkerchief and he completed his task with one minute to spare. The man rested for a minute and then proceeded to entertain the assembled crowd with feats of strength without any signs of tiredness.

A report on the event in the *Meath Herald* a few days later described the man as an Englishman and 'an old traveller, as both his arms were tattooed all over, and in addition to being much browned by the sun, he wore small earrings'.

6 May

Allen's Court Nunnery

A notice in the *Hibernian Journal* on 6 May 1772 read:

'A shopkeeper in New Row [Dublin] is requested by a female correspondent to choose a more proper place for letting his horse to mares, than in the view of the windows of Allen's Court Nunnery, as such an indelicate sight must necessarily shock the modesty of the religious ladies who live there.'

7 May

Crime in Dungarvan

The Justiciar of Ireland Thomas Fitzmaurice was a busy man on 7 May 1295 when he hanged eight men and one woman for a range of petty crimes in Dungarvan, County Waterford.

Nicholas, the baker, was hanged for stealing malt and oats worth four shillings, while Walter Oteruey suffered the ultimate sanction for sheep stealing. Maurice Oshynny, Thomas Saus, Thomas le Waleis, Crachyn Galgaryg, Aulef O'Donegan and Donkud O' Huroc all suffered the same fate for a range of non-violent crimes.

There was no discrimination on the grounds of gender. Fitzmaurice also hanged Alice le Lunt who was found guilty of stealing money from her father and other robberies.

8 May

VE Day in Dublin

As millions of people gathered all over Europe to celebrate the end of World War II on 8 May 1945, the nights following VE Day in Dublin were anything but peaceful.

The incidents began on 7 May when some pro-British Trinity students hoisted a Union Jack, a Russian flag, the French tricolour and a bedraggled and dirty Irish tricolour on the flagpole at Trinity – with the Union Jack on top and the Irish national flag at the bottom.

Approximately one hundred students had assembled on the roof of the college and a large crowd – which included future Taoiseach Charles Haughey – quickly gathered outside on College Green. Insults were traded back and forth and two young men climbed a lamp post on the green and set fire to a Union Jack. The students on the roof retaliated by singing 'God Save the King'.

By that time, the crowd outside had swelled to several thousand, and an attempt was made to storm the college gates. It was repelled by the Gardaí and Trinity security staff. The students then took down the flags and set fire to the tricolour on a parapet. They threw it down behind the Oliver Goldsmith statue, but one young man retrieved the flag, doused the flames and hung it on the college railings.

Throughout the next day, there was sporadic scuffling in the city when Trinity students, wearing red, white and blue ribbons, periodically clashed with their University College Dublin counterparts, who wore green, white and orange colours.

Trouble broke out again later that night when thousands gathered again on College Green following a number of provocative flag displays from the Trinity students. Union Jacks being periodically flown from windows at the college invariably met with a hail of stones and bottles from the outside. Many windows were smashed, and a large number of protesters were arrested.

The rioting spilled over into other parts of Dublin, and the windows of the *Irish Times* offices in Westmoreland Street were broken. The windows of the British Representative's Office and the American Consulate General were also smashed.

The demonstrators eventually dispersed at 10.00 p.m. when a thunderstorm broke out. Six young men were later charged with minor offences, ranging from disorderly behaviour to stone throwing, and all received fines or were given the benefit of the Probation Act.

9 May

Colonel Blood

Meath man Colonel Thomas Blood will go down in history as the man who stole the Crown Jewels from the Tower of London on 9 May 1671 and lived to tell the tale.

Blood, who owned a small house in Dunboyne, County Meath was born in in 1617 or 1618. He spent much of his early life in England, and when the English Civil War broke out in 1641, Blood initially fought on the side of Charles I, but later abandoned him to join Oliver Cromwell's parliamentarian army.

Blood was involved in a number of daring schemes during his life, including a failed plot to seize Dublin Castle and kidnap Earl of Ormond and Lord Lieutenant of Ireland James Butler in May 1663. However, Blood embarked on his most audacious scheme in May 1671 when he attempted to steal the Crown Jewels from the Tower of London. The jewels were kept in the basement of the Tower where they were guarded by Talbot Edwards, assistant keeper of the Crown Jewels, who lived in the Tower with his family.

Blood went to the Tower disguised as a parson and using the pseudonym Doctor Ayliffe. He managed to gain the confidence of Edwards over a period of time. The 'parson' eventually suggested a match between Edwards' daughter and his own 'nephew', who was in fact his son Thomas. On 9 May 1671, the 'parson' and his 'nephew' and two other men arrived at the Tower. While Thomas junior was chatting to Edwards' daughter, the elder Blood suggested that the keeper take him and his friends for a private viewing of the Crown Jewels.

When the unsuspecting Edwards let the men into the room where the treasure was kept, he was overpowered and knocked unconscious. Blood grabbed the crown, crushing it flat so that he could conceal it under his cloak. His accomplices took the sceptre and orb and they all prepared to flee.

However, while they attempted to make their escape, Edwards regained consciousness and managed to raise the alarm. Following a short struggle, during which several shots were fired, Blood and his accomplices were captured and imprisoned in the Tower.

During questioning, Blood refused to talk to anyone else but King Charles II, and to everyone's amazement Charles agreed to his request and met him three days later. Nobody knows exactly what transpired during their meeting, but Blood, instead of being hanged by the neck as everyone expected, was freed three months later. Even more astonishingly, he received a full pardon and was given lands in Ireland worth £500 per annum.

It's not exactly clear why Blood was treated so leniently, but it is believed that he acted as a spy for the king in later years and provided him with intelligence on his former Cromwellian friends.

He died at his home in Westminster on 24 August 1680 at the age of sixty-two and was buried at Tothill Fields in London.

10 May

Palmerstown axe man

On 10 May 1310 Richard le Noble stood trial for chasing Robert Makartan through the streets of Palmerstown in Dublin with an axe. The reason for the attack is not given in the court records, but le Noble is stated to have struck the victim a blow with the axe out on the street. When the terrified victim locked himself into his house for safety, le Noble broke down the door with the axe and chased him to Avelan le Hore's house nearby. He broke one of her windows in an attempt to get at the injured man, but he was prevented from doing any further damage by some locals who went to Makartan's aid. Le Noble was found not guilty by the jury and acquitted.

11 May

Derry suicide

The *Ballyshannon Herald* of 11 May 1832 reported on a coroner's inquest held at Craghadoes near Derry into the suicide of eleven-year-old William Devany. The coroner John Miller said that it was the most appalling case he had ever witnessed. Devany – who worked as a labourer – had just returned home from a day's work. His mother, seeing him carrying a rope, asked what he was doing. The boy told her that he needed it to do a job for his master.

Devany then walked away from the house, tied the rope to a hawthorn tree at the side of the public road and hanged himself.

12 May

Hiring fair

The great hiring fair in Newry took place on 12 May 1881. It was reported in the *Belfast Morning News* that it was a fine day in Newry, with little drunkenness despite the large number of servants in the streets.

Despite the fact that many servants left the fair without getting employment, a considerable number of agreements were entered into. Ploughmen were taken on at rates of between five pounds, ten shillings and seven pounds per half-year; active women were paid two pounds, fifteen shillings to three pounds, ten shillings; young girls, twenty-five to thirty shillings; and boys, two pounds, two shillings to three pounds, five shillings.

13 May

Wreck of the Maria

At midnight on 13 May 1849, the sailing ship *Maria*, which had left Limerick 6 weeks earlier with 10 crew and 111 emigrants on board, collided with an iceberg in the St Lawrence Gulf, killing all but 12 people on board.

The *Maria* had set out from Limerick on 2 April on a voyage to Quebec in Canada. Most of the passengers were small farmers, labourers and their families, who were fleeing from the awful effects of famine in Ireland.

The ship, skippered by Michael Hedigan, who was said to be a skilled an experienced sailor, slammed into a large iceberg only fifty miles from its destination. The bow of the ship caved in almost immediately. Piercing screams were heard from below, and the *Maria* sank within minutes of the collision.

Some twenty passengers and crew managed to escape in a small boat, while others clung to wreckage or clambered onto the ice floes. Only the lucky ones who had made it to the boat survived; the rest perished in the freezing cold temperatures. The survivors – nine passengers and three crew – survived a whole day in the freezing temperatures before being picked up by the *Roslyn Castle*, which took them to Quebec.

14 May

Killed by a fish

Galway, 14 May 1767:

'We hear from Connemara, that an old experienced fisherman, who was at the taking of a sunfish on that coast about ten days ago, had received so violent a stroke on the small of his back from the tail of the fish, as totally to sever his back bone, and killed him on the spot.' (*Leinster Journal*, 20 May 1767)

15 May

Great hurling match

A 'great hurling match' took place on Crumlin Commons in Dublin on 15 May 1749. The game, which was played between the hurlers of Munster and Leinster, went on all day and only ended when 'night obliged them to give over', according to the *Dublin Courant*, 16–20 May 1749.

Crumlin Commons was a popular sports venue in Dublin until it was enclosed in the nineteenth century. It was also a popular spot for Ireland's horse-racing fraternity, but the local people found it to be a bit of a nuisance and they tried to put an end to the races in 1789. Backed up by the local magistrate and a strong force of soldiers, they attempted to move the race goers on and tear down their tents and stalls. However, the race goers ignored their attempts and carried on with their racing which lasted for several days.

16 May

'Biggest Irishman since Finn McCool'

The *Hibernian Journal* of 16 May 1787 recorded the death and burial of Roger Byrne at Rosenallis in Queen's County (Laois). Described by the newspaper as the largest Irishman since Finn McCool's time, Byrne, from Borris-in-Ossory, was said to have weighed in at a staggering forty-five stone. Others claimed that he actually weighed fifty-two stone.

The coffin was carried on a very long bier by thirty men who had to be relieved at regular intervals. It was reported that Byrne – whose waistcoat could comfortably fit seven of Borris-in-Ossory's largest men together – died at the age of fifty-four from 'suffocation occasioned by an extremity of fat which stopped the play of his lungs'.

17 May

The white castle

On 17 May 1784 the *Hibernian Journal* reported:

'The White Castle in Naas, County Kildare, was blown down on the previous Thursday night during a gale, killing at least one man. The man, George McDermot, died when the falling castle demolished two adjoining houses. Another eight people were rescued alive from the rubble but five of them were so badly injured there are no hopes for their recovery.'

18 May

Croke Park cross-dressers

Two unusual events occurred in Dublin on 18 and 19 May 1896, when an English women's football team togged out against an representative Irish women's side in a series of games at grounds in Jones's Road. The grounds were then known as the 'City and Suburban Racecourse and Amusements Grounds' and were subsequently purchased by the Gaelic Athletic Association to become known as Croke Park. The English women also took part in a novelty game against an Irish men's team, who wore women's skirts for the occasion.

A crowd of around a thousand people turned out to watch the two exhibition games, which had to be postponed for two days when the English women missed their ferry.

The Irish representative side, kitted out in red jerseys, won the first match 3-2, while the second was a 2-2 draw. The *Sport* reporter said that the crowd hadn't expected to see 'such a vigorous exhibition from the weaker sex' and the games were described by him as being played with 'the greatest openness and rivalry'.

Curiously, one of the teams had a man playing in goal, but we are not told who he was or even which team he was playing for. It was revealed, however, that when the keeper – 'a well-known international' – was smartly beaten in goal, he came in for his share of 'jeering remarks' from the crowd.

The two games were deemed to be a great success, so much so that another set of games was arranged for 23 May. On that occasion, the English women played against a men's team, which was put together by the unnamed 'well-known international'. The men's team, advertised as Mr Morrogh's XI in the *Irish Times,* comprised of several 'well-known names' from the football world. The men rather bizarrely agreed to wear 'fancy skirts' for the occasion in order to play on level terms with the women.

The final score of this game was not given in *The Irish Times*, but it was reported in advance of the match that it was usual practice in this type of contest for the 'gentlemen' to let the women win.

19 May

Limerick man and Queen Victoria

One Saturday afternoon in May 1849, a young Queen Victoria was returning to Buckingham Palace after a carriage ride in Hyde Park with her children and her husband Prince Albert. As the carriage approached the bottom of Constitution Hill, a man emerged from a small group of onlookers and fired a pistol in the direction of the carriage. No one was hurt in the incident, and the culprit was apprehended by a park keeper and a number of onlookers. Some of the spectators tried to attack the man before he was quickly bundled into a cab and taken to King Street Police Station.

It later transpired that the gunman − described by the *London Observer* as 'an ignorant, half-starved Irishman, occupying one of the lowest stations in society' − was a 22-year-old bricklayer's labourer named William Hamilton from Adare in County Limerick. Hamilton had been living in London for the previous five years at a boarding house in Pimlico.

The notion that Hamilton was an assassin was quickly dismissed by the police, and Fleet Street papers described him as an attention seeker or a lunatic. The *London Observer* said that he was 'beyond the possibility of possessing a motive for the destruction of the Queen of England' and speculated that he had pulled the stunt in order to be transported to another country.

It also emerged that there were no bullets in the pistol, only gunpowder. Hamilton had borrowed the rusty miniature pistol from Bridget O'Keefe, his landlady, earlier that morning and had sent one of her children to buy him a penny's worth of gunpowder.

After firing the pistol Hamilton made no attempt to escape and he was quickly disarmed by the park keeper. No one suffered any injury in the incident, and Hamilton was later sentenced to seven years' transportation. He was never heard from again.

20 May

Savage killing

Hue and Cry, 20 May 1847:

'Description of John Savage, who stands charged with having, on the 17th day of April, at Quay-lane, in the city of Limerick, parish of Saint Mary, stabbed a boy named James Kiarney with a knife in the left side, from the effects of which he died in the city Infirmary on the 30th day of April: 14 years of age, 4 feet 10 inches high, slight make, dark complexion, brown hair, blue eyes; wore a blue cap, barragon jacket, corduroy trousers; is a native of Johnsgate, city of Limerick.'

21 May

Ivy dies in bush battle

On 21 May 1765 John Ivy of Swift's Alley in Dublin died from wounds he sustained on 1 May in a battle over a May bush (see entry for 1 May) .

22 May

Famine death

On the evening of 22 May 1849, Inspector Fox of the Royal Irish Constabulary saw a corpse being carried through Ballina, County Mayo on a cart with a piece of sacking thrown over it. He sent for the county coroner Charles Atkinson and held an inquest into the circumstances of the death.

The dead man was Murtagh Loftus, a native of Ballina, married with three daughters. The family, said to be in a wretched state of poverty, were living on the outdoor relief scheme and supplemented their meagre income by selling brooms made from gorse, which brought in about a shilling a week.

The family had been in the workhouse in Ballina a few months earlier, but had left after a fortnight, preferring to work under the outdoor relief scheme instead. One of the daughters had gone back into the workhouse by early May.

A few days before his death, Loftus and his wife had been seen leaving Ballina carrying a load of their homemade brooms. His wife went to Killala with her load and Murtagh Loftus walked to Bartra. On the morning of his death some cockle gatherers at Bartra saw Loftus fall over and when they went to help him, they found that he had died.

Loftus's youngest daughter was sent for, and she went to Killala to find her mother. The two women returned to Bartra and they were forced to carry the dead man's corpse until they had almost reached Ballina, where a cart was found to bring the unfortunate man home.

23 May

A costly indiscretion

Extract from the *Dublin Sunday Observer*, 27 May 1832:
'Dublin Police, College Street Office –

'Rather a laughable, and assuredly a constructive event, was disclosed at this office on Wednesday, furnishing another proof that experience teaches most men not until they have personally felt the fruits of individual indiscretion. The singular part of this case is that the sufferer is not a Christian but 'a Jew' – a veritable Jew .... Now this descendant of 'Father Abraham', Mr. Louis Nathaniel, 'like all the tribe' having a sneaking kindness for the sex, was induced to make love to Miss Elizabeth Pepper, from Dame Street, on Monday night. They laughed and quaffed and drank old sherry – they talked about all sorts of politics, until the drowsy god asserting his influence over Jew and Gentile, laid the gentleman prostrate and snoring. The watchful Pepper no sooner noted this than she arose and ... sacked everything she could lay her hands on ... a handsome repeating watch with corresponding guard ... a diamond ring which she coaxed from the Levite's forefinger ... next vanished a musical snuff-box, which played all sorts of tunes, 'Garryown', 'the Boyne Water', and 'Moll in the Wad', then followed a chased ring .... The lady could not find her own clothes, and accordingly put on the Jew's pantaloons, investing her shoulders with short vest, coat and cloth; she mounted the new hat, 'adopted' a pound note found in the vest pocket, and placing a neat silk umbrella under her arm, left her friend to sleep on, and dream of Paradise Regained …. She was found by the watchman marching not very steadily down Wood Street …'.

24 May

Bunclody atrocity

On the night of Saturday, 24 May 1775, near Bunclody in County Wexford, the home of a Protestant man named Ralph was attacked by a number of Whiteboys. Ralph, who lived at Ryland near Bunclody, had been forced to hand over a gun to the men some nights earlier, but he had hidden the gun's firing mechanism before handing it over.

The Whiteboys returned to punish Ralph for his deception, but he saw them coming and escaped out through the back window. His poor wife wasn't so lucky, however, as the raiders cut off both of her ears before wrecking every piece of furniture in the house.

25 May

Ringrose the highwayman

The notorious highwayman John Gowny's life of crime finally came to an end on 25 May 1749 when he was captured at Birr in King's County (Offaly) and taken into custody by Sir Laurence Parsons. Gowny, whose stamping ground was in the hills around Woodford in County Galway and Mountshannon in County Clare, had been wanted for murdering Galway servant John Cushin. Gowny, who was also known by his nickname Ringrose, was tried at Galway Assizes in September 1749 and was hanged and gibbeted at the scene of his crime.

26 May

White Quakers

On Monday, 26 May 1845, Dublin man Michael Dunn was committed for trial for stealing a horse, the property of Quakers Samuel Jacob and Abigail Beale. When he was committed, Dunn was dressed in the uniform of the White Quaker sect – an extreme breakaway group of the Quakers. Dunn, who was originally a Roman Catholic, is reported to have joined the White Quakers after he had heard that they were well fed and had nothing to do all day. He had a previous conviction for horse stealing and was a known Ribbonman.

The White Quakers were so called because they only wore white clothing and painted all of their furniture white. They followed a simple and extremely frugal lifestyle and no symbols of pride or ostentation, such as mirrors, clocks or new-fangled inventions, were allowed in their homes. Occasionally, the White Quakers were known to dispense with the wearing of clothes altogether and they were sometimes seen parading through the streets of Dublin naked.

27 May

The scourge of emigration

Dundalk Express, 27 May 1865, 'Emigration from Dundalk':
    'It would appear that the emigration mania is increasing. Upwards of 400 persons passed through this town in the

last fortnight en-route for[sic.] America. Those leaving are generally of the small farmer class, and in many cases each group consists of the entire family – the aged parents and their children, most of the latter being in the prime of life. In fact the bone and sinew of the land are going, and no one need be surprised if, in the course of a few years, Ireland becomes a scarcely populated country. Those staying at home are the young, the aged, and the infirm, many of whom in due course, will take up their abode in the workhouse, and thus become permanent burdens on the rates….'

28 May

The poitín makers

A government report in the newspapers on 28 May 1864 shows that the illicit trade in poitín making was thriving in Ireland. A Revenue return for the fiscal year ending March 1863 showed that 1,980 illicit poitin-making stills were found, with 287 successful prosecutions. There was a rise in the figures for the year ending March 1864, with 2,743 discoveries and 411 convictions. The stills were mostly found in the counties of Donegal, Galway, Mayo and Sligo. Poitín was generally produced in remote rural areas far from the watchful eyes of the law.

29 May

Waterford suicide attempt

When it came to suicide or cases of attempted suicide in the early part of the twentieth century, newspaper editors showed little restraint or sensitivity in their reports. Readers were often treated to a blow-by-blow description of the events, and very little was left to the imagination. This report of an attempted suicide in the *Waterford News* on 29 May 1924 was a case in point:

'Richard Hamilton a young ex-British Navy man aged about 28 years, made an unsuccessful attempt to end his life by cutting his throat with a razor on Saturday night last. From the facts it would appear that at about 8 o'clock, Hamilton and a younger brother aged 18 years were in their home at No. 4 New Street. The younger boy went out to fetch a bucket of water, and on his return he was horrified to find the older man lying on the floor in a pool of blood. There were five separate gashes from which blood flowed copiously on the left side of the unfortunate man's neck between the end of the ear and the top of the shoulder. He was in a collapsed and very weak condition, and was only semi-conscious. A priest and doctor were quickly summoned and the latter ordered the man's immediate removal to the Waterford Co. and City Infirmary. At the latter institution it was found that the wounds were not as serious as at first supposed and after his injuries had been dressed Hamilton was certified to be insane and was transferred to the Waterford Mental Hospital where he now remains…'.

30 May

Extreme weather in Antrim

A number of Irish newspapers reported on a storm of astonishing ferocity that occurred in Antrim on 30 May 1788. A letter written in Ballycastle on the day following the storm provided details of torrential rain and ferocious thunder and lightning:

'…Many accidents have happened, the Old Rookery of Bonnymargy, adjoining Knocklade is totally destroyed;

added to which, the woods of Gartmaddy have suffered much, many trees being torn up from their roots. But our fears were very much increased in the evening by a most uncommon noise from Knocklade [Knocklayde Mountain], the top of which burst, and the discharge of burning matter and hot stones from it was truly alarming … several cattle [were killed] in the adjacent fields, many cabins were thrown down and several people are missing (among whom are the dissenting minister and parish priest of this place), supposed to have been overtaken by the burning matter which was thirty perches in breadth, and ran near a mile and a half. I really believe such a phenomenon was never before seen in this country, and to complete our misfortunes, the rain, which had it been moderate would have been a blessing, has come down in such quantities that it raised a flood in our river, which carried off the west pier of our quay and the draw-bridge.'

There were similar incidences reported in parts of England at that time too. Many birds were killed in lightning strikes and hailstones 'as big as gooseberries' destroyed chimneys and killed some sheep near Broughton.

31 May

Burned by a pig

Hibernian Journal, 31 May 1771:

'Last Thursday, a woman at Kilrush [County Clare], going to wash clothes, left an infant in a cradle, when a pig drew the cradle to the fire, by which means the child was unfortunately burnt to death.'

JUNE

1 June

Shower of fish

To the editor of the *Patriot*, by E.S., Crossmolina, County Mayo, 1 June 1815:

'Sir – A very extraordinary occurrence, which reached my ears, is said to have taken place one day in the latter end of last April, upon the peninsula that separates the two harbours of Black Sod and Broad Haven, called the Mullet …. Some labourers employed in setting potatoes about half a mile from the sea shore, were surprised by a sudden shower of herring fry falling around the place where they stood, which, on reaching the earth, immediately began to spring about with vivacity, as fishes usually do when thrown upon land …. It was at noon of a heavy dark day, that this singular occurrence happened; a smart shower of rain preceded the descent of the fishes. The gentleman, my informant, saw some of them dead, and declares that, as incredible as the story may appear, he knows no motive whatever that can have induced the country people to tell a falsehood in this matter. Without pretending to account for the phenomenon; I have only to observe, that the fact itself is not unworthy of credit, as I know from undoubted authority that in the East Indies small fishes are frequently seen to descend in the same manner from the clouds, at a considerable distance from the sea.'

2 June

Pomeroy Fair

On 20 June 1828, the *Dublin Evening Mail* reported on the Pomeroy Fair, which took place on 2 June that year – a terrifying affair, by this account:

'The fair went on as usual till between one and two o'clock, pm, when immense numbers of idle fellows from the neighbouring parishes arrived in town, each possessed of a good cudgel, and soon commenced sham fighting opposite the police barrack ....The police came out of their barracks in a very steady manner ... to quell the riot; they soon made prisoners, who were nearly as soon rescued, and maltreated the police very much. After the police had retired to their barrack, the mob again commenced, to the great terror of every Protestant in the town, when the police appeared the second time, and were instantly attacked with short bars of iron, stones, etc., and [were] soon ... surrounded. Seeing themselves in imminent danger (for they were all severely wounded already), they loaded their pieces with blank cartridge, which the leaders of the mob observed, and [which] only made them more fierce and determined; they then loaded in good earnest and fired, when unfortunately a man of good character, named O'Brien, brother to Priest O'Brien, of Killeshal, was killed, and three men and a woman severely wounded...'.

3 June

Idle and disorderly persons

At a meeting of the City Assembly of Dublin on 3 June 1740, it was reported that 'the peace of this city has been of late disturbed by numbers of idle and disorderly persons assembling themselves in many parts thereof, on Saturday night last and the three following days, and violently broke open the houses of several of the inhabitants, and forcibly took their goods.'

The Lord Mayor of Dublin responded to the crisis by issuing a proclamation offering a reward for apprehending and convicting those involved, with a reward of twenty pounds for the first person convicted and ten pounds for those subsequently convicted.

On Friday, 20 June four men, identified as ringleaders of the rioting, were tried at the Court of the King's Bench. One was acquitted, while Morgan Bracken was publicly whipped and fined nine pence and two other defendants, Henry White and Peter Sweetman, were fined four shillings and nine pence each and sentenced to transportation.

Two weeks later another three men, Patrick Moore, Charles Foy and Matthew Spencer, were tried for the same crime. Moore and Foy were found guilty of stealing meal and bread and sentenced to a whipping, while Spencer was sentenced to seven years' transportation.

All of those being transported later escaped when they managed to overpower the ship's crew off Waterford and make good their escape to dry land. One of these – the above-mentioned Henry White – made his way back to Dublin and was rearrested in September 1740 for assaulting a gardener in Dirty Lane. He was hanged two months later.

4 June

Don't shoot the messenger

On 4 June 1832, several Irish newspapers reported on the details of a duel that took place between Mr S. Costigan of Ely Place, Dublin and John Sheehan, editor of the *Comet* newspaper. The duel took place at the four-mile stone on the Ashbourne Road the previous morning. The two men exchanged a number of shots without hitting each other. The duel ended when the police arrived.

The dispute arose because Costigan had objected to an article Sheehan had written in the *Comet* about a royal review in the Phoenix Park. Costigan claimed that the piece had offended his family.

The *Comet* was an anti-establishment, pro-O'Connell, anti-tithe newspaper and it folded after Sheehan was jailed for perverting the course of justice in 1833.

5 June

The Jewish gunslinger from Dublin

The Jewish gunslinger Jim Levy was born in Dublin in 1842; he emigrated to the US with his parents at a young age. As soon as he was old enough, Levy travelled west in search of work and he ended up in Pinoche, Arizona, where he found employment as a miner.

Levy had his first gunfight in 1871 after he had given evidence in court against Michael Casey, who had shot dead a man named Tom Gasson. Casey went looking for Levy after the trial and challenged him to a gunfight. Levy accepted the challenge and shot Casey dead. However, Levy didn't emerge from the fight unscathed. A friend of Casey shot him in the face, scarring him for life and knocking out several teeth.

Levy gave up mining afterwards and became a professional gambler, moving all over the West Coast and earning a formidable reputation as a gunslinger. He had at least sixteen gunfights, winning them all. The gunfight that made Levy's reputation as a gunslinger occurred in March 1877 when he shot and killed the famous gunfighter Charlie Harrison in Cheyenne, Wyoming following a disagreement in a bar.

Levy's luck finally ran out on 5 June 1882 when he got into a row in Tucson, Arizona with a card dealer named John Murphy. The two men had agreed to a gunfight, but Murphy and two of his friends decided to kill Levy beforehand when they heard about his superior fighting skills. They shot him dead as he was leaving the Fashion Saloon in Tuscon. He was unarmed.

6 June

Erin go Bragh

On Wednesday, 6 June 1849 the aeronaut Mr Hampton ascended from the Rotunda Gardens in Dublin in his hot air balloon, the *Erin go Bragh*, on his flight to Harold's Cross. Hundreds gathered inside and outside the gardens to witness Mr Hampton's first flight of the season. He was joined on his voyage by Miss McQuade and John Whitty, a Carlow engineer.

The balloon took off from Rutland Square (now Parnell Square) at 6.00 p.m. to great applause and cheering from the spectators. It was a fine sunny evening and the *Erin go Bragh* rose to a height of almost a mile and floated gently across Dublin.

After a short flight lasting half an hour, the balloon landed at its intended destination in a field beside Harold's Cross, where a great crowd, marshalled by a large body of police, had turned up to see Hampton and his passengers descend safely.

7 June

Violence in the streets

The Dublin newspapers ran a number of court reports on 7 June 1899 which highlighted the difficulties experienced by the Dublin Metropolitan Police in their dealings with drunk-ards. The *Freeman's Journal* of that day reported on a number of such cases heard a day earlier in the Dublin police courts.

Kate Kelly, described in court as a woman of no fixed abode, was found drunk on the previous evening at Hardwicke Place and arrested. She refused to go to the police station with the constable and punched and kicked him several times. She was fined ten shillings for her drunkenness; if she failed to pay, she would face a week in prison. Her sentence for the attack on the policeman was a month in jail with hard labour.

Also charged at the same court was New Street flower seller Rose Keegan, who had been arrested on Upper Leeson Street for using 'objectionable language'. Constable 51E gave evidence that after he had arrested Keegan, she threw herself on the ground and refused to move. The constable called for a stretcher to transport his reluctant prisoner to the Bridewell, but this only seemed to infuriate her further and she hit him and spat in his face. Constable 41E tried to intervene, but Keegan punched him in the face, giving him a black eye for his trouble. She was fined twenty shillings and jailed for six weeks with hard labour.

In the days before the invention of the 'black maria' or police car, the stretcher was the standard method of immobilising and conveying troublesome prisoners to jail.

8 June

Fed a child to the pigs

Richard de Cantolup – a thoroughly nasty and corrupt individual by all accounts – was hauled before the courts at Ardfert, County Kerry on 8 June 1295, charged with two instances of murder and a number of other crimes.

De Cantolup, who was a king's sergeant, or barrister, was accused of being involved in the killing of a man on the 'bridge of Limerick' and the murder of Richard de Hereford in Ardfert. He was also accused of manipulating juries to his own advantage and imprisoning people, only releasing them if they 'gave him a gift'. He was charged with robbing the Bishop of Emly, harbouring villains such as Tadhg O'Henehan and his son, and, according to the *Calendar of Justiciary Rolls* for that year, 'living upon poor persons for a week or more, to the injury of the whole country'.

It got worse. De Cantolup was further accused of allowing his pigs to eat a child, who was believed to have been his own son, and preventing the local coroner from taking away the pigs to examine them.

De Canolup was acquitted on all of the major charges. He was fined twenty marks and allowed to go.

9 June

Elephant runs amok at Dublin Zoo

The *Evening Herald* editions of 10 and 11 June 1903 gave details of the tragic killing of a zookeeper at Dublin Zoo by an elephant. On Tuesday, 9 June the unfortunate keeper James McNally was trampled to death by Zita, an elephant from India, which had been one of Dublin Zoo's main attractions for over twenty years.

McNally and his son had been tending the elephant, which had an infected foot, when the animal ran amok and attacked the keeper, first knocking him to the ground with her trunk and then pinning him there by placing her foot on his head. The elephant stayed in this position for a considerable period, and by the time staff eventually managed to lure her away from McNally it was too late. The keeper had died from massive injuries to his head inflicted by the sheer weight of the creature.

The elephant was shot the next morning by two policemen supervised by Inspector General Neville Chamberlayne, who was said to have considerable experience of elephant hunting in India.

With the loss of Zita, Dublin Zoo also lost its right to claim ownership of the largest elephant in Ireland or Britain. Zita, who weighed over five tonnes and stood twelve feet high at the shoulder, arrived in Dublin from India in 1882. McNally had looked after the elephant from that time and taught it several tricks, including the visitors' favourite where Zita danced on a raised platform while McNally whistled a tune.

This was not the first time a keeper had been killed at Dublin Zoo; another keeper had been gored to death by a stag there twenty years earlier.

10 June

The Dublin Watchmen

The *Dublin Evening Post* of 10 June 1732 reported on an attack on the New Street Watch house in Dublin in which a watchman was killed. A number of young men passing through New Street had thrown stones into the watch house, striking one of the watchmen. The watchmen gave chase to the youths and, in the ensuing battle, one of the watchmen was killed. Some of the rioters were captured and taken to Newgate Prison, and two young men named Farrell and Linney were executed in July for murdering the watchman.

In the days before we had an organised police force in Dublin, it was left to the individual Protestant parishes to make provision for their own policing needs. The local churchwarden was effectively the chief superintendent of policing in his area and the police force – known as the parish watch – was stationed in watch houses and watch stands all across the city. The watch was generally comprised of old retired soldiers and it was seen as being a corrupt and ineffective method of policing.

11 June

The Pretender's birthday

Dublin Intelligence, 11 June 1726:

'Yesterday being that celebrated by several in this city as the Pretender's [James III] birthday, in the evening a great mob gathered at Stephen's Green …. [T]hey, to begin some game, fell to toss[ing] dead dogs and cats about, which being near the Right Honourable the Lord Abercorn's house, his Lordship, ordering they might disperse, which it seems was not their intention without mischief, for they with abundance of insolence threw one of the dead creatures to the window in order to hit his Lordship in the face and then persisted in their evil intentions with stones and bats with which they broke the windows in a very riotous manner…'.

12 June

Rail Disaster

Ireland's worst rail disaster occurred on 12 June 1889 when eighty-eight people were killed and many more injured in a collision between two trains in County Armagh. One of the trains, consisting of fourteen carriages, two guards vans and close to one thousand passengers set out from Armagh Station at 10.00 a.m. on an excursion to Warrenpoint, a popular seaside destination on the shores of Carlingford Lough.

The excursion had been organised by the Armagh Methodist Church and the vast majority of the passengers were children and young people who attended Sunday schools in the Armagh area.

The train wasn't long out of Armagh Station when it stalled on a steep gradient close to Killeoney Bridge due to the heavy passenger load. The driver Thomas McGrath and fireman Henry Parkinson decided to bring half of the fourteen carriages to Hamilton's Bawn Station, a couple of miles further up the line, and come back for the rest of the carriages. Eight carriages and one guard's van were uncoupled and secured with stones, in a practice that was known as 'cogging', while the driver and fireman headed off to Hamilton's Bawn with the first half of the train.

However, the gradient was too steep to hold the other half of the train and the stones soon gave way. The guard and the brakesmen tried to slow the carriages down, but, despite their efforts, the train began to gather pace and it was soon flying uncontrollably back down the track to Armagh.

The driver of the 10.25 a.m. train out of Armagh Station saw the uncoupled carriages of the excursion train hurtling towards him. There was nothing he could do to avoid the collision. Passengers jumped from both trains in an effort to escape, but eighty-eight people died and scores more were injured.

Some had miraculous escapes. One little boy, Frank Moore, was found alive and unscathed on an embankment after someone had thrown him out the window of one of the carriages. Another man named Reilly avoided death when he leapt from the train just before the crash. An Armagh woman named Sloane, who was travelling on the later train, had a miraculous escape. She saw the carriages hurtling towards her and she threw her three children out of the window before jumping out after them. All escaped serious injury.

13 June

Cholera

Ireland – already reeling from the effects of famine – was further devastated by a major cholera outbreak in 1848 and 1849, which claimed thousands of victims. One of these was the Dublin poet James Clarence Mangan, who died from the disease at Meath Hospital on 13 June 1849.

Cholera victims were supposed to be buried immediately after death to avoid spreading the disease, but Mangan's funeral was delayed for three days while his friends tried to find a coffin. The epidemic had killed so many people in Dublin that there weren't enough coffins or hearses to go round. Mangan's remains were interred at Glasnevin Cemetery on 23 June and the funeral was attended by only five of his closest friends.

14 June

Blessed are the cheesemakers

On 14 June 1789 the *Duke of Leinster* left Dublin bound for Nova Scotia with 127 convicts on board. One of these was the notorious Fr Patrick Fay, who served both as a Catholic priest and a Church of Ireland chaplain in Dublin, but was better known in the city for his other activities such as violent assault, embezzlement, wrestling and boxing.

Fay was also a successful property speculator and ran a lucrative practice as a couple-beggar. A couple-beggar was an unscrupulous priest or minister of varying religious persuasions, who would marry any couple regardless of their age or status, once they could afford to pay an exorbitant fee. Fay was particularly prolific in this regard and it was said that he married up to half a dozen couples per day, charging them a guinea for the privilege.

Fay had been sentenced to death in September 1788 for swindling money from two farmers and the high sheriff of County Meath, but he managed to have the sentence commuted to transportation for life instead. Along with fourteen cartloads of prisoners, he was taken from Newgate Prison on 13 June to the ship at the North Wall. There was consternation when the cart overturned near Capel Street. Some of the prisoners tried to escape in the confusion, but were subdued by the soldiers guarding them. Fay himself was injured in the incident.

Although Fay was on board the *Duke of Leinster* when it left Dublin on 15 June, he wasn't on it for very long. It appears that he bribed the captain to allow him to escape on board a fishing boat somewhere off Wicklow Head. Fay subsequently settled at Bordeaux in France, where it was reported he had established a successful cheesemaking business.

15 June

A lucky escape

Saunders' Newsletter, 15 June 1815:

'It has been repeatedly insisted upon, that the custom of too hastily interring human bodies, has frequently proved the cause of death to persons whose life might be preserved for some time longer. A most striking instance in support of this assertion occurred on Tuesday evening in Cork. A soldier of the 93rd regiment, quartered in the barracks, was looked upon to be dead, and after having been laid out in the usual way during two days, was conveyed to the place of interment (St Nicholas's Churchyard) on yesterday evening, when on lowering the body into the grave, the soldiers assisting heard the noise of struggling in the coffin, and on examination, found the man, whom they were in the act of burying, endeavouring with his hands and knees to force up the lid. To their great astonishment, they found their comrade still alive, and conveyed him home in the open coffin. This should prove an additional warning against premature interment.'

16 June

'A most savage act'

The *Evening Freeman*, 16 June 1836, Passage West, Cork:
    'A most savage act was perpetrated at Passage-West, on Friday night last, the particulars of which, it is our painful duty to lay before our readers [in] this post. It appeared that the deceased, Anastacia Twomy, and her husband, quarrelled while on the road from Cork to their own house, the evening of this dreadful occurrence, and that he, becoming exasperated, commenced striking her with a stick, blows from which he continued to inflict until he got her into his own stable where he leaped upon her body in such a manner as shortly to deprive her of existence. Her cries in this place drew her children to the spot, and as they witnessed the cruelties of the father, their testimony on his trial, corroborated as it will be by others who witnessed them on the road, will, it is believed, convict him upon

the most indubitable evidence. An inquest was held before Richard Foot, Esq., coroner, on Saturday and continued by adjournment until Monday morning when the jury found as follows: 'That the deceased, Anastacia Twomy, came by her death by violence committed upon her head, body and limbs by her husband, Jeremiah Twomy.'

17 June

The Umbrell-ometer

If you thought an umbrella was just for keeping you dry, think again. According to the *Kilkenny Journal* on 17 June 1857, an umbrella could tell you an awful lot about a man's character, for example, if he was mean, cruel to animals, or likely to be a miser. No need for psychologists in mid-nineteenth century Kilkenny. Just watch the way he handles his umbrella.

'We think the umbrella can be taken as a very good test of a person's character. The man who always takes an umbrella out with him is a cautious fellow, who abstains from all speculation and is pretty sure to die rich. The man who is always leaving his umbrella behind him, is generally one who makes no provision for the morrow. He is reckless, thoughtless, always late for the train, leaves the street door open when he goes home late at night .... The man who is always losing his umbrella is an unlucky dog, whose bills are always protested, whose boots split, whose 'change' is sure to have some bad money in it. Be cautious how you lend a thousand pounds to such a man! The man who is perpetually expressing a nervous anxiety about his umbrella, and wondering if it is safe, is full of meanness and low suspicions, and [with] whom it is best not to play at cards, nor drink a bottle of wine. He is sure to suspect you are cheating him, or that you are drinking more than your share…'.

18 June

A row in the town

Athlone Independent, 18 June 1834:
'Yesterday evening a regular set-to took place among the stall-keepers, bacon-huxters and green-grocers in the Main Street. Knives, cleavers, stools and wattles were in active requisition, and shouts, screams, oaths and curses were dealt about as plentifully as blows. After half an hour's close encounter, which was warmly contested by both parties, a strapping Amazon decided the fortune of the day by a well-directed and scientific blow, laid in between the eyes of the leader of the opposition side, which quickly placed him *hors de combat*, and by the club law of our club-footed legislator, Billy Glass, who spared neither friend or foe on the occasion, order and tranquillity were restored among the belligerents.'

19 June

Capel Street poisoning case

In Dublin on Saturday, 19 June 1830, Mary Connor approached night watchman John Proctor in Capel Street at midnight and offered him a drink of punch. Proctor gratefully accepted the drink from the woman but he had only drunk a small amount when his mouth and throat began to burn.

'I took a sup of it,' he said, 'and directly I felt a burning in my throat; it had not the same taste as when I tasted it first; it tasted very bitter .... I could hardly swallow my spittle ...'. It later emerged that the drink contained enough poison to kill four men.

Connor was caught soon afterwards and charged with the attempted murder of Proctor. During the trial it emerged that Mary Connor, alias Curry, had attempted to poison the watchman because he had arrested her 'fancy man' Mosey Connor and lodged him in Newgate Prison. Connor was subsequently found guilty and transported to Australia.

Mary Connor was found guilty of the attempted murder of the watchman and, to her horror, the judge sentenced her to death. The execution date was fixed for 28 July, but just three days before she was due to be hanged her sentence was commuted and she was transported to Australia instead.

20 June

'He would have done much evil'

The Tyrell brothers of Castleknock in County Dublin were in hot water in June 1305 when both appeared in court on a number of charges. First up was William Tyrell, who was fined and jailed for running his cattle through Richard Manger's corn and assaulting him. Also jailed on the same day was John Tyrell who had assaulted members of the Deuswelle family.

John Deuswelle and his brother were sitting in a garden minding their own business when they were confronted by Tyrell. Tyrell, who was 'angered against them', attacked one of the Deuswelle servants before turning his attention to John Deuswelle, who managed to fend him off with a dagger. Tyrell went to his brother's house in Castleknock where he tooled up. Then he pursued the Deuswelle brothers to their mother's house, where they had taken refuge.

When he couldn't get in, Tyrell began to throw rocks over the wall at the Deuswelles, and he was only prevented from doing further damage when the brothers' neighbours responded to their cries for help.

The court heard that Tyrell 'would have done much evil' if he hadn't been restrained. Tyrell was found guilty and jailed for an unspecified period. He was also jailed for stealing meat, bread, fish and other goods from a number of poor men in Dublin. When he was arrested, Tyrell stole an axe and escaped from custody, but the Mayor of Dublin had him rearrested and took his horse to pay for the goods stolen.

21 June

'A common strumpet'

At a sitting of the Kilmallock Court in Limerick on 21 June 1300, the Chief Justiciar John Wogan sat in judgment on a case involving miller Walter de Capella and his boss John Thebaud of Fersketh, County Limerick.

The dispute arose when Thebaud's mistress called de Capella a thief and he replied by calling her a 'common strumpet'. The row escalated and de Capella fled the area after Thebaud's mistress threatened to have the miller killed.

He took refuge at the home of Henry de Cogan, but Thebaud pursued him and had him put in the stocks. De Capella managed to escape but Thebaud recaptured him and 'tore out his eyes'.

The court heard that a remorseful Thebaud had promised to feed and clothe de Capella for the remainder of his life, but despite this he was jailed and made to pay a fine of one hundred shillings.

22 June

Killarney Kate

The Register, Adelaide, South Australia, 22 June 1922:

'Ellen Cahill, an elderly woman, known locally as Killarney Kate on account of her singing the Irish song 'Killarney [Lakes]' in the streets, was charged at Prahran (Victoria) on Monday with being an idle and disorderly person, and having no visible lawful means of support. The records of Melbourne Gaol showed that Cahill has been convicted of being drunk on 156 occasions....'

Killarney Kate was a well-known character and busker on the streets of Melbourne who specialised in the singing of Irish ballads. She was born in Castlecomer, County Kilkenny in 1863 and emigrated to Australia during the 1870s with her parents, who went on to run a hotel in Melbourne. Cahill began her musical career by singing at her parents' hotel and at charity concerts.

It's not entirely clear when or why she decided to take to the roads, but she seems to have established herself as a street performer sometime around 1910. She was a familiar sight on the streets of Melbourne and she also sang on the city's trams. She also had a penchant for bursting into song in the middle of the road on occasion and refusing to move until she had finished her performance.

Although she had a wonderful singing voice, Cahill was a troubled soul and she was as famous for her brushes with the law as she was for her musical performances. She could be – as reported in one newspaper – 'an exuberantly hilarious individual', but she had her dark side too. She had dozens of convictions for petty crime. Most of these were for being drunk and disorderly, but some were for theft and she was also renowned for her quick temper and use of strong language.

She was admitted to Melbourne Hospital in late December 1933 suffering from pneumonia and she died there on 3 January 1934. Hundreds turned out on the streets of Melbourne for her funeral, which was paid for by a celebrity who chose to remain anonymous.

23 June

Grinning through horse collars

Dublin Courant, 23 June 1747:

'Tomorrow, being the 24th of this Instant June, there will be a Smock Race, run for by the Women on the Strand near the Brickfields. At the same Place, a Hat is to be Cudgeled for, Tobacco grinned for, and several other entertaining Diversions.'

This type of a day out was very popular in mid-eighteenth-century Dublin, and 24 June, the feast day of St John the Baptist, was a big day in the social calendar for the city's poorer classes.

'The strand near the Brickfields' is today better known as Sandymount Strand. 'Cudgeling' was a kind of friendly stick fight where you had to hit your opponent over the head with a wooden sword-like stick to score points. The 'tobacco grinned for' was a reference to the bizarre practice of grinning through horse collars. This was a contest where participants would put on a horse collar and the man or woman who managed to pull the ugliest face won the prize.

24 June

1798 mail robbery

On 24 June 1807, William Garland, with an address at no. 5 Bride Street in Dublin, was charged with forging an endorsement on a twenty-guinea banknote that had been stolen nine years earlier during the 1798 Rebellion. The note – issued by the Bank of Ireland – had been stolen on the night of 23 May 1798 when a group of rebels armed with pikes and muskets held up the Galway mail coach at Lucan and made off with several mail bags.

Garland – who was apprehended after attempting to change the note at a Kevin Street grocery shop owned by a Mr Fleming – claimed that he had found it concealed in a bed mat. However, he was acquitted after the grocer, and others, spoke up for him and told the court that Garland had only been eleven years old at the time of the robbery and could not have played a part in it.

25 June

How to deal with mad people

If only our eighteenth-century practitioners of psychiatric medicine had bothered to read the *Hibernian Journal,* there would have been no need for straitjackets, lobotomies, lunatic asylums or any of that nonsense. On 25 June 1772, the *Journal's* resident medical 'expert' summed up in one paragraph the exact way to handle what he termed the 'many evils and unfortunate accidents arising from the fury of mad people'.

The advice from the 'expert', known only as 'A lover of mankind', was as follows:

'Upon entering the room where the mad person is, your eyes must be fixed firmly on theirs: Upon theirs dropping, which they will do in a little time, you must continue yours with the steadfastness you at first made your attack. If they attack you a third time, you must still oppose them with the same strength. This is the period at which they always find themselves overcome, and never renew the attack, and always retain an awe of you.'

26 June

Bread thieves

The *Drogheda Conservative Journal* of 26 June 1847 – at the height of the Great Famine in Ireland – gave details of a number of convictions handed down for stealing bread at a Drogheda court earlier that week.

John Cavanagh was one of six hungry people who were handed jail sentences for stealing loaves of bread from bakeries and bread carts in the town. Cavanagh was sentenced to three months' imprisonment with hard labour, for stealing bread from a bakery owned by Mary Branagan. It was his second conviction for stealing bread and the prisoner begged the court to transport him instead. The keeper of the jail at Drogheda raised a laugh in court when he announced that the poor man was 'an enormous glutton', who was subject to epileptic fits and therefore had to be fed on 'white bread and new milk' at great cost to taxpayer.

27 June

Attempted murder of parish priest

On 27 June 1804, Counsellor Charles Frazer Frizell, barrister-at-law, was tried in Dublin for burglary, assault and the attempted murder of the parish priest of Rathfarnham.

During the weeks and months following Robert Emmet's attempted rising in 1803, the British military and local yeomanry were particularly active in Rathfarnham and surrounding areas. There was a curfew in force in the district and all lights were ordered to be extinguished by 9.00 p.m. each night. Locals were constantly harassed and homes were raided on a regular basis.

One of these raids, which occurred on the night of 3 February 1804, resulted in Frizell – a member of the Rathfarnham Yeomanry Corps – being charged with conspiracy to murder Dr William Ledwich, parish priest of Rathfarnham.

At 10.00 p.m. on the night in question, Ledwich, who was staying at the home of his aunt, Catherine Byrne, in Rathfarnham Village, was reading in bed when he heard a commotion downstairs. When he looked out the window he saw Frizell and Lieutenant Costley of the Rathfarnham Yeomanry Corps outside.

Frizell demanded that the priest accompany him to the guardroom, but Ledwich refused. Frizell called him out a second time and Ledwich decided to close the window. As he was in the act of closing it, a sword was thrust through the opening, narrowly missing the priest. Ledwich, fearing for his life, escaped out through the back of the house and spent the night out in the open in his night clothes.

In the meantime, Frizell ordered his men to open fire on the house and they unleashed a volley of shots, breaking all the windows in the process. The yeomen smashed their way into the house, assaulting the priest's niece Ann Ledwich and threatening to decapitate the priest.

At the trial, Counsellor Egan, speaking in defence of Frizell, said that on the night in question 'Frizell had been heated by wine' and had only asked Ledwich to accompany him to the guardroom because he had breached the 9.00 p.m. 'lights out' rule. He also accused the witnesses of exaggerating the attack on the priest's house and asked the jury for an acquittal.

Although several residents of Rathfarnham had witnessed the attack, the night was dark and no one could definitively say whether it was Frizell or Costley who had attacked the priest with a sword. Subsequently Frizell was acquitted on all counts.

However, in view of the circumstances of the case, the judge bound over Frizell to keep the peace, particularly in respect of the Ledwichs and Catherine Byrne, and he was ordered to pay a personal bond of £500 along with two independent sureties of £250 each.

28 June

Hibernian Marine School

On 28 June 1766, the *Freeman's Journal* announced that 'The Governors of the new charitable institution of an Hibernian Nursery for the Marine have taken a house at Ringsend, which is now fitting up, where they propose to lodge, diet, clothe and instruct 20 Boys, the Orphans or Children only of decayed Masters of Ships, or of Mariners…'. Three years later, the Marine school relocated to a larger building at Sir John Rogerson's Quay.

Admission to the Marine School in Dublin was strictly on the understanding that the boys would be educated in the Protestant faith, even if they were from Catholic families, and this rule led to difficulties on occasion.

Early in April 1829, one of the pupils, an eleven-year-old Ringsend boy named Doran, died at the school. The Master, Mr Baker, sent word to the Reverend Wall, assistant chaplain at St Matthew's Protestant Church at Irishtown, to prepare for the boy's funeral the following afternoon.

The deceased boy had previously been a Catholic and some of his family and friends were unhappy at the idea that he would be given a Protestant funeral. When the funeral procession arrived in Ringsend, it was joined by a large crowd of local people led by the Doran family. The Marine School contingent was pushed away and, once the procession reached Irishtown, the coffin was seized and carried three times around the churchyard in the customary fashion.

The coffin was then carried to the open grave in the churchyard and John Doran – the boy's uncle, who was filling the grave – told the Reverend Wall that there would be no Protestant prayers read in the churchyard that day. Doran threatened to break Wall's head with a spade while his wife Elizabeth attempted to take Wall's bible from him.

While all this was going on, the deceased boy's friends were trying to fill in the grave and two policemen made a vain attempt to arrest John Doran. In the ensuing melee, the side of the grave fell in, and stones and clods of earth were thrown in the churchyard. Wall was eventually forced to withdraw for his own safety.

John, Elizabeth and John's sister Margaret Doran were later found guilty of riot and assault at Irishtown and were each fined one mark as punishment. The Dorans were unable to come up with the money, but were spared a prison sentence when the jury and members of the public had a whip-round to pay the fine.

29 June

Putrefied corpses for landfill

There was shock and outrage expressed in Dublin on 29 June 1789 when it was discovered that labourers working on a public building at the Little Green near Halston Street were digging up dead bodies from a graveyard and using them as landfill in another part of the city. 'Bones, skulls and putrefied carcasses' were taken in an act of 'sacrilegious indecency' and thrown into carts for use in another unnamed building project across the city.

30 June

'The illegitimate son of Henry VIII'

Sir John Perrot, born sometime around 1527 in Wales, was president of Munster from 1571 to 1573, and also served as lord deputy of Ireland from 1584 to 1588. He was reputed to have been the illegitimate son of Henry VIII, to whom he was said to have borne a very close resemblance.

Perrot was a man of immense physical strength and was known to have had a fondness for drink. He also had a violent temper. On one occasion during his tenure as lord deputy, he actually thumped the Knight Marshal Sir Nicholas Bagenal during a debate in the council chamber.

Perrot was appointed lord deputy of Ireland in 1584 and he received the sword of state from Archbishop of Dublin and Lord Chancellor of Ireland Adam Loftus in June of that year. Perrot was no sooner in the job when he became embroiled in a row with Loftus. Perrot asked Lord Walsingham for permission to convert St Patrick's Cathedral into a courthouse and the adjoining residential buildings into a courthouse, infuriating the archbishop. To add insult to injury, he suggested that funds from the archbishop's estate be diverted to build two colleges in Dublin.

Elizabeth I removed Perrot from the position of lord deputy, and he surrendered the sword of state on 30 June 1588. Perrot was later accused of high treason and was lodged in the Tower of London in 1591. He died there in September 1592, before the conclusion of his trial.

JULY

1 July

Mass evictions in Galway

The *Tyrawly Herald* of 1 July 1852 reported on a mass eviction of poor families in County Galway a few days earlier. In the townlands of Barnacranny, Ballagh and Tonabrucky, 42 families were evicted, leaving a total of 203 people homeless and destitute. The vast majority of these people were forced to seek refuge in the workhouse.

2 July

A spree on bonfire night

Reporting on Galway Court of Petty Sessions proceedings on 2 July 1859, the *Galway Express* gave details of a case concerning eleven-year-old Amby Sheridan and James Glynn, who was a year younger.

Sheridan had accused the younger boy of stabbing him in the shoulder with a knife at a bonfire on the night of 23 June. Glynn claimed that he and his friends had been on a 'spree' on the night in question and that a drop of whiskey had been taken.

While Glynn was drinking from the bottle, the older boy slapped him on the back, nearly choking him, and said, 'more power to you'. The defendant said that he remembered pushing Sheridan away, but could remember nothing more as they were all 'blind drunk'. Sheridan, whose arm was bandaged, told the court that the stab wound was an inch deep. The case was heard at the Galway Assizes later that month and the ten-year-old Glynn pleaded guilty as charged and was jailed for six months.

3 July

Dolly disaster

On Monday, 3 July 1905, Dubliners awoke to the dreadful news that a small pleasure boat with six passengers aboard – all members of Shelbourne Football Club – had sunk in a squall on Dublin Bay close to Poolbeg Lighthouse the previous evening.

The craft in question – the *Dolly* – was owned and skippered by Ringsend man James Waddock. Waddock's five companions, including a nine-year-old boy John Purdy, were all from Ringsend; all six perished in the tragedy. The other victims were Peter Redmond, James Owens, Robert Cunningham and John Polhill. Young Purdy was particularly unlucky to be aboard as he was only picked up from a rowboat downriver after begging the men to let him come with them.

The *Dolly* left Ringsend early the previous Sunday morning for a day's fishing off Howth Head. Initially the sea was calm and the weather pleasant. Later that evening, however, as the Dolly was making its return journey to Ringsend, the weather began to turn nasty.

As the little craft approached Poolbeg Lighthouse, the winds strengthened and two men who were out walking near the lighthouse saw that it was struggling against the squalls. The boat appeared to have been struck by a gust of wind, which capsized it. The two witnesses later said that they observed two of the men struggling in the water, but they disappeared after twenty minutes. They saw a small dog, which had been on board the *Dolly*, nearly make it to the shore, but he gave up and sank within twenty yards of the sea wall.

A lifeboat was launched from the Pigeon House and it was joined by the Ringsend Coastguard in a desperate attempt to save the men. However, despite an extensive search, they were unable to find any trace of the boat or the missing men. The only items found were James Waddock's gallon jar, which he used to carry porter on his fishing expeditions, and an oar from the boat.

James Owens, one of the victims, was the father of Shelbourne Football Club Captain Jackie Owens, and the club launched a disaster fund for the families affected by the tragedy.

4 July

Ardee transvestite

The *Dublin Evening Post* of 4 July 1732 informs us that, during a duel in Dublin, Mr Burnside, who was a writing master, shot Mr Cashell in the left breast, killing him instantly. The dispute arose after Cashell had taunted Burnside on Bachelor's Walk in Dublin, calling him a 'Buttermilk Beau'. Burnside immediately fled Dublin.

In its next issue, the *Dublin Evening Post* claimed that Burnside had been arrested at Ardee in County Louth, disguised in women's clothing. However, the *Post* edition of 18 July issued a correction of this information, stating that the man captured was not Burnside at all but a 'fellow that has affected that dress since his childhood, and we hear, has served as a maid servant in several houses'.

5 July

A Dublin Riot

On the night of 5 July 1886, a serious riot took place in Dublin in which one man died, at least fifty were injured and eight-five were arrested by the city police. The rioting

occurred following the election of the Nationalist candidate Edmund Dwyer Gray as MP for the St Stephen's
Green ward of Dublin city.

About 8 o'clock in the evening, bands celebrating
Gray's victory began to parade in the area and soon
attracted a huge crowd. Later, an estimated crowd of two
to three thousand of Gray's supporters converged on York
Street, just off Stephen's Green, which was then home
to the Nationalist Workingmen's Club, the Conservative
Workingmen's Club and an Orange Hall.

The bands halted outside the Conservative Club –
which was packed with Orangemen – and they began to
play a selection of rousing Fenian tunes. When asked later
to describe exactly what these tunes were, Police Inspector
Talbot said that he didn't know but commented wryly that
he was sure they weren't playing 'God save the Queen'.

When the Nationalists began to sing 'God Save Ireland',
the Orangemen inside the club responded by booing and
hissing. The crowd then began to hurl bottles, stones and
bricks at the building, and an unsuccessful attempt was
made to set the front door on fire.

At the height of the rioting, a number of shots were
discharged from inside the Conservative Club and some
of the demonstrators were taken to the nearby Mercer's
Hospital with gunshot wounds. One man, James McConn,
died while running from the scene directly after the
shooting, but it was established afterwards that he had died
from a heart attack.

The crowd quickly dispersed after the shooting, and
a large force of police entered the Conservative Club.
Police later arrested eighty-five Orangemen, most of
them armed with cudgels. Fourteen rioters were arrested
outside the club, but were not detained. Inside the club,
police discovered a number of iron bars, and in a yard at

the back of the house they uncovered two revolvers that had recently been fired and a quantity of ammunition.

Three Dublin Orangemen, Archibald Cruickshank, Robert Clarke and William Ward, were charged with firing into the crowd, but were later acquitted, as were the others arrested in the Conservative Club.

Sporadic rioting continued around the city for the next three nights. On 7 July a large number of nationalists again gathered in York Street, this time to defend the Nationalist Club against attack from students of Trinity College, who had threatened to 'capture the Fenian flag in York Street'. The students never carried out their threat although they were involved in a few minor incidents throughout the city.

The bell-ringers of St Patrick's Cathedral had the last word in the matter at midnight on 8 July. After ringing the midnight hour, they rang out the tune of 'Rule Britannia'. However, no one responded to this act of provocation and the streets remained calm.

6 July

'An unfortunate boy'

This missing person's ad from the *Dublin Evening Post* on 6 July 1809 gives voice to every parent's nightmare:

'An unfortunate boy, who left his parents' house, with an intention of walking into the country for his amusement, on Wednesday, 31st May last; and although every enquiry has since been made respecting him, yet no certain information has been received. It is, therefore, hoped that any humane person, who may have met him, or knows where he may be found, will have the goodness to send information by letter, or otherwise to No.3

Townsend Street – and any reward or expense, which may be required, will be thankfully given. As his long absence may induce him to think he may be punished for his misconduct on his return, he may rest assured, that on the contrary, he shall be treated by his unhappy relations with every kindness and affectionate regard. The above boy is between 16 and 17 years of age, slender made, about five feet, five inches high, light complexion, fair hair, blue eyes, with a slight cast, high nose, holds his head to one side, and walks with one shoulder forward – his legs feeble, and his right knee rather large – had on him a blue cloth coat, with flat-plated buttons, a red waistcoat, with black spots, and a black one under it – nankeen pantaloons, and a pair of blue cloth under them. It has been supposed he went towards Kilkenny.'

7 July

Drowned in the Liffey

There were two cases of drowning reported in the *Freeman's Journal* on 7 July 1788. The first concerned a ten-year-old boy who fell into the River Liffey at Coal Quay on the previous day. On the morning of 7 July, the body of a woman was taken from the river at George's Quay. The woman had been stabbed several times and it was reported that she had been working as a prostitute 'in that hotbed of iniquity' at Stocking Lane near Townsend Street.

It was also reported on the same day that a woman, who was caught in the act of stripping a child in Cook Street, was seized by a mob, given a severe ducking under a pump and taken to the police watch house on the Old Bridge over the Liffey.

8 July

Death of Sarah Atkinson

Sarah Atkinson, the philanthropist and writer, devoted much of her spare time to charitable work in Dublin. She was particularly prolific in her efforts to help young Dublin girls who had found themselves in the city's many work-houses and institutions during the mid-nineteenth century.

Sarah Atkinson, née Gaynor, was born in Athlone in 1823 and was the eldest of five daughters. She moved to Dublin with her family when she was fifteen. In 1849 she married doctor and proprietor of the *Freeman's Journal* George Atkinson.

In 1856, aided by her friend and neighbour Ellen Woodcock, Sarah established St Joseph's Industrial Institute in Drumcondra for the training and rehabilitation of young women who had been released from the South Dublin Union Workhouse. Many of the girls taken on by Atkinson and Woodcock had been born in the workhouse and were considered to be 'untameable', having spent long periods in solitary confinement for unnamed misdemeanours in a place called 'the cage' at the South Dublin Union Workhouse.

In a memoir of Sarah Atkinson penned after her death, her friend Rosa Mulholland, wife of Sir John Gilbert, related that Sarah had particular success with a group of girls in the workhouse who were known collectively as the 'Gypsy Band'. According to Mulholland, these girls conducted such a violent reign of terror in the workhouse that even the governor was afraid of them.

Amongst other crimes attributed to the Gypsy Band were rioting, stealing from and assaulting their fellow inmates and, on one occasion, even trying to set fire to the workhouse. Atkinson is credited with completely reforming these girls at her Drumcondra school so that, as Mulholland put it, 'they became docile and industrious, and in many cases happily lived to distinguish themselves by their virtuous conduct.'

Many were eventually retrained and sent abroad to England, Australia and the US, where they were given a new start in life. However, Atkinson and Woodcock's works came to an abrupt end when the government refused to grant them any further funds to keep the school going.

Sarah Atkinson died on 8 July 1893 in Drumcondra and was buried in Glasnevin Cemetery following a large funeral.

9 July

Orange riots in Liverpool

Extract from *The Telegraph* (Dublin), 9 July 1852:

'After I dispatched my letter yesterday, a rumour prevailed that St Patrick's chapel in the park had been attacked by the Orangemen, as they went in that direction from the procession, with band playing and colours flying. I at once went to the place, but happily the rumour was not correct so far as the chapel was concerned, but I found that there had been a serious riot, in which several persons had been severely injured ….The row originated (as a matter of course) in consequence of a drunken Orangeman, who was at the rere[sic.] of the procession, insulting some women who sold fish and oranges at Saint James's Market, or near the top of Park Lane. The women naturally returned the insult by throwing a stone or two at the ruffian, when he called out 'to hell with the bloody Pope, and damnation to holy water and the priests.' This, I need hardly say, caused a row, and a fearful one followed, in which the parties above alluded to were hurt. The police, horse and foot, soon arrived and quieted the disturbance, but the locality was in a state of great excitement and agitation almost all the night.'

10 July

'Fiends of hell'

The *Freeman's Journal* of 10 July 1839 contained an interesting report of a Dublin dog-biting case. An old Quaker woman named Alicia Napier Wilson Boyle was charged at the Dublin Police Court with having a dangerous dog. James Hanlon told the court that the woman's dog had bitten one of his children.

When asked by the judge – Alderman Darley – why her dog had bitten the child, Boyle replied that Hanlon's children were 'fiends of hell' who were always annoying her. A police sergeant told the court that the poor woman was insane. When asked to explain, the sergeant told the court that she called her home *Shamrock Villa*, 'which consisted of one room, where a cow, a goat, two dogs, and herself are located, and she also has a coffin in it'.

The judge was going to allow the woman to keep the dog if she promised to keep it muzzled, but Hanlon objected saying that the dog was too dangerous. The judge decided that the dog must be destroyed and the old woman left the court in a very distressed state.

11 July

Charles Macklin, comedian

The famous eighteenth-century comic actor Charles McLoughlin – born in Westmeath in 1690 – was better known by stage name of Charles Macklin. His family was originally from Derry, and one of his proudest boasts was that he had thirteen uncles at the Siege of Derry – ten inside with the Williamites and three outside besieging the walls with the followers of King James.

Macklin was apprenticed to a saddle maker as a teenager, but he ran away to Dublin after a few years. He was first seen on the stage in England in 1725, where he became a comic actor and author of note, and he had a meteoric rise through the ranks of the acting profession. His career nearly came to a dramatic end when he was charged with the murder of one of his colleagues at the Old Bailey in 1735.

Macklin was accused of slaying Thomas Hallam at the Drury Lane Theatre during a dispute that began over a wig. A row broke out in the dressing room when Macklin accused the dead man of wearing his wig. 'Damn you for a blackguard, scrub, rascal,' said Macklin. 'How durst you have the impudence to take this wig?' When the hapless victim tried to answer him back, Macklin jumped out of his chair and thrust a walking stick into Hallam's eyeball, fatally wounding him.

Luckily for Macklin, the Old Bailey jury only found him guilty of 'manslaughter without malice aforethought' and he was given only a token punishment.

Macklin continued to tread the boards until 1753 when he opened a school for oratory. This venture failed soon afterwards. He returned to the stage and had great success in London and at Crow Street Theatre in Dublin. He gave his last performance in Drury Lane in 1789 and he died on 11 July 1797. He was buried at St Paul's Church in Covent Garden.

12 July

A seventy-year-old orphan

Clearly a case of a writer with a sense of humour, this obituary on the death of a Fermanagh woman first saw the light of day in the *Fermanagh Reporter* in July 1851 and was republished in the *Daily Express* on 12 July that year:

'On Sunday last, one mile south of this town, at the very advanced age of 107 years, Peggy Kavanagh, who retained all her faculties while she retained her breath. The youngest of her family, an orphan lad of 70, still survives her, and is yet unprovided for.'

13 July

Swarm of bees

There was an unusual report in the *Munster Journal* on 13 July 1749 concerning a swarm of bees at the Royal Barracks [now Collins Barracks] in Dublin. The bees had flown into the barracks a few days earlier and had swarmed all over a young servant boy. The boy was forced to stand in the one spot without moving while a beekeeper was summoned.

It was reported that the boy stood on the same spot for hours with bees clinging to his face, arms and legs. He was about to collapse when an officer made him take hold of a branch of a tree, and, fortunately for him, some of the bees flew on to the branch. The rest flew into hives brought by the beekeeper.

Amazingly, the boy was only stung once during the entire ordeal and the beekeeper gave him a guinea for his trouble.

14 July

Refused to 'plead her belly'

When a woman was sentenced to death in Ireland during the eighteenth century, she could apply to the court to have her sentence commuted if she could prove that she was pregnant. This was known in common parlance as 'pleading her belly'.

One woman who refused to do this was Dublin woman Mary Costelloe who, along with her husband Edward, was hanged at St Stephen's Green for doctoring coins. The newspapers reported on 14 July 1750 that, after the judge had passed the death sentence on her, Mary Costelloe refused to 'plead her belly', saying that she would rather die in the arms of her husband.

15 July

'The evil effects of drink'

Writing in 1888, the *Evening Telegraph* columnist Michael McDonagh summed up the life of the County Clare-born poet Thomas Dermody as 'a black record of the evil effects of drink; of lost opportunities; of rank ingratitude to friends who had ever a helping hand extended to save him from his gloomy fate…'.

Born in Ennis in 1775, where his father taught the classics, the young Dermody was teaching Greek and Latin by the time he was nine years old.

Dermody left home and walked to Dublin in 1787, living on raw turnips that he picked along the way. He lived rough on the streets of Dublin for a time until he was taken in by Dr Houlton, an eminent physician, who discovered him reading a Greek classic in a bookshop. Houlton later described Dermody as a 'little lowly country boy, meanly habited and evidently not more than ten years old'.

Houlton was to be only one of a long list of benefactors to recognise the young Dermody's talents. Another of these, the Reverend Gilbert Austin, paid to have a book of Dermody's poetry published in 1792. Dermody was drinking very heavily at that stage and soon left Reverend Austin's household. He had several more wealthy patrons, including the Dowager Countess of Moira, and he managed to fall out with all of them.

Irish MPs Henry Grattan and Henry Flood also held Dermody in high esteem and occasionally gave him money. Grattan was so impressed with his poetry that he sometimes quoted passages from Dermody's work during speeches at the Parliament House on College Green.

Dermody decided to go to England to seek his fortune, but he got so drunk at a hostelry in South Great George's Street that he was captured by the press-gang on three separate occasions on his way to the boat and had to be rescued by his friends. He eventually made it to England in 1794 and he enlisted in the Wagon Corps. He rose to the rank of second lieutenant and retired on half pay in 1801.

However, he soon resumed his heavy drinking habits and the years of debauchery and ill-health finally took their toll. He was found dying in a derelict cottage in Sydenham, Kent by his friend John Raymond, who later published the young poet's biography. Thomas Dermody died on 15 July 1802 and he is buried in Lewisham Churchyard.

16 July

Sir Walter Scott in Dublin

On 16 July 1825 the *Freeman's Journal* welcomed the novelist Sir Walter Scott on his one and only visit to Dublin, saying: 'there is no Prince except our own that should be welcomed to this island with greater enthusiasm than Walter Scott, for there is no author who has been more generally read and admired in Ireland than he has been.'

Scott had arrived in Dublin two days earlier and stayed with his son Walter at no. 9 St Stephen's Green, which later became the Stephen's Green Club. The younger Scott was, at that time, an officer in the 15th Hussars Regiment of the British Army, which was then stationed in Dublin.

Although Scott had earlier stressed that this was to be a private visit, the Dublin newspapers reported that he had hardly closed the door behind him before a steady stream of visitors began to arrive. Invitations poured in from all over the city for the famous author, most of which 'were politely but firmly declined'.

He was a huge star in Dublin and his every move was chronicled in the newspapers. Wherever he went, Scott was surrounded by a large number of Dubliners, all eager to catch a glimpse of the great man. Businesses came to a standstill as shopkeepers and employees rushed out onto the pavements to applaud him, and it was reported that 'even the mob and boys huzza'd [cheered] as at the chariot wheels of a conquerer' as he passed by in his carriage.

During his brief stay in the city, Scott visited many of its public buildings, such as Christ Church and St Patrick's Cathedral, and spent some time in Marsh's Library where the librarian showed him the desk where Scott's friend and fellow novelist Charles Maturin —who had died nine months earlier – had worked for many years. He also paid a visit to Maturin's widow to sympathise with her on her bereavement.

17 July

Strolling beggar

Advertisement in the *Dublin Courant,* 17 July 1744:
    'Broke out of the City Work-house, the 17th day of June last, WILLIAM MADDEN, a Strolling Beggar, aged

36 Years or thereabouts, about five Feet ten Inches high, well made, of a pale complexion, wore his own black slim Hair, has an Issue [a wound] in his right Arm (which he blows up to a large size to excite compassion), and on his left Hand a big Bile; he went off in a brown coloured Body Coat, and old light coloured Great Coat. Whoever secures the said Madden, so as to bring him to the said House, shall have five Guineas Reward, to be paid by the Treasurer thereof. Signed by Order, THOMAS EATON, Register.'

18 July

Suffragettes in fire alert

'Theatre Royal on Fire'; 'Hatchet Thrown at Mr. J. Redmond'; 'Explosive Material Found in a House'– these were just some of the headlines which appeared in Dublin's newspapers on 19 July 1912. The headlines referred to an attempt by English suffragettes to burn down the Theatre Royal in Hawkins Street, along with other misdeeds, as part of an ongoing campaign to secure voting rights for Irishwomen.

In the weeks previous to the attack on the theatre, members of the Irish Women's Franchise League and others had taken part in a number of protests around Dublin and Ireland, which included a window-smashing campaign on Sackville Street.

However, the protests were taken to a new level when, on the night of 18 July 1912, three English suffragettes made a determined attempt to set fire to one of Dublin's premier entertainment venues during a visit to Dublin by the British Prime Minister H.H. Asquith.

The incident at the Theatre Royal began after 8.30 p.m., just as the early evening show was ending. One of the suffragettes attempted to set fire to reels of highly flammable cine-films and also set fire to a seat in the dress circle. Meanwhile, another suffragette had started a fire in a private box close to the stage, set fire to the stage curtains and hurled a blazing chair into the orchestra pit.

Theatre staff and a number of soldiers in the audience rushed forward to subdue the flames and one of the protestors was arrested on the spot. The woman in the private box managed to flee from the theatre but left behind a box containing a whiskey bottle half full with petrol. A bag containing gunpowder, matches and firelighters was also discovered at the scene.

The Englishwoman arrested at the theatre was Gladys Evans of Muswell Lodge, London; Mary Capper from Manchester and Lizzie Baker from Liverpool were apprehended later. All three were charged with conspiracy to inflict grievous bodily harm and to cause an explosion in the Theatre Royal.

Another militant, Mary Leigh, who refused to give her address, was also charged with taking part in the plot and with throwing a hatchet at Prime Minister Asquith's carriage on the same evening, wounding John Redmond M.P. in the head.

Evidence was given that Leigh rushed at the Prime Minister'carriage near Prince's Street and flung a hatchet in through the window. Inside the carriage were Asquith, his wife, the Lord Mayor of Dublin and John Redmond. Luckily for Redmond, the hatchet bounced off a policeman's helmet before hitting him and he received only minor cuts to the ear.

The four women were tried for the crimes in early August. Mary Capper was acquitted of all charges laid against her and released, while Lizzie Baker was given a sentence of seven months' imprisonment with hard labour. Evans and Leigh didn't get off so lightly, however, and each was given a prison sentence of five years.

19 July

Attacked with a slash hook

A twelve-year-old boy appeared at the Louth Summer Assizes on 19 July 1864 on a charge of cutting and wounding a little girl with a slash hook. He was acquitted due to lack of evidence.

Also on trial that day was Hugh Flynn, who killed John Larkin during a drunken brawl at a pub in the seaside village of Blackrock in County Louth. Flynn was found guilty of the manslaughter of Larkin and was sentenced to twelve months in prison with hard labour.

20 July

Pretend whipping

The perceived lenient treatment towards two women, who had been punished for shoplifting in Dublin on 20 July 1776, provoked an angry and sarcastic response from a writer in the *Hibernian Journal* a few days later. The two women had been whipped from Newgate Prison to College Green for stealing linen from a shop in Nicholas Street, but, in the writer's opinion, the man doing the flogging had gone far too easy on them.

'The two females who were whipped (or rather pretended to be whipped) last Saturday, for shop-lifting, present their respects to Mr. Sheriff Beasly who attended on the occasion, and with the deepest sense of gratitude return him their humble thanks for his extraordinary lenity and tenderness in not suffering the sentence of the law to be executed on them without even the smallest degree of rigour; therefore hope that through his recommendation, they and the rest of the worthy corporation of shop-lifters will be permitted to pursue their honest calling unmolested for the future. They at the same time beg leave to return the humane and worthy hangman their sincere thanks for the gentle manner in which he performed the operation.'

21 July

The servants are too well fed

Saunders' Newsletter, 21 July 1814: Samuel Donegan was found guilty of assaulting Arabella Crosby at her home at no. 92 Dorset Street in Dublin. Donegan – a servant – had previously been a lodger at Crosby's house and he had returned on 20 June to pick up some of his things.

While he was at the house, a dispute developed and Donegan grabbed Crosby by the hair and tried to drag her to the ground. She was rescued by her neighbours, and Donegan was arrested and charged with assaulting Crosby and provoking a riot.

Finding Donegan guilty on the assault charge, the judge sentenced him to three months' imprisonment and commented: 'The servants have now become so insolent from being too well fed; it will become necessary to punish such ruffians.'

22 July

Battle over the ball alley

General News-letter, Dublin, 22 July 1771:
'Sunday evening, about eight o'clock, a number of fellows from Crosse-Lane went to a ball-alley at the sign of the Cherry tree on Drumcondra road and insisted to have the alley immediately cleared for them; but the persons who at that time employed it refusing to comply, a battle

ensued which lasted a considerable time – to the great terror of the inhabitants of the neighbourhood and to the innocent people who were walking that way to take the benefit of the air. During the engagement, the numbers having considerably increased on the Drumcondra side, the Crosse Lane heroes thought it most prudent to make their retreat, which they effected with much difficulty, as showers of stones were instantly thrown after them till they reached Dorset Street. We do not hear that any lives were lost, but many were wounded…'.

23 July

'Prepare a Holland shirt for your poor Jack'

On 23 July 1784, the *Hibernian Journal* reported on the case of John Keenan, who was hanged at Gallows Hill near Kilmainham two days earlier for robbing Captain Withers, an army officer, in January of that year. Keenan had been sentenced to death on six previous occasions, but had managed to cheat 'Jack the breath-stopper' each time by giving information to his captors in relation to other crimes.

He nearly managed to escape from Newgate Prison before his trial by sawing through the bars, but he was caught by the jailer. On the evening before his execution he wrote a last letter to his wife:

'My dear Polly, I am down at last. I now must die, prepare a Holland shirt for your poor Jack, which shall be the last …. My friend at Harold's Cross holds a cup, two watches and six copper-plate papers of mine – I would advise you to marry him … he will never see you want whilst there is powder and shot …. Adieu, my sweetheart…'.

24 July

Hanged for a crime they didn't commit

Three men were hanged at Gallows Hill in Dublin after they had been wrongly accused of robbing a man of his watch and coat outside the Royal Hospital Kilmainham.

The three men, Henry Binns and brothers John and Peter Mullen, vehemently protested their innocence before they were executed on 24 July 1784. Their innocence was only proven the following year when John Hugan, who was being hanged for another crime, made a sworn statement that he had been responsible for the robbery at the Royal Hospital.

25 July

Dublin dosshouses

On 25 July 1906 an intrepid newspaper reporter from the *Evening Herald* wrote of his adventures while sampling life in the city's dosshouses disguised as a tramp. He spent his first night in place known as the 'Leather Lodge' next door to the stage entrance to the Theatre Royal. The price of a bed at the Leather Lodge – so called because of the rough leather quilts handed out to guests – was 'a deuce' (two old pence) and the beds were mainly occupied by shoeblacks and sandwich-board carriers.

The kindest thing our man could think of to say about the place was that 'the Spartan simplicity of the accessories of the twopenny doss would rejoice the austere soul of the most self-denying ascetic.' Check-in time at the Leather Lodge was 6.00 p.m., and guests had to be up and out by 6.00 a.m. the next morning.

Slightly better accommodation was to be had at the 'Men's Shelter' in Peter Street, where the fourpenny entrance fee included a cooked breakfast of bacon and eggs. One of the regular visitors to the Peter Street shelter was a poet who made his living by selling poems to love-sick shop boys, students and apprentices, who would then pass them off as their own.

The crème de la crème of the dosshouses, as far as our friend was concerned, was the Iveagh Hostel in Bride Street, which he described as a 'first-class hotel, conducted on the most up-to-date lines'. In addition to a wash house, drying room and cookhouse, the Iveagh contained a library and a billiard room, and lodgers had their own private sleeping accommodation.

26 July

Hanged for a coat

Drogheda man Edward Kelch was taken before Drogheda Crown Court on 26 July 1790, where he was charged with robbing Bryan Leoland of a coat and seven shillings. The robbery took place seven weeks earlier at 11.00 p.m. at night outside the Dublin Gate in Drogheda. Kelch and a companion held the victim up with a pistol. Despite evidence given to the court by Kelch's sister and brother-in-law, the jury took only a few minutes to find him guilty and he was sentenced to be hanged on 7 August.

27 July

Four young women dead in Killarney

The *Leinster Journal* of 27 July 1768 reported on the deaths of four young women at a house in Killarney, County Kerry. The four women – who were said to have been in perfect health – went to bed in the same room in the house and all four were found dead the following morning. Dr Thadee Cronin, who examined the women, said that they had died from smoke inhalation.

28 July

MacRobespierre of Kilkenny?

During the French Revolution, one of the leading lights in the terror was one Maximilien Marie Isidore de Robespierre, who was born in Arras in France on 6 May 1758. Robespierre is one of the best-known and most controversial leaders of the French Revolution and he was largely responsible for the Reign of Terror, during which thousands of opponents of the Revolution died in prison or were executed.

Although no documentary evidence exists to prove it, and there has been no rush in this country to claim him as 'one of our own', there have been persistent tales of Robespierre's alleged Irish ancestry. One source claims that Robespierre's grandfather went to France with King James after he had fled Ireland and settled in Arras, but French historian Jules Michelet, in his *History of the Revolution*, has claimed that the Robespierre family might have been in France from as early as the year 1600.

Another book, *Ireland and Irishmen in the French Revolution*, written by Richard Hayes, suggests that the name Robespierre was originally Fitz Roth Piers, of which there were several Catholic families during the sixteenth and seventeenth centuries. According to Hayes, some of these were landowners and holders of municipal office in Kilkenny until their land and titles were confiscated during the Elizabethan and Cromwellian periods.

Hayes also gives details of the Kilkenny Fitz Roth Piers family that was recorded in Irish state documents during the sixteenth and seventeenth centuries. For instance, one document written in 1594, during the reign of Elizabeth I, gives details of various lands in Kilkenny which were granted to an undertaker [property speculator or land agent], including 'the rent of a garden which John Routh Fitz Piers had owned'.

In 1648 a house and surrounding lands owned by the Mayor of Kilkenny Robert Rothe were confiscated and he and his family were banished to Connaught. Rothe's wife was a Fitz Piers and they both eventually settled in France. One of their sons, Robert Rothe Fitz Piers also settled there. Hayes suggests that this Kilkenny Fitz Roth Piers family took on the French name of Robespierre because it was nearest phonetically to their own.

However, all of this is in the realm of rumour and innuendo and to date there is no concrete evidence that the architect of the Reign of Terror had any Irish links at all.

29 July

Crime watch

The *Hibernian Journal* reported on wide variety of crimes in Ireland on 29 July 1771. In Dublin, a man was pilloried at the Tholsel [courthouse and council chambers] for running a brothel, while a blind man was lashed from the gate of the Phoenix Park to Chapelizod Bridge for robbing the 'turnpike desk'. At the time there were a number of turnpikes in the city. A turnpike gate was the early equivalent of the toll bridge.

In other news, a young gentleman managed to fend off a footpad, or a highwayman operating by foot, who attacked and tried to rob him in William Street. He was slashed four times but the footpad ran off when members of the public went to the young man's aid.

A coroner's inquest was held into the death of Thomas Street publican Andrew O'Brien. The inquest heard O'Brien had died from a broken skull some time previously following an assault by his wife. His wife absconded after the incident.

Meanwhile, in Tipperary, Michael Halpenny was sentenced to a term in Clonmel Prison for stealing sheep – the property of Creagh Butler of Kilmoyler in Tipperary.

30 July

Detective Smyth – first Dublin Metropolitan Policeman to die during War of Independence

The first member of the Dublin Metropolitan Police (DMP) to be killed in the War of Independence was Detective Sergeant Patrick Smyth, who was shot near his home at no. 51 Millmount Avenue in Drumcondra on 30 July 1919. Smyth was originally from Cavan and was the father of eight children.

Detective Smyth – who was attached to the G Division, a vital cog in the British government's intelligence network – left Dublin Castle shortly before 11.00 p.m. that night and took a tram to Drumcondra, getting off at the Tolka Bridge. He had nearly reached his home when he was approached by two men who opened fire on him with revolvers, shooting him four times.

Smyth – who didn't die until sometime later – said that the men shot him again as he lay on the ground. On hearing the commotion, Smyth's eldest son Francis rushed outside to his father's aid, while another son, aged eight, rushed from the house saying that he was going 'to catch those who had shot his dada'.

An ambulance was called, and Smyth was taken to the nearby Mater Hospital where – although his condition was described as 'very serious' – he didn't appear to be in any immediate danger of dying. However, Smyth never recovered from his wounds and he died in the Mater on 8 September.

No one was ever charged with the killing of Smyth, but it later emerged that he had been killed by Michael Collin's elite hit squad that later became known as the Twelve Apostles. Collins had set up the squad in order to take out DMP detectives attached to the G Division at Dublin Castle.

Smyth had been active in pursuing republicans under the Defence of the Realm Act, and was considered to be a marked man by his colleagues. The squad had threatened Smyth earlier in the year to force him to drop charges against a republican, but Smyth had ignored the threats.

It was not the first time that Collins' men had tried to kill Smyth. They had lain in wait for the detective for several nights before they finally caught up with him. Smyth was the squad's first victim.

31 July

Execution of Mullingar brothers

Tuesday, 31 July 1849 saw the public execution of two Mullingar brothers – Martin and Denis Curley – for the murder of their uncle James Curley in March of that year. The two men were executed on the gallows outside Mullingar Jail in what proved to be the last public hanging in the town.

At the trial for the murder some weeks earlier, Martin Curley caused a commotion in court when he put a curse on the presiding judge, telling him that neither he nor anyone who had given evidence against him would have a moment's peace. Another member of the Curley family was also imprisoned for trying to intimidate a juror during the trial, telling him that he was measuring him up for a coffin.

On the morning of their execution, the Curley brothers rose at 6.00 a.m., having slept soundly the night before. They went to mass in the prison chapel and were said to have dined heartily on tea, bread and butter afterwards in their cells. They spent the rest of the morning in prayer and emerged at the front of the prison at midday dressed in their grave shrouds, ready for execution.

Before they were hanged, both men were given the chance to make a final declaration. Denis went first and fully acknowledged his part in the murder, saying that he hoped his punishment would act as a deterrent to others. Martin, however, was not so penitent. He swore that he had had no hand, act or part in the murder of his uncle. Both men then forgave their prosecutors and Martin said that 'I was never a sworn party man and I am innocent of the murder for which I am now going to suffer'.

The brothers then stepped forward to the gallows. The executioner placed the ropes around their necks and drew the bolts on the platform, and both men plunged to their deaths. Martin's death was instantaneous, while his brother took a few minutes to die.

Afterwards, both men were lowered into coffins and buried in the prison graveyard.

AUGUST

1 August

Beware of the ferret

Animal lovers were urged by the *Dublin Courier* to exercise caution when dealing with ferrets after a Westmeath man was viciously attacked by his pet ferret on 1 August 1760. The man, who lived in Tully, was said to have been extremely fond of his ferret, so much so that the animal was given free run of the bedchamber. However, while the man was asleep on the night in question, 'he had his face very much mangled by the ferret, and would in all probability have been otherwise greatly hurt had he not luckily killed the animal.'

2 August

Cherry Mulally 'pleads her belly'

Unlike Mary Costelloe, who was hanged in Dublin in July 1750 after refusing to 'plead her belly' (see entry for 14 July), the exotically named Cherry Mulally had no such qualms while facing a similar charge in the Dublin courts a few weeks later, on 2 August 1750.

Cherry Mulally and Valentine Magee were prosecuted for stealing cloth valued at thirteen pounds from Mr Overstreet Grogan's shop in Dame Street. Both faced the death penalty if convicted. Magee was acquitted after a long trial, but Mulally was found guilty as charged. She managed to avoid the death penalty by 'pleading her belly' and she was judged to be pregnant by a 'jury of matrons'.

3 August

Lost dog

It is somewhat refreshing and quite unusual to find a little bit of humanity among the tales of violence, murder and all kinds of mayhem in our newspapers over the years. This advert, placed in the *Dublin Courier* on 3 August 1761, related to a lost and obviously very-much loved dog:

'Strayed from on board a gabbard at the Custom house quay, a black dog of a mongrel breed, something of the greyhound make and answers to the name Tide-waiter, is remarkable for fawning and licking the spittle of any person who takes notice of him; is apt to fasten himself on gentlemen until they are obliged to kick him off; and is very fond of being caressed by the ladies, but if they make free with him, always babbles and never fails to bite them. Any person who brings or sends him to the watch-house on the Custom-house quay, shall have the thanks of the whole corps or officers of the tide, as they are greatly distressed for want of the entertainment he generally afforded them.'

4 August

James Henry's lucky number

It was reported in the *Newry Examiner* on 4 August 1832 that fifteen prisoners from Armagh Jail had been transferred to Newgate Prison in Dublin in preparation for their transportation to Australia. Among the prisoners was James Henry, who had been transported thirteen years earlier for stealing thirteen hens. He returned to Ireland after serving his sentence. On this particular occasion he was being transported for stealing thirteen sheep.

5 August

'Destroyed her illegitimate child'

A Wicklow woman ran afoul of the law in 1845 when she was charged with killing her child.

On 5 August 1845, *Hue and Cry* published the following report:

'Description of Ellen O'Brien, who stands charged with having, on or about the 25th day of April, at Calary in the barony of Rathdown, and parish of Calary, destroyed her illegitimate child: 23 years of age, 5 feet, 5 inches high, slight make, fair complexion, light brown hair, high nose, limbs clumsy, good looking; is a native of the county of Wicklow. She is well educated for her station in life, good manners, and dressed respectably, usually wore a black Orleans mantle.'

The *Hue and Cry* was an early, printed, version of TV programmes like RTÉ's *CrimeCall* or its predecessor *Garda Patrol*, in which the public were alerted to be on the lookout for various criminals or malefactors wanted for questioning by the authorities.

6 August

Ballincollig gunpowder explosion

Five workers died in a catastrophic explosion at the Royal Ballincollig Gunpowder Mills in Cork on 6 August 1859. It is not known how the accident happened, but the men had just returned from their breakfast when disaster struck. Mr Somerville, a superintendent at the plant, described seeing a column of flame shooting forty feet into the air, while others reported hearing the explosion in Cork city and at Passage, twelve miles away.

Many houses in nearby Ballincollig were badly damaged in the blast. Windows were blown out and some houses lost their roofs. Trees were torn out of the ground and hurled eighty feet in the air and the banks of the local canal were badly damaged.

The five workers who died that day were torn apart in the explosion, and many body parts were found scattered up to a mile away, so great was the force of the blast. An inquest was held into the men's deaths, and the jury returned an open verdict on the tragedy.

7 August

'The offensive spectacles'

There was a story in the *Dublin Courant* on 7 August 1744 about the enormous begging problem on the streets of the capital city. All kinds of methods had been undertaken by the city fathers in an effort to deal with the problem, including the jailing of beggars and forcing them to wear badges.

Another scheme to try and get beggars off the streets was the opening of the Hospital for Incurables on Lazar's Hill (Townsend Street) in 1744. However, the hospital was unable to cope with the huge influx of beggars, and its directors declared in the *Courant* that they would only be able to take in limited numbers in the future. They announced that only the 'offensive spectacles', i.e. the objectionable-looking beggars, were to be taken in in the future, and they warned the citizens not to obstruct the 'Porter of the said Hospital, the Person employed by the said Directors to seize them'.

8 August

Death of Lord Powerscourt

While the Powerscourt family is chiefly known in Ireland for its magnificent estate at Enniskerry in County Wicklow, it was also responsible for the erection of one of Dublin's finest and largest dwelling houses, Powerscourt House at no. 59 South William Street. This townhouse of palatial proportions, built between the years 1771 and 1774, cost £8,000 and was designed by James' Street stonemason Robert Mack. It was built using Wicklow granite from the Powerscourt estate in Enniskerry.

When Lord Powerscourt, Richard Wingfield, died 'following a painful disposition' on 8 August 1788, he lay in state in the parlour of Powerscourt House for two days before being taken to the family tomb in Enniskerry for burial. On 11 August 1788, his remains were escorted to Wicklow by a large number of gentlemen in carriages as well as many of his lordship's tenants in coaches and on horseback, and a detachment of the Powerscourt Volunteer Horse.

The *Freeman's Journal* later erroneously reported that an unseemly incident had occurred at Powerscourt House while Wingfield's remains were on public view. According to a report written in that newspaper on 12 August, some members of the Powerscourt Volunteer Horse had arrived at William Street to form a guard of honour around the coffin of their dead leader, but were denied access to the house by the commander of the Dublin police.

The writer went on to say that the militiamen eventually managed to sneak into Powerscourt House through a back door with the help of a servant, and they took possession of the room where their master's body lay. The report in *Freeman's Journal* further asserted that they gave the commander of the police and his men a good hiding before throwing them unceremoniously out on the street.

However, the editor of the *Freeman's Journal* was forced to issue a retraction of the story in his newspaper two days later, and to state that it was completely untrue.

9 August

Assault victim urged to give up the drink

In this assault case heard at Belfast's Court of Petty Sessions on 9 August 1881, the judge acquitted a man who admitted to a charge of beating his wife and urged the victim to give up the drink because she was only antagonising her husband.

George Nesbitt, an elderly man from Mackey Street in Belfast, was charged with assaulting his wife at their home on the previous evening. Mrs Nesbitt gave evidence that, during a row about money, her husband had knocked her to the ground, cutting her head. George Nesbitt agreed that he had assaulted his wife, but he claimed that she had provoked him into hitting her because she was in the habit of drinking too much. Apart from that, said George, 'there was no better woman.'

Judges Ward and Thompson dismissed the charge against Mr Nesbitt and 'expressed a hope that the woman might take the temperance pledge' (*Belfast Morning News,* 10 August 1881).

10 August

Showing a rookie hangman the ropes

On 10 August 1775, the *Freeman's Journal* reported on the almost farcical execution of William Wardell at St Stephen's

Green in Dublin. Wardell, who was hanged a day earlier, had been sentenced to death for stealing a considerable amount of jewellery and silver from the home of Lady Parsons. Before the execution, Wardell got up in front of the crowd and said his last few words. He was said to have, 'behaved with a contrition and decency befitting his unfortunate situation'.

He stepped up to the gallows and the rookie hangman, instead of making the usual noose, proceeded to wind the rope around the condemned man's neck 'in an awkward bungling manner'. However, the day was saved when a member of the crowd, who had witnessed many executions, stepped forward to show the new man how things were done. Poor Wardell was dispatched 'according to the rules of art'.

11 August

'A picture of human misery worthy of Carl of Carlsberg'

Between the years 1828 and 1829, the colourfully named German prince and travel writer Hermann Ludwig Heinrich Von Pückler-Muskau toured extensively in Ireland and recorded his adventures in a series of letters. They were subsequently translated and published in 1832 under the title *A Tour in England, Ireland and France*. His writings contain many interesting references to living conditions in mid-nineteenth-century Dublin, and record his impressions and observations on some of the people who he met during his stay in the capital in 1828.

Prince Pückler-Muskau (1785–1871) arrived in Dublin on 11 August 1828 on board a steam packet from Holyhead. He obviously wasn't too enamoured of this relatively new mode of transport as he reported that he had spent the ten-hour journey being 'tossed about and sick to death' from the smell and heat of the ship's boiler. He described the voyage as 'a picture of human misery worthy of Carl of Carlsberg'.

When he had recovered from his ordeal, the prince set out to explore Dublin. He wasn't too impressed and described the city as having a 'dirty air', although he did concede that it contained 'many magnificent palaces and broad streets'. He also loved the natural features of Dublin, such as the bay, the Hill of Howth, and the Dublin and Wicklow mountains.

He was particularly taken with Three Rock Mountain and he rode out to it from his lodgings one morning, having risen 'earlier than usual' to make the trip. On reaching the top of Three Rock, the prince found himself 'on a large and naked plateau' and described the three rocks as 'witch's stones rearing their heads' in front of him.

Pückler-Muskau also portrayed in vivid detail the poverty that existed on the dirty streets of Dublin, describing them as being 'crowded with beggar-boys, who buzz around one like flies, incessantly offering their services' and wearing rags that were 'beyond belief'.

The Prince visited Dublin's famous Donnybrook Fair, an annual event that went on for a week each August, and he was evidently horrified by the drinking and fighting that he experienced at the fair. He noted that the 'poverty, dirt and wild tumult' was matched in equal measure by the 'glee and merriment'. There were hundreds of tents and booths at the fair 'all ragged like the people and adorned with rags instead of flags', and the prince was appalled to note that one tent had 'hoisted a dead and half putrid cat as a sign'.

Prince Pückler-Muskau left Dublin soon afterwards and embarked on a whistle-stop tour of Ireland. He returned to the city briefly in December 1828 and left the country for good on 14 December on board the Howth steam packet bound for England.

12 August

Kilmainham Jail

On this day in 1796, Kilmainham Jail in Dublin opened its doors to receive prisoners for the first time. *Faulkner's Dublin Journal* announced: 'On 12th August 1796 ... the new County Gaol was completely finished and fit for the reception of the prisoners; the several persons confined in the old were conducted to the New Gaol under a strong military guard.'

13 August

Tallaght tea

Customs and Excise officers uncovered a bizarre counterfeiting operation in Dublin in August 1818 when Dublin farmer John McDermott was arrested for manufacturing fake tea at his farm on Killinarden Hill in Tallaght, County Dublin. Two Englishmen had also been involved in the illicit – and highly dangerous – operation, but had managed to escape from the clutches of the law.

Excise man Richard Fitzgerald found large quantities of the illegal tea at the farm and several hundredweight was discovered in shops around Dublin. The enterprising McDermott had been using a number of home-grown materials to make his illicit brew, but the problem was that some of these were extremely poisonous. Along with the leaves of potato stalks and mountain sage, the farmer also used deadly nightshade, which is highly toxic, and ivy leaves, alder leaves and a herb called robin-run-the-hedge, an extremely potent laxative. The process was then finished off by colouring with verdigris – a hazardous material – for the green tea, while copperas or iron sulphate was used to finish the black tea.

It's not known if anyone was harmed from drinking the tea, but it was reported that the manufacturing operation had been going on for several months before it was discovered.

14 August

Esteemed Army surgeon revealed to be a woman

On 14 August 1865 the Dublin newspaper *Saunders' Newsletter* reported – under the headline 'A female army combatant' – the death of Dr James Barry, army surgeon and inspector general of army hospitals. It revealed that Barry, who had held various medical posts in the British Army for over forty years, was in fact a woman.

The real truth about 'James Barry's' origins have never been adequately resolved and, despite the attempts of several biographers, we don't even know what her real Christian name was. However, it seems likely that her father was Cork man Jeremiah Bulkeley, who was confined in a Cork debtor's prison.

In 1809 Mrs Bulkeley and her daughter went to Edinburgh where the child, who was only ten years old, enrolled at the university as a medical and literary student. At that time girls were barred from third level education, so she entered the university dressed as a boy and using the name James Barry for the first time, which was the name of her uncle, an artist.

She was awarded with an MD three years later and moved to London in 1812, where she was apprenticed to a surgeon at St Thomas's Hospital. In 1813, still disguised as a man, she joined the British Army as a hospital assistant.

Barry was sent South Africa in 1816. In 1817 she was appointed as personal physician to the Governor of Cape Town's household. At that time Barry was described as 'a fragile looking ghost in British military uniform' with red hair and high-heeled shoes, and as having shoulders that appeared to be padded with cotton wool.

Barry was promoted to the post of colonial medical inspector in 1822 and was sent to Mauritius in 1828. This was followed by stints in Jamaica, St Helena, the Windward and Leeward Islands, Malta, Corfu and the Crimea, where she had a falling out with 'the lady with the lamp' Florence Nightingale.

Barry's final posting was to Montreal in 1857, where she was promoted to the rank of inspector general of army hospitals, the highest rank obtainable by a medical doctor.

She retired from the army two years later and returned to London, where she resided until her death with her West Indian servant John and her dog Psyche. Barry contracted dysentery in 1865 and died on 15 July that year.

It was only after Barry's death that her secret was finally revealed, when the woman who was laying her out for burial made the discovery that James Barry was in fact a woman.

When the deception was uncovered, the British Army abruptly abandoned its plans to give her a military funeral. She was buried soon afterwards at Kensal Rise Cemetery in London and her friends saw to it that her military title was inscribed on her gravestone.

15 August

Whiteboys in Rathkeale

On the night of 15 August 1821, two hundred Whiteboys, many of them on horseback and dressed in white shirts, dragged the tithe-proctor John Ives from his home near Rathkeale, County Limerick and warned him to stop collecting tithes in the area.

The police at Rathkeale, under the command of Thomas Doolan, had been tipped off about the operation and were waiting nearby. Doolan ordered the Whiteboys to surrender, but they started firing on the police instead. A policeman named Thomas Manning was shot dead during the opening skirmish.

The police fired back and several Whiteboys were said to have been killed or injured in the clashes that followed. Three days later, the *Limerick Chronicle* reported that several dead bodies had been hidden in the area afterwards:

'Those found by the Police, in the first instance, were taken to Rathkeale, where they were interred on Thursday, without coffins, in a large hole dug up by their companions, in a piece of waste ground, near the Guard-house. The two prisoners were compelled by Mr. Going to perform all offices at the burial – after digging the hole, they were obliged to bear the bodies and place them beneath, and afterwards to shake quick-lime plentifully over them...'.

16 August

Those wicked Whiteboys – again

Hibernian Journal, Carrick-on-Suir, County Waterford, 16 August 1773: A large number of 'those wicked people called Whiteboys, 'many of them armed and dressed in white uniforms', gathered at Carrick-on-Suir Green where they proceeded to strip naked a weaver named Laurence Wall and 'beat him in a cruel manner'. The Whiteboys tied Wall to a stake in the middle of the green and left him there for the whole night until he was freed the following morning. 'Strange infatuation! That neither the laws of God or man will deter them from such barbarous practices and nocturnal meetings.'

17 August

'His body seemed a moving mass of worms'

A man was found beside Mr Gosson's lime kiln near Finglas, Dublin, on 17 August 1809. He was discovered lying face down by a passer-by, who initially thought he was dead. On turning him over to examine him, he discovered that the man was not dead but, according to a report in the *Times* of London on 22 August:

'[T]he whole surface of his body seemed a moving mass of worms ... and from every aperture of his head, his eyes, ears, mouth and nose, poured innumerable worms as if the interior of the skull was entirely filled with them. His eyes were dissolved, and the cavities, as well as those of his ears, mouth and nose, were filled with a white moving mass, more horrid and disgusting than it is possible for imagination to conceive.'

The poor man was taken to a nearby barn where he lingered until the following day and died in a 'state of total putrisolution'.

18 August

Savage sentencing

On 18 August 1790 details were given in the *Hibernian Journal* of the savage and downright disproportionate sentences handed down by Judge Hamilton at Armagh Assizes a few days earlier.

Peter Kennan was found guilty of murdering John Toner of Ballintemple and sentenced to death. Two men, Edward Connolly and Anthony West, who had given evidence for Kennan during the trial, were found guilty of perjury, and both were sentenced to be pilloried, jailed for six months and transported for seven years. Judge Hamilton, who wasn't finished with the two men, inserted a sadistic little twist to their punishment. In addition to being publicly humiliated at the pillory, the judge ordered that both men were to have their ears nailed to the pillory for the duration of their punishment.

The good judge obviously wasn't in great form that day. Next to appear in the dock was seventy-year-old Margaret Steenson, who was charged with stealing fifty yards of linen from the bleach yard of Jackson, Eyre and Co. of Maydown. Steenson, who had been up before the courts before on similar charges previously, was found guilty and Hamilton ordered that she be hanged on 7 September.

Another man, John Tole, was found guilty of rioting and sentenced to three months in prison and to be whipped through the streets of Armagh.

19 August

The men who robbed the Wicklow mail

Two infamous Dublin highwaymen were captured in 1802 and the 19 August edition of the *Dublin Evening Post* had the details.

The outlaws John Foy and James Griffin, who had robbed the Wicklow mail three times, were arrested at their lodgings at South Earl Street. The men were found to be in possession of bank notes stolen from the mail coach the previous morning. The proceeds from several other robberies were also recovered, along with many items stolen from various houses around the city.

20 August

Dungarvan Eviction

20 August 1851: Two hundred poor women and their children were left to fend for themselves when they were evicted from the overcrowded Dungarvan Workhouse. It was reported in some newspapers that the women and children were forced to take refuge in ditches around the town. The cries of the frightened and hungry children were said to have been particularly heart-breaking.

21 August

Strangled by the hangman

On Saturday, 21 August 1784, according to the *Hibernian Journal,* an enormous crowd gathered at St Stephen's Green in Dublin to witness the very unusual execution of Mary Fairfield, who was sentenced to death for the murder of a wet nurse named Mary Funt. Fairfield was taken to the Green from her cell at Newgate Prison on the back of a cart and escorted through the streets of the city by a detachment of the Dublin Police. There she was strangled by the hangman who then flung her lifeless body onto a blazing fire.

Fairfield had been convicted of stabbing Funt to death in Dublin in December 1783 and was originally sentenced to be burned at the stake. However, Fairfield 'pleaded with her belly', telling the court that she was going to have a baby. As was normal in such cases, she was examined by a jury of matrons who accepted that she was pregnant and she received a stay of execution. As time went on, however, it became clear that Fairfield wasn't pregnant and she was passed fit for execution.

22 August

Criminal correspondence between his wife and a neighbour

On 22 August 1722 it was reported, in the *Dublin Coruant*, that James Kelly of Clonleigh, County Carlow, suspecting that his wife was having a 'criminal correspondence' with one of their male neighbours, followed them. "[T]hinking their friendship was protracted beyond the bounds of decency', Kelly picked up a saw and broke his neighbour's skull with it.

23 August

Sea monster sighted

The *Freeman's Journal* of 23 August 1850 reported a sighting of a 'sea monster' off the coast of Kerry a few days earlier. The crew of Irish Fishery Company boat the *Lord Nelson* was fishing in the Blasket Sound when they saw the head and neck of a serpent, which 'filled the minds of the sailors with indescribable terror'.

The 'monster' thrashed around on the surface of the water for a while, and, snorting like a steam engine, plunged back into the depths of the sea. The terrified fishermen then made their way back to Dingle, where they 'recounted their escape from the marine monster, and it is to be feared they will not be induced to visit that part of the coast for some considerable time'.

A Dingle-based ichthyologist (fish scientist), told the *Freeman's Journal* that the monster was in fact the *Ictheus Megacoddensis* (giant cod), 'which was not infrequently seen some centuries since on the Irish coast'.

24 August

The death of Napper Tandy

United Irishman James Napper Tandy was born in the Cornmarket area of Dublin in 1740. His father John was an ironmonger and a serving member of the Holy Trinity Guild of Merchants. Very little is known about Tandy's early life in the Cornmarket. In 1962 Dublin Corporation removed a plaque commemorating Tandy from no. 7 High Street before demolishing the building.

Tandy worked in the family business of ironmongery for a time, but later went into business as a land agent and rent collector. He was elected to the Dublin city assembly in 1777 as a representative of the merchant's guild and he served the city in this capacity for nearly eighteen years. He was active in many initiatives at that time, including a campaign against the relocation of the Custom House from Wellington Quay to its present location. Tandy and the merchants of the city were against the proposed move on the basis that it would lead to greater expense and inconvenience to them.

Later on, Tandy became secretary of the Dublin branch of the United Irishmen, whose membership included Wolfe Tone, Thomas Russell and Oliver Bond. The United Irishmen were proscribed in 1792 and Tandy was forced to flee to the US during the following year after falling foul of the police. He continued to work for the United Irishmen in the US.

Tandy went to Paris in 1797 where he managed to persuade the French to take part in an invasion of Ireland. The French made him a general, and in September 1798 he landed in a French brig, the *Anacreon*, at Rutland Island off the coast of Donegal. On landing, Tandy raised an Irish flag and issued a proclamation that was optimistically dated 'The first year of Irish Liberty'. On learning of General Humbert's defeat at the Battle of Ballinamuck in County Longford on 8 September 1798, Tandy withdrew and sailed for Norway. He eventually made his way to Hamburg, Germany, where he was captured and extradited back to face trial for treason in Ireland.

He was sentenced to death after his trial at Lifford in Donegal, but was released following the intervention of Napoleon Bonaparte. He returned to France where he was awarded a full general's pension and he died in Bordeaux on 24 August 1803.

25 August

'White is sick, Grey is fled, now for Black Fitzwilliam's head'

The Battle of Glenmalure in the Wicklow Mountains took place on 24 August 1580 during the Desmond Rebellions. The English forces – under the command of Lord Deputy of Ireland Arthur Grey – in their heavy armour were taught a lesson in guerrilla warfare by the much more mobile and lighter-clad rebels led by Fiach McHugh O'Byrne and Viscount Baltinglass.

Sir William Stanley, who was present at the battle, wrote a letter to Sir Francis Walsingham, Chief advisor and spymaster to Queen Elizabeth I, outlining the events of the day. Stanley said that it was the 'hottest piece of service' that he had ever seen and it was clear that the English soldiers were not fit for the task at hand. Colonel Moore, who was an English commander in the field that day, was described as a 'corpulent man' who was not able for hardship, and Stanley said that some of the soldiers died climbing the steep sides of the glen, 'being so out of breath, that they were able to go no further, being not hurt at all'.

Stanley claimed that only thirty English soldiers died that day, but it does seem that the actual death toll was much higher. Depending on which source you believe, estimates vary from three hundred up to eight hundred dead. The battle is commemorated in the song 'Follow me up to Carlow'.

26 August

Tarring and feathering committee

On 26 August 1784, the remains of a Dublin wool comber named Condron were carried from the Liberties in Dublin by a 'vast concourse of people' and buried at Churchtown Cemetery. Condron had been shot dead two days earlier during a riot in Francis Street. The riot occurred during the public whipping of Garret Dignam, who had been found guilty of tarring and feathering a butcher. The punishment, which was carried out with 'unexampled severity', involved Dignam being tied to a cart and whipped all the way from the Tholsel beside Christchurch, up Patrick Street, along Thomas Street and back to the Tholsel via High Street.

There had been a spate of tarring and feathering in Dublin by weavers and other tradesmen involved in the linen trade during a campaign against the importation of foreign goods and materials, and the authorities were determined to make an example of Dignam.

The cart carrying Dignam was accompanied by all the watchmen of Dublin as well as a strong military force. A huge crowd had gathered at the junction of Patrick Street and Francis Street and some stones were thrown at the soldiers. The soldiers retaliated and opened fire on the crowd, killing Condron and wounding three or four others.

27 August

Whipped

Nicholas Reily was whipped from Kilkenny Jail to Watergate on 27 August 1744 for attempting to pass a counterfeit guinea in Edward Oldfield's shop in Kilkenny. The punishment was repeated on 31 August and 3 September.

28 August

The Donegal Jackal

It was reported in the *Hibernian Journal* on 28 August 1772 that a vampire-like animal 'resembling a jackal' was on a killing spree near Lifford in Donegal. The 'jackal' had apparently killed several sheep and lambs around Lifford by biting them on the neck and sucking the blood from their carcasses without doing any further damage.

29 August

Yeoman of the cat

Two job descriptions that you will definitely not see in any of today's newspapers were mentioned in this report in the *Freeman's Journal* on 30 August 1810. I'm not sure if there's too much demand for a 'flogger in ordinary' or a 'yeoman of the cat' these days, but those were the dubious titles held by this Carlow carpenter during the 1798 Rebellion.

'Mansion House, yesterday. Two men named Guy and Heavy, both Hibernians, were charged by a countryman named Kinshela, a journeyman carpenter, with having put him in danger of assassination with reports they had propagated of him. The report was, that he had been a private in the Carlow Militia during the rebellion (1798); and that he had hired himself to come to Dublin to officiate as Yeoman of the Cat, or Flogger in Ordinary to one of the flagellating tribunals which the circumstances of the rebellion rendered necessary to establish in that city. Mr Kinshela complained that this report was propagated by the defendants amongst his countrymen in London, and particularly at a public-house in Grub Street; that he was everywhere treated by them with insult, and that he was hourly in danger of losing his life. Mr Guy, who assumed the office of spokesman in the defence, said – If he did say such a thing it was true enough, for he had ocular demonstration of it; and while he himself was in confinement upon suspicion of being one of the Croppies, he had frequently seen the complainant (Kinshela) flogging the suspected men at the triangles and dipping his cat in the brine at every stroke, literally rubbing salt in the wounds. The Lord Mayor advised the parties to retire and make up their quarrel amongst themselves.'

30 August

A fishy tale

Extract from *Pue's Occurrences*, Dublin, 30 August 1755:

'A Fishwoman in the Ormond-Market, well known by the name of Miss Biddy, was taken into custody by order of the Right Hon the Lord Mayor for forestalling a great quantity of herrings, to the great prejudice of the poor. She was put into a chaise, which with the horse, were adorned with several herrings hanging to them, and in that manner (attended by a vast concourse of spectators) was carried through several of the markets and street of this city. She afterwards sat for three hours in the stocks at the Market House, was fined forty shillings, and the herrings distributed among the poor.'

31 August

This mansion of infamy

Dublin policemen got more than they bargained for when they raided a gaming house in Smock Alley in August 1790. According to a report in the *Dublin Chronicle* on 31 August, the police were searching for a large sum of money stolen from a countryman by a gang of sharpers, or swindlers, a few days earlier. The police discovered a human skeleton and several other bones in the cellar of the gaming house which, the newspaper speculated, probably belonged to 'some unfortunate person ... [who] was first plundered and afterwards murdered by the abandoned frequenters of this mansion of infamy and danger.'

SEPTEMBER

1 September

Prizefighting

Two men named Savage and McLoughlin were charged with attempting to organise a bare-knuckle boxing match in Dublin on 1 September 1861. On the day in question, Sergeant O'Neill of the Dublin Metropolitan Police was patrolling in Great Britain Street (now Parnell Street) when he noticed an unusually large crowd gathering in Moore Street. The police dispersed the crowd, but the men – followed by one hundred eager spectators – made their way to Glasnevin where they tried to get the fight on at Cory Lane. Sergeant O'Neill and seven policemen attempted to move the men on again, and O'Neill was assaulted in the ensuing tussle. Eighteen were arrested in the melee that followed.

2 September

Murder at Stepaside

One night in May 1893, Bernard Cox, an insurance collector employed by the Prudential Assurance Company, was robbed of fifteen pounds and bludgeoned to death. Cox, a native of County Cavan and sixty-five years old, was attacked while returning from his rounds to his home at Stepaside in South County Dublin, two doors from the local police barracks.

Cox had been collecting insurance premiums at Enniskerry, County Wicklow earlier that day and he was last seen alive at 8.30 p.m. On his way home the victim stopped off at Deering's public house at Golden Ball, where he drank a glass of whiskey before heading back to Stepaside, a half mile away.

Cox never reached home and the following morning his body was discovered by the side of the road at St Patrick's Well by a local farm labourer who was on his way to mass. The insurance collector had been beaten to a pulp and the murder weapon – a heavy iron bar – was discovered nearby.

A local tramp, 35-year-old James Reilly, was arrested at Stepaside on the day after the murder and subsequently charged with the killing of the insurance collector. At his trial for murder on 2 August 1893, Reilly was found guilty as charged and sentenced to death.

The sentence of death by hanging was duly carried out on 2 September at Kilmainham Jail, and the *Freeman's Journal* of 4 September 1893 carried a detailed report on Reilly's execution.

The paper reported that a large crowd – 'the percentage of ragged little boys being particularly large' – had gathered at Kilmainham to witness the customary hoisting of the black flag that was raised after a hanging had taken place.

As the hour of execution approached, an expectant hush fell over the crowd. Less than a minute after eight, 'the black flag was hoisted, after which there was a murmur of sympathetic awe from the crowd. That was all people had come to see; and having seen it, everyone went his way, and the surroundings of the jail looked as deserted as if nothing at all had happened.'

3 September

Onward Christian Soldiers

There was very unChristian like behaviour displayed in Dublin on 3 September 1906 from Salvation Army preacher Weldon C. Graham of Lombard Street West, who was charged with using indecent and profane language in the city. Graham had been preaching to a small gathering of children when he suddenly began to abuse passers-by. When Sergeant Lennan of the Dublin Metropolitan Police attempted to arrest him, Graham tried to throttle him and tore his tunic. Graham was found guilty as charged and ordered to pay a fine of ten shillings plus damages; failure to pay would mean a month's imprisonment.

4 September

Eaten by his own pig

Reported in the *Newry Examiner*, 4 September 1833:

'DONNYBROOK FAIR – HORRIBLE ACCIDENT. – A man about 68 years of age, returned home in a state of drunkenness, on Sunday morning, to New Street. In this condition he was left alone by his family, who went to indulge in the demoralizing festivities of the fair. The unfortunate man became so overcome, from the effects of liquor, that he fell into a completely drunken stupor. On the return of his son-in-law and daughter, between nine and ten o'clock at night, he was found lying on the ground in the following most appalling situation: his nose, cheeks and lips, and in fact the entire front of his face, were eaten away, together with the left hand, which was gnawed, and the bones crushed in a frightful manner, by his own pig, The miserable man is now lying in the Meath Hospital, and probably such an awful case has not been admitted into any similar institution for many years. Accustomed as the medical gentlemen of that hospital have been to see dreadful accidents, such a horrible spectacle as this they never witnessed.'

5 September

Runaway apprentices

5 September 1767, *Finn's Leinster Journal*:'Run away on Tuesday night last, from the service of William Watters, of Newland, in the County of Kilkenny, two apprentice boys; one named PETER MOUTRAY, about 15 years of age, with white hair, a pale face and well made but thin. The other named PATRICK HARRISON, squat made, with black hair and pock marked, same age. They both had on black velvet caps, light coloured coats with green cuffs and capes, green waistcoats, etc. They stole five shirts and several other things. Whoever secures them and lodges them in any of his Majesty's jails shall be paid a guinea reward by me, WM. WATTERS.'

It is interesting to note that on the same day, another Kilkenny man, Richard St George, offered the same reward of a guinea for the safe return of his two dogs that had strayed.

6 September

Executioner executed

On Thursday, 6 September 1770, a man was hanged for murder at Philipstown in what is now County Offaly. The execution – attended by a huge crowd – was unusually quiet but, when it was over, the onlookers stoned the hangman to death and left his body lying under the gallows for a number of days. The hangman, believed to a man named Darby Brahan, had officiated at the execution of Catholic priest Father Nicholas Sheehy four years earlier.

7 September

Marching for bread

On Monday, 7 September 1846, over five hundred starving people marched in silence to the workhouse in Boyle, County Roscommon to plead with the local magistrates and board of guardians for work. A man at the head of this sombre procession held aloft a pole with a loaf of bread stuck on the top of it. Finding that the magistrates and guardians were holding a meeting at the Sessions House in the town, the people made their way to the Crescent where they handed in a number of petitions asking for work.

Stating that no more than twenty of their number had eaten anything that morning, the people informed the magistrates that, since the potato crop had failed, they were unable to feed themselves, and they made a dignified plea for some work to tide them over. The authorities agreed to write to the Lord Lieutenant about their case and the Boyle Relief Committee asked the Board of Works to reinstate the outdoor relief works which had ended some days earlier.

8 September

The Irish Giant

On 19 September 1806, several British newspapers announced the death of Patrick O'Brien, aka 'The Irish Giant', at his lodgings in Bristol on 8 September. O'Brien had died from a combination of 'liver and lung diseases' at the age of forty-six.

O'Brien was said to be over eight and a half feet tall and his real name was Patrick Cotter. Originally a Kinsale bricklayer, he was taken to England by a showman who agreed to pay him fifty pounds per year for the privilege of showing him at various exhibitions around the country.

However, when the greedy showman attempted to effectively sublet Cotter to another agent, Cotter resisted and was thrown into a Bristol debtor's jail on a trumped-up charge. He was eventually released from prison following the intervention of a benefactor, William Watts, who also managed to free Cotter from his contractual obligations with the showman. Cotter was just eighteen at the time.

With the help of his benefactor, Cotter was then able to set himself up in the famous fair of St James', where he was said to have made a substantial amount of money for himself.

He made his home in Bristol where he became so well known that it was impossible for him to venture out in daylight, and he would only go out at night to take the air. Once, while out for a walk in Bath, Cotter frightened the wits out of a policeman by taking the cover off a street lamp and lighting his pipe from the flame.

Cotter seems to have been the archetypal gentle giant, and all who knew him described him as a friendly and unassuming type. Known as an inoffensive and charming man, Cotter loved good company and was fond of the occasional glass of wine.

When Cotter died he was buried under twelve feet of solid rock underneath a Catholic chapel in Trenchard Street, Bristol in order to prevent his remains being stolen by bodysnatchers. One month prior to his death, Cotter – who was afraid that his corpse would be dug up and exhibited in a museum – had given £200 pounds to the church to ensure that this, his last wish, was carried out.

9 September

Wanted for embezzlement

Hue and Cry, 9 September 1843:

'Description of Peter Keenan, who stands charged with having, on the 15ᵗʰ day of August instant, at Louth, in the Barony of Louth, and Parish of Louth (being an indentured servant to Michael M'Geough, a Baker residing in the Village of Louth), absconded, having embezzled the sum of 17s. 6d, the property of his Master. A warrant is in the hands of the Police at Louth for the apprehension of Keenan: 19 years of age, 5 feet 8 inches high, slender make, fair complexion, brown hair, blue eyes, large flat feet, walks awkwardly, long features, and fresh complexion; … is a native of the County Louth. Travelled in the Mail Car to Drogheda on the 15ᵗʰ instant, in company with a young woman who represents herself to be a foreigner, and states she cannot speak English. This girl is about 20 years of age, middle size, well looking, dark brown hair, wore a pink frock, straw bonnet covered with blue silk, and a black scarf. It is supposed those persons have gone to Dublin, and [are] likely to stop at the lodgings of Anthony Hoy, a Shoemaker, residing in a Cellar at No. 76. Bride-street.'

10 September

A hurl on the head

Extract from a *Dublin Courant* letter from a gentleman, near Cashel, County Tipperary, 10 September 1744:

'Last Sunday near a hurling pitch at a place called Glounanere in this neighbourhood, a most melancholy accident happened. Two young men having a dispute, one James Broughelly came up with an intention of separating them, when one of the heroes, without any provocation, struck him with his hurl on the head, of which he died in a few hours.'

11 September

Woman shot dead at a hurling match

The *Dublin Evening Post* of 11 September 1733 gave details of a tragic incident at a hurling match played near Athy in County Kildare. One spectator attacked another with a horsewhip and both men fired pistols at each other. While neither of the two protagonists was injured in the incident, a passing female spectator was killed instantly, and another man had his teeth shot out and his lower lip torn off.

12 September

Botched execution

John Tierney was hanged in front of the county jail in Nenagh, County Tipperary on 12 September 1849 for the murder of a respectable Thurles tailor named Burke.

At 12.30 p.m. on the day of the execution, Tierney was led out of the jail to the gallows, which was surrounded by a detachment of the 79th Highlanders Regiment of the British Army and a strong force of police.

The condemned man walked firmly towards the gallows carrying a crucifix in one hand and a handkerchief in the other. The hangman – who caused great excitement in the crowd by not wearing a disguise – quickly stepped forward and placed the rope around Tierney's neck and put a white hood over his head. He drew the bolt and Tierney plunged through the trapdoor. The unfortunate man didn't die immediately, however. The executioner had tied the knot under his chin instead of underneath his ear and he writhed and kicked as he was slowly strangled at the end of the rope.

Eventually Tierney's struggles ceased and he was cut down. His body was put in a coffin and brought back into the jail for burial.

13 September

Notorious Ned

Notorious Ned Jordan was Canada's first pirate. He was also Carlow's first pirate, but it's a fairly safe bet that he didn't serve his piracy apprenticeship sailing up and down the River Barrow.

Edward Jordan was born somewhere in Carlow in 1771 and he took part in the 1798 Rebellion on the side of the rebels. Following the Rebellion, he was given an amnesty and set out for the US with his wife Margaret Croke and their four children. He eventually ended up in Halifax, Nova Scotia, where he had a brief career as a fisherman. However, he soon ran into debt, and his boat, the *Three Sisters*, was repossessed. A small crew led by captain John Stairs took possession of the boat to bring it back to Halifax in September 1809. Stairs made the fatal mistake of allowing Jordan and his family back to Halifax with them on the boat. Three days later, on 13 September, Jordan murdered two of the crew and reclaimed control of the boat.

Captain Stairs managed to escape and raise the alarm, and Jordan was captured a few weeks later. He was tried for murder and piracy in Halifax on 15 November 1809 and executed on 25 November. It was Canada's first piracy trial, and Jordan was tarred and hanged in chains at the entrance to Halifax Harbour.

14 September

Diddlers

The bizarre practice of shop sign stealing has been around for a very long time, and it seems that there are very few places in the world that haven't been subjected to these peculiar thefts. Two hundred years ago, Dublin had its very own gang dedicated to this pursuit, as can be seen from a newspaper article published in the *Freeman's Journal* on 14 September 1805. The columnist was so enraged by an outbreak of sign stealing in central Dublin that he urged the authorities to hang the perpetrators!

The gang in question were known as the Diddlers, so called after a villainous character named Jeremy Diddler in a popular eighteenth-century play called *Raising the Wind*. The Diddlers were described in less than glowing terms in the *Freeman's Journal* as 'low clerks, shop boys .... torturers of cat-gut who call themselves musicians, and the graceless children of improper parents'.

As well as being involved in thieving and rioting in the city, the writer accused the Diddlers of reviving the craze for stealing shop signs, doorknockers and figures from over shop doors. These pranks had seemingly been carried out some years earlier by another Dublin gang, but the practice died out after several were jailed for other offences and some were even hanged.

Nothing was safe from the Diddlers. Shopkeepers, publicans and householders awoke to find their knobs and knockers and emblems of trade missing. Boot scrapers, iron grills and even railings were sometimes carried off at night. Several premises in George's Street and Dame Street had been attacked, and the writer not only urged shopkeepers in the area to be vigilant against further outbreaks of 'diddling', but he also called on them to defend themselves with firearms if necessary.

The gang had actually been caught in the act by the Dublin Watch earlier that week and one of them was arrested and taken to the watch house. However, when news of his arrest spread, his companions emerged from a nearby tavern and rescued him, bringing him back to the hostelry in triumph. The man and one of his companions were eventually rearrested and charged with assaulting the watchmen. The owner of the tavern where the gang congregated was fined ten pounds for having his pub open after midnight.

The writer urged the authorities to hang the perpetrators of the pranks, saying that justice in these cases would be best served by a 'wholesome castigation from Jack Ketch'. (Jack Ketch was a common euphemism for the hangman).

The Diddlers were in trouble again at the end of September when it was reported that several of their number had bathed nude at the Grand Canal near Charlemont Street, offending the modesty of local residents there and pelting them with stones and other missiles.

The *Freeman's Journal* warned that they knew who the perpetrators were but wouldn't publish their names 'in hopes that they will desist from such disgraceful improprieties'.

This obviously had no effect on the Diddlers, as four of them were arrested a few nights later while making off with the public water trough and spout on Grafton Street.

15 September

Robinson Gang

On Saturday, 15 September 1792, George Robinson from the Liberties – leader of a gang of notorious murderers and highwayman – was hanged along with three other gang members at Kilmainham Commons. Between 1790 and 1792, Robinson and his gang had been active in the Dolphin's Barn area of Dublin and many of the crimes committed in that area during the period were attributed to them.

Robinson and his three companions, John Cunningham, William Norton, and Charles Brooks, were sentenced to death for the murder of retired merchant Benjamin Lyneal at his home in Dolphin's Barn. Another gang member, John Conran, gave evidence against them in order to save his own skin.

Robinson hatched a plan to rob Lyneal at a tavern in Back Lane. At first, the other gang members were reluctant to carry out the robbery in the heart of Dolphin's Barn, where the locals were described as 'people of resolution'. Despite their misgivings, the gang pressed ahead with their plans. On the night of the murder, Lyneal was playing cards in a room at the back of his house with his two daughters and his nephew Reverend Crane, when the gang – heavily armed with pistols and swords – broke into the house.

On hearing the commotion at the front door, Reverend Crane bravely attacked the gang with a poker, but Brooks stabbed him in the chest with a sword. Crane should have died in the attack, but he had a lucky escape when the sword broke in two. Lyneal tried to grab Conran's pistol during the struggle, but it went off, killing the merchant.

The gang fled the scene, but Robinson and Conran were arrested soon afterwards during a botched attempt to rob a tavern in the city centre. The Dublin police put pressure on Conran to give evidence against his comrades in return for his freedom and he eventually agreed to the deal. Cunningham and Norton were soon picked up and the four men were tried and convicted for the murder of Lyneal at the end of August 1792.

The executions took place at Kilmainham Commons on 15 September 1792 and thousands of Dubliners turned out to see the hangings. Before they were dispatched, the men confessed to several other crimes for which several innocent men had already been hanged.

16 September

Miracle at Lourdes

Thousands of Irish pilgrims made the annual trip to Lourdes in September 1913, and on 16 September, the *Irish Independent's* special correspondent wrote of 'indescribable scenes' during the long train journey across France and on Irish day at the shrine. As you might expect, there was much praying and singing of hymns during the train journey as pilgrims from the four provinces of Ireland converged on Lourdes. The correspondent also reported on members of the clergy shaving themselves with the aid of bottles of Vichy mineral water, but the main topics of his report were a number of 'miracles' and 'improvements' concerning Irish people at the grotto in Lourdes.

The greatest cause célèbre at the grotto that year related to 21-year-old Grace Moloney of Killaloe in County Clare. According to the writer, Moloney entered the baths at Lourdes a cripple, but walked firmly away. When she cried out with joy, Moloney was nearly killed in the ensuing crush and had to be rescued by priests and bath attendants.

She had been suffering from tuberculosis of the knee for the previous eleven years.

It was also reported that two deaf priests from County Meath had recovered their hearing, while three people from Belfast – all members of the same family – were able to throw away their crutches after visiting the grotto. Eight-year-old James Downey was first to be cured. He had just left mass at the grotto when he suddenly threw down his crutches and shouted: 'Look, I can walk without them!' Michael Downey, who had to be carried on and off the ship and trains on the journey to Lourdes, also threw down his crutches after visiting the grotto, and his nephew James McAllister, aged nine, found no further need for his crutch after being immersed in the water for half an hour.

17 September

'A young man of good education'

On 17 September 1773, as it approached Dublin, the Drogheda stagecoach was held up at the 'wall of Santry' by two highwaymen. The robbers were described as being between sixteen and twenty years old and both were dressed in blue overcoats. The young men, said to have been well bred and remarkably polite, stripped the passengers of their cash and pocket watches. On learning that one of their victims was a priest, the highwaymen gave him back his purse.

Soon afterwards, a young man named Fleming – 'a young man of good education' – was arrested near Stradbally (County Laois) and charged with the Santry robbery. Fleming confessed to having taken part in that robbery as well as several others, implicating his fellow gang members in the process. He also showed the authorities where the loot from the robberies was hidden in return for immunity from prosecution.

18 September

Female cannibal

A woman described as a tigress, a vampire and a cannibal was arrested in Charlemont, a small village in County Armagh, on 18 September 1845 for attacking pawnbroker David Alderdice. Alderice had a row with the woman about a forfeited pledge and matters quickly turned nasty.

The *Armagh Guardian* reported that Alderice tried to throw the woman out of his shop but 'the infuriated tigress sprung on the old gentleman with a savage growl' and bit him severely on the hand. We are also told that the pawnbroker, who was in his seventies, was 'obliged to pummel the vampire', before he was rescued by the police. The 'female cannibal', as she was described, was then hauled up before Judge Olpherts J.P. who committed her to Armagh Jail.

19 September

Buried alive

On 19 September 1778 *Finn's Leinster Journal* reported on a horrific event that occurred at Bully's Acre Cemetery in Dublin some days earlier. Some people who were attending a burial in the cemetery noticed that the soil on a nearby grave appeared to be moving. On closer inspection it was discovered that a small baby – no more than four months old – had been buried alive under the mound. The child was still alive when it was rescued by the mourners, but it died soon afterwards.

20 September

Monaghan mystery

There was more to this bizarre 'kidnapping' mystery than meets the eye, but victim James Gillanders wasn't too perturbed about the incident when interviewed by reporters afterwards. Gillanders, an attendant at Monaghan Mental Hospital, was found tied to the front gates of the asylum early on Sunday, 20 September 1931.

According to a report on the incident in the *Irish Press*, Gillanders had been 'placed under arrest', blindfolded and held in a room at the hospital on Saturday night. He was moved to various parts of the building throughout the night and was taken out early on Sunday morning and tied to the gates. Gillanders told the *Press* reporter that he had been well treated during his ordeal and was 'provided with tea and whiskey, and had as good a night as if he was at a dance'.

21 September

Runaway horse

Reported in the *Freeman's Journal* on 21 September 1821:

'Last week, at the races of Letterkenny, a most dreadful accident took place. One of the horses bolted from the course, and struck down two men in the crowd; in passing over them, he set his forefeet exactly on the windpipe of one man, who expired instantly; his hind feet struck the breast of another man so violently, that the ribs were separated all along on one side from the spine. It is though he cannot survive.'

22 September

Charles McCready

An estimated crowd of three to four thousand people, many of them 'females of the lower classes of society', turned up at a field beside the county jail in Cork on 22 September 1856 to witness the execution of Private Charles McCready of the 68th Light Infantry Regiment of the British Army, based in Fermoy.

McCready had been sentenced to death for shooting his sergeant, Eoin Guinny. The condemned man – a young Englishman – was attended in his last hours by two Catholic priests and he was said to have 'prayed long and fervently to heaven for mercy'.

The job of hanging McCready was given to an unnamed young fellow soldier who had been imprisoned for robbing an officer. He was said to have handled the execution like a professional, and the hanging went off without a hitch.

23 September

Shot, as a warning to the otters

There was great consternation in Dublin in September 1956 when it emerged that a mystery killer had been doing away with Dublin Zoo's rare bird population. The killer only operated under the cover of darkness and there were daily news bulletins on the efforts made to capture the perpetrator.

The killings first came to light when 'Blackie', an Australian black swan, and his companion were found dead in the lake with their necks broken on 23 September. Blackie had been in the news just three weeks earlier when he had briefly escaped from the zoo. He was recaptured soon afterwards near Naas, County Kildare.

Fourteen other rare birds at the zoo were slain in a similar fashion in the days preceding Blackie's killing. This led the authorities to believe that an otter from one of the lakes in the Phoenix Park was responsible.

Zoo attendants and keepers were issued with shotguns and ordered to shoot the perpetrator on sight. All the zoo's rare birds were moved to a guarded enclosure, where they were to remain until the culprit was found.

On 25 September, the *Evening Herald* reported that the zoo authorities had drafted in bloodhounds in an attempt to flush out the 'mysterious night menace'. The bloodhounds searched every corner of the zoo, but no trace of the killer was found. Zoo officials were cautiously optimistic that the culprit had moved on, but a spokesman vowed to continue the search until the killer was identified.

There was further consternation the following day, when it was revealed that the 'Dublin Zoo killer' had turned its attention to the president's swans in the grounds of Áras an Uachtaráin. Six of the swans were killed, along with a dozen small fowl. A number of small deer were also killed in the Phoenix Park, and suspicion soon turned to the park's fox population. Park rangers were ordered to shoot as many foxes as possible, and one fox was shot dead in the grounds of the Áras. Many believed that this fox was in fact the 'zoo killer', but it was pointed out that many of the dead birds had been found in the water.

There were several bizarre suggestions from the public as to how the zoo authorities should go about catching the killer, including one novel suggestion from a resident of Dublin who suggested that electrified wooden geese decoys should be deployed on the lake so that the killer would be electrocuted when he tried to bite one.

The killings eventually came to a halt in mid–October when armed detectives and otter hunters shot a pair of otters in the grounds of Áras an Uachtaráin.

24 September

'Brian Cooney's birthday

Charles Bianconi, the earliest developer of an efficient integrated transport service in Ireland, was born Joachim Carlo Giuseppe Bianconi on 24 September 1786 at Tregelo near Lombardy in Italy.

When Bianconi turned sixteen he was, by his own admission, 'a dunce and a very wild boy' and he was apprenticed to Andrea Faroni, a dealer in cheap religious pictures who was to bring him and three other boys to make and sell his wares in London. Faroni and his four apprentices walked over the Alps to Switzerland and from there they made their way, not to London, as they had originally planned, but to Temple Bar near Essex Bridge in Dublin, where they arrived in the summer of 1802.

Faroni took lodgings in Temple Bar and immediately set to work making small leaden frames for his pictures so that his apprentices could sell them on the streets of Dublin.

In time he was ordered to travel further afield to Wexford and to Waterford, where his pictures of Napoleon Bonaparte and his generals went down very well with the locals.

After a period of eighteen months plodding the highways and byways of Leinster and Munster, Bianconi decided to go into the picture-selling business for himself with money that his father had given him. He spent the next few years peddling his pictures around Munster, and in 1806 he opened a carving and gilding shop in Carrick-on-Suir, County Tipperary. He moved on to Waterford for a short time before finally settling in Clonmel, where he was christened 'Brian Cooney' because the locals couldn't pronounce his Italian name.

He took his first steps into the transport business on 5 July 1815 when he ran his first horse and car service between Clonmel and Cahir with a single horse and two-wheeled car, carrying passengers, goods and mail. Although it was slow to take off, Bianconi gradually expanded his car service to take in Tipperary and Limerick and, by 1832, he had three hundred horses and was ferrying passengers and goods throughout the country, mainly in the south, midlands and west of Ireland.

In 1833, Bianconi managed to expand the business further when he won a lucrative mail contract. By 1845 he had 1,500 horses, 100 coaches, 100 drivers and 140 coach stations, and he served 23 counties throughout Ireland. This marked the high point of Bianconi's coach business as from then on the railways gradually encroached on it.

Bianconi married Elizabeth Hayes in 1827 and they had three children together. He was a devout Catholic and a staunch ally and supporter of Daniel O'Connell. He played an active role in Liberal politics and was a member of the Repeal Movement. He was also deeply involved in local politics and was twice elected mayor of Clonmel, in 1844 and 1845. He was appointed deputy lieutenant of Tipperary in 1863 and he was also a founding member of the Catholic University in Dublin. Bianconi purchased Longfield Estate near Cashel in 1846, where he lived until his death in 1875 from a stroke at the age of ninety.

25 September

Rum overdose

Cork Evening Post, 25 September 1758.

'Friday night a porter who had been left to watch a parcel of rum on the Custom-House Quay, drank so immoderately of the liquor as to kill himself before morning.'

26 September

Torn to pieces by a sow

The *Tyrawly Herald* of 26 September 1852 reported that an unattended child was torn to pieces by a sow at a house in Mass Lane in Sligo. The child's mother tried to drive the pig off, but she was badly mauled in the attempt.

27 September

Chalking Act

Daniel Lynch had the dubious distinction of being the first Cork man to be charged under the Chalking Act, for stabbing a woman named Catherine Collins to death with a penknife and mutilating her body. Lynch was hanged at Gallows Green in Cork on 27 September 1784. Under the terms of the Chalking Act, his body was denied a Christian burial and was given up for dissection instead.

28 September

Cruelty to a mule

Three men, Francis Brien, John Kelly and Patrick O'Toole, appeared at Kells Court of Petty Sessions in County Meath on 28 September 1857, charged with 'cruelly beating a mule' and assaulting Sub-constable Myers on 15 September that year.

Myers told the court that he had seen Brien beating the mule 'very unmercifully' with an iron bar and he gave evidence that O'Toole and Kelly had also beaten the animal. Myers also told the judge that Kelly had struck him when he went to remonstrate with the men and O'Toole had threatened to 'smash him with an iron bar'.

The judge dismissed the charge of animal cruelty on the basis that the mule had a long track record of kicking people, but he found the men guilty of assaulting Sub-constable Myers and fined them ten shillings each with costs.

29 September

Dublin's first female mayor

Kathleen Daly Clarke, the first female lord mayor of Dublin, was born in 1878 into a prominent nationalist family. One of ten children, she was the niece of John Daly, a member of the Irish Republican Brotherhood, and she was married to Thomas Clarke, one of the leaders of the 1916 rebellion, who was executed at Kilmainham Jail.

Kathleen, a founder member of Cumann na mBan, the women's Republican organisation, was elected as a TD on two occasions, in 1918 and 1927. She was a Fianna Fáil senator during the 1930s and she was also a member of Dublin Corporation. She was elected as the first female lord mayor of Dublin in June 1939.

At her inauguration, Kathleen was offered the chain of office, which had been presented to Dublin Corporation by William of Orange. She refused to wear King Billy's chain and was instead invested wearing another chain which was used for everyday mayoral duties.

As soon as she got into the Mansion House, Kathleen set about removing a large portrait of Queen Victoria from the entrance hall. She declared that she would not be able to sleep in the Mansion House until the offending picture was removed as she (Victoria) 'had been so bitterly hostile to Ireland and everything Irish'. While she was at it, the new mayor decided to remove several other paintings of British monarchs which she found hanging around the house.

When her term as lord mayor ended, Kathleen left Fianna Fáil. She ran as an independent candidate in the next corporation election, but was not re-elected. In 1948, she stood in the Dáil elections for Clann na Poblachta, but she failed to win a seat.

Kathleen Clarke died on 29 September 1972 at the age of ninety-four. She was given a state funeral in the Pro Cathedral in Marlborough Street and was buried in Deansgrange Cemetery.

30 September

Death of Denis Kerin

On Monday, 30 September 1850 nearly one hundred inmates of the auxiliary workhouse in Miltown Malbay, County Clare were sent to be inspected by the Ballvaughan Board of Guardians at Ennistymon Workhouse. The inmates, mainly boys, set out at 5.00 a.m. from Miltown and walked all the way to Ennistymon – a distance of nine miles – where they were kept until five or six o'clock that evening. The boys, who were between six and fifteen years old, were ordered to return to Miltown and they set off without having eaten anything for the entire day.

It was an unusually wet and windy night for that time of year. Many of the boys succumbed to hunger and exhaustion on the return trip and were unable to make it back to Miltown. Some of the lucky ones found refuge in houses along the way, but on the following morning at roll call in the Miltown workhouse, twelve boys were found to be missing.

One of these was eleven-year-old Denis Kerin, whose body was found on the roadside at Clonbony Bridge, a half mile from Miltown Malbay. He had wounds on the front and back of his head, and it was supposed that he had received his injuries 'by being frequently dashed against the walls' by the strong winds.

An inquest into the boy's death was held at Miltown Malbay on 3 October and it was found that, 'Denis Kerin, aged eleven years, came by his death, on Monday night, September 30th, on his way from the Ennistymon workhouse to the auxiliary at Miltown, from exhaustion for want of food and exposure to cold, from the neglect of the officers connected with the parent house and auxiliary, together with the neglect of the Ballyvaughan Board of Guardians.'

OCTOBER

1 October

Parnell Monument

Although his name doesn't immediately suggest an Irish connection, Augustus Saint-Gaudens, sometimes described as the US's 'foremost sculptor', was in fact born at no. 35 Charlemont Street in Dublin in 1848. He was the son of a French cobbler, Bernard Paul Ernst Saint-Gaudens, and Mary McGuinness from Ballymahon in County Longford.

In the years following the death of the 'uncrowned king of Ireland' Charles Stewart Parnell in 1891, steps were taken to build a fitting monument in his honour. In 1898 a fundraising committee was formed to raise the necessary money, and the foundation stone for the Parnell monument was laid at the top of Sackville Street (O'Connell Street) in October 1899.

Saint-Gaudens was approached to design the monument and, following lengthy negotiations, he agreed to take on the project for a fee of £5,000. The Parnell statue, eight feet high and cast in bronze, arrived in Dublin in 1907 and was immediately put on public display at an Oireachtas art exhibition. This proved to be one of Saint-Gaudens' last major works as he died on 3 August that year.

Because of his Irish background, Saint-Gaudens was said to have shown great enthusiasm for the Parnell project and he went to great lengths to make sure that it was right. He had a model made of the buildings on the proposed site of the monument in Sackville Street and Great Britain Street to ensure that the scale was right, and he also built a full-scale wooden model of the monument in a field near his studio.

He even went to the trouble of having replicas created of Parnell's last suit of clothes made by his Dublin tailor.

The Parnell monument was eventually unveiled twenty years after his death on 1 October 1911 by then leader of the Irish Parliamentary Party John Redmond. Thousands gathered for a march from St Stephen's Green to the monument and the crowd was so vast that it took nearly an hour and a half to pass through Grafton Street. So great was the crush at the monument that railings, erected just days previously to protect it, collapsed.

On the day after the unveiling, Dublin Corporation changed the name of Great Britain Street to Parnell Street.

2 October

The tramp class

Mary Devlin and Mary Boylan, described in the *Irish Independent* on 2 October 1908 as 'two women of the tramp class', were jailed after a special court hearing in Newbliss, County Monaghan for assaulting Hugh Finnegan who kept a lodging house there. Police Sergeant Young gave evidence that the two women had beaten Finnegan with iron cooking implements and said that there had been up to twenty tramps in Newbliss at the time of the attack. Sentencing Devlin to six weeks' imprisonment and Boylan to four weeks', Resident Magistrate Moore observed that 'in his experience, nearly all the tramps that came before him were from Co. Cavan.'

3 October

Perished from want

Extract from a letter from Boyle, County Roscommon, published in the *Longford Journal*, 3 October 1846:

'The little Cunningham's father is dead. Poor man! He perished from want: he had to go three miles every day to his work on the public roads, and three more back, for eight pence a day. He had eight in [his] family to support on this slender means, with oatmeal at its present enormous price. On returning from work on Thursday evening last he was so exhausted that he fell into a bog-hole, where he remained a considerable time until he recovered some strength, when he crawled out and sat by a turf-bank until the moon shone out. With great difficulty he made his way home to Tullaghan bog. That night he was taken very ill, and swelled up very much in the morning. In the course of the following day this swelling had abated, and he died at seven o'clock the same evening.

'I wanted the family to go into the workhouse; but as the two little boys have now got work on the road near Lavin's, they have thought better to remain as they are – the poor widowed mother preferring to hold on [to] her poor miserable cabin, under any circumstances, rather than *unhouse* themselves. The little baby died yesterday, which, though it added to her affliction, lightened her care.'

4 October

The Jolly Beggarmen

An anonymous scribe penned a letter to the *Times* 'Letters to the Editor' page, published on 4 October 1856, in which he made the astonishing claim that, far from being penniless and destitute, the beggars of Dublin were in fact a highly organised and disciplined political group run by a number of organisations that he called the 'Hell Committee', 'Brat-lending Club', 'Brothel-house Committee' and 'Swallow-tail Club'.

Using the pseudonym 'Nuncio', the anonymous scribe – who appears to have been a British spy – related that he had been sent to Dublin some thirty years earlier to keep an eye on agitation associated with the cause of Catholic emancipation. While performing these duties in Dublin, Nuncio said that he became aware of an organisation known as the 'Corporation of Jolly Beggars', which met on a regular basis 'in a room not forty yards from the centre of Sackville Street'.

Nuncio learned that the 'Jolly Beggarmen' were to meet on the evening of St Patrick's Day sometime during the 1820s and — being a spy — decided that he'd like to take a closer look to satisfy his curiosity. He bribed the owner of the tavern where the meeting was to take place to let him hide in the roof space in order to eavesdrop on the proceedings below.

From his vantage point in the attic, Nuncio observed the arrival of '83 respectably dressed men and women' who sat down to a lavish three-course meal washed down with beer, stout, ale, 'five kinds of wine', brandy and poitín.

After dinner came the speeches and toasts, and our spy ace Nuncio cleverly deduced that the assembly below were Catholics because they first raised a glass to Daniel O'Connell followed by a toast to 'his holiness' the Pope.

Next came the business end of the meeting. The city was strictly divided up into lots, and every beggar or thief had his or her own patch. No one was allowed to enter the territory of another and any transgression of this rule was punishable by expulsion.

The chairman, described as a failed novelist by Nuncio, then called the meeting to order, and reports from the various 'schools' were read out. First up was a spokesman from the Hell Committee, who gave details of brushes with the police and complained of interference from gamblers who weren't affiliated to the Jolly Beggars.

Next in line was the Brat-lending Club, which allegedly hired out children to beggars who were used to 'excite compassion by shivering, screaming, sobbing, etc.'. This was followed by a contribution from the Brothel-house Committee, but Nuncio didn't elaborate on the details of the speech.

Last to address the floor was a speaker from the Dublin Swallow-tail Club, representing the city's pickpockets. Nuncio tells us that the pickpockets were called the Swallow-tail Club because the swallow-tail was apparently the part on a gentleman's coat that was easiest to rob.

The session ended with more political speeches and singing. Nuncio commented that, while the rest of Ireland seemed ungovernable, the Jolly Beggars were as well organised as the 'hierarchy at Rome'.

5 October

Mad cat attack

'A Mad Cat Savagely Attacks a Boy' was the sensational headline in the *Irish Independent* in October 1894. The boy in question was sixteen-year-old Patrick Rigney, who lived at Clonlyon, Belmont in King's County (now Offaly). Young Rigney had been on his way home on the evening of Friday, 5 October when he noticed two cats – one alive, one dead – lying in a ditch.

Rigney was poking at the dead cat with a stick when the live one attacked him savagely, biting him on the leg and hands and clawing at his clothing. The youth managed to fend the cat off, but it returned to attack him again and again until Rigney eventually managed to strangle it. The dead animal was inspected by a vet who confirmed that it had rabies. The injured Rigney had suffered numerous severe bites and scratches in the attack, so arrangements were made to send him to the Louis Pasteur Institute in France to be vaccinated against rabies.

6 October

Drumkeeran Fair

At the Leitrim Assizes on 6 October 1832, Revenue policeman William Donnelly was acquitted on a charge of murdering Leitrim man Patrick Judge at Drumkeeran Fair. The Revenue Police had been at the fair to seize illegal poitín. The police were attempting to arrest a woman and a man named Kelly when a riot started. Missiles were thrown at the police and they retaliated by firing into the crowd, killing Judge.

There was conflicting evidence given during the trial. A Drumkeeran school teacher Michael McTernan told the court that he had heard some shots fired and witnessed Donnelly kneeling down and firing two shots at the dead man. Another witness, Owen Doherty, claimed that there were no stones thrown at the police that day and no rioting.

Another school teacher, Edward Taylor of Enniskillen, insisted that there had been huge disorder in the village that day and he had heard a rioter shout: 'Come on ye cowardly rascals – prepare to pelt them with stones boys.' Another witness claimed that the police had said that they were going to 'take down the Connaught Paddies like sparrows'.

Having heard all the evidence, the trial was speedily concluded and the jury acquitted Donnelly without leaving the box to deliberate.

7 October

Unlawfully opened a grave

In October 1829 the Dublin newspapers were awash with reports of bodysnatching from the city's graveyards. The anatomists at the Royal College of Surgeons and Trinity College paid handsomely for a fresh cadaver, and Dublin's 'sack-'em-up' fraternity were only too happy to meet the demand.

In early October, Maynooth man Thomas Myland was arrested after the body of a four-year-old boy was found in a pub in Frederick Lane in Dublin. The boy was the son of a Maynooth cobbler named Michael Mee, and Myland had been at his funeral on the day before he was arrested. He said that he came up with the bright idea of becoming a bodysnatcher at the funeral, and he returned to the cemetery later that night and dug up the child's remains with the aid of a billhook. Myland bundled the corpse – 'grave clothes and all' – into a sack and headed off towards Dublin with his grisly package.

He went into the pub on Frederick Lane where he had a few drinks. Then he went on his way, but forgot to bring the body with him. The pub owner and a waiter found the child's body and called the police. Myland was arrested later when he returned for the body.

On 7 October 1829, Michael Askins was convicted of stealing the body of a two-year-old girl from Merrion Churchyard in Dublin with the intention of selling it for money. Askins was spotted carrying the child's body at the corner of Mercer Street and North King Street by a night watchman who challenged him. Askins dropped his bundle, took off his shoes and fled the scene, but he was caught soon afterwards in Digges Lane.

He was found guilty as charged and committed to Newgate Prison for three months.

8 October

Athlone tong-lashing

On 8 October 1834, the *Athlone Independent* reported on a court case involving local women Bridget Hopkins and Eliza Griffin, in which Griffin hit Hopkins over the head with a metal tongs. Hopkins gave evidence to the court that Griffin had become involved in a row with her brother, and had worked herself into such a fury that she began to break up Hopkins' furniture and smash all the delph in Hopkins' kitchen dresser.

When Hopkins tried to calm her down, Griffin turned on her, 'called her an old whore [and] swore she'd make her hold her chat'. She then grabbed a metal tongs and hit poor Hopkins 'such a tip of it as nearly silenced her for ever-and-aye'.

Griffin, who was extremely remorseful, was fined three pounds or faced six weeks in Roscommon Jail in default.

9 October

Bodies wrapped in copies of the Irish Times

A man named Walsh, who lived at a house called Sloperton in Monkstown, County Dublin, was walking in his garden on 9 October 1880 when he came across a newspaper parcel concealed in the bushes. On opening it, he found that the parcel contained the bodies of two newborn babies.

Later that day, a man named Barnes was out walking in Monkstown when he found a bundle containing a live baby who was about two months old. The baby was taken to the police barracks at Kingstown (Dún Laoghaire) and was then removed to the Loughlinstown Workhouse.

An inquest into the deaths of the two infants discovered by Mr Walsh was reported on in the *Dublin Evening Mail* two days later:

'The jury first proceeded to view the bodies. They were those of pretty twins, and had been born only four days. Round each throat was a string of calico, tied tightly as possible. The little bodies were swollen and presented a pitiful sight. They were found wrapped up in three copies of the *Irish Times* of June 7th ...'.

10 October

Hangman caught stealing a cow

'Jack Ketch in Jeopardy' ran the sensational headline in the *Freeman's Journal* on 10 October 1831. The original Jack Ketch was the nickname of a famous London hangman named John Price, and any hangman that came after him in England or in Ireland became known in common parlance as 'Jack Ketch', 'Jack the breath stopper' or 'Jack the Struggler.'

In this case, the *Freeman's Journal* was referring to John Foy, the Kilmainham hangman, successor to the notorious Tom Galvin. Foy had been spotted a few nights earlier driving a cow through High Street by a night watchman. The watchman called the police, who arrested Foy and held him in custody overnight. The next day, it emerged that the cow was the property of Michael Cavanagh, a Kilmainham pub owner. Foy was committed for trial and the only excuse that he could give for his behaviour was that business was bad in the hanging trade.

11 October

Pitch barrel

On 11 October 1760, servant Elizabeth Fairly was executed at Gallows Hill in Downpatrick, County Down for the murder of her mistress Rose Seawright. Before the execution took place, the condemned woman had to listen to a sermon from a Reverend Bailie in which he impressed on her the wicked nature of her crime. Fairly then spent some time praying, and it was reported that she was genuinely repentant for what she had done.

Her execution was not a straightforward one. First, she was hung over a barrel of pitch and, once the 32-year-old woman had been suspended for a 'proper time', the barrel was set on fire.

12 October

A woman scorned

On 12 October 1790, the *Dublin Chronicle* contained a report on the stabbing of a 'genteel young man', as he emerged from St. Anne's church in Dawson Street with his wife. The attacker, described as being a female of 'tolerably decent appearance', stabbed the man in the arm and was about to stab him again when he tore the knife from her grasp.

It emerged afterwards that the man had once been in a relationship with his assailant and had promised to marry her and that 'her present desperate conduct was the result of jealousy and despair'. No charges were pressed, and the woman was allowed to go on her way.

13 October

Professional hurling in Galway

It was a rare thing to see a sports report in an Irish eighteenth-century newspaper, and reports on hurling matches were almost non-existent. Hence, it was a real pleasure to discover this report in *Pue's Occurrences* on 13 October

1759, even if the hurling match itself is hardly referred to. It's also interesting to note that the game was played 'for a considerable sum of money'.

'Country News, Galway: There was lately a grand match in the neighbourhood of Gort in this county, for a considerable sum of money between the counties of Clare and Galway. The hurlers of the latter made a very handsome appearance; they marched from Gort to the Turlagh, two miles distant, preceded by a band of musick, a French horn, a running footman, and a fellow in an antic or Harlequin dress. None of the hurlers were in the least hurt, the greatest harmony having subsisted. The county of Clare hurlers were elegantly entertained at Crusanahane the night following, and one hundred guineas was proposed to be hurled for, but the time and place not yet agreed on. The above procession closed with many carriages and horsemen, the numerous company at the Turlagh made a fine appearance.'

14 October

Kidnapped and raised as a chimney sweep

There was an unusual court case reported in the *Freeman's Journal* on 14 October 1829 when three master chimney sweeps, Christopher Long, Andrew Behan and William Brennan, were brought before the Dublin Magistrates for the kidnapping of a young Glasnevin boy Alec O'Donnell.

The boy's mother told the court that three years earlier she had sent her son to live in Wicklow with his uncle, Daniel Fitzsimons. She heard nothing more about her son until a woman living in Clonskeagh told her that she had seen Alec in a Dublin street, 'clothed in sweeps apparel, following one of the sooty tribe, who appeared to be his master'.

Shortly afterwards, Mrs O'Donnell was walking through Kevin Street when a small boy covered in soot approached her saying, 'Mother, Mother, how are you?' After a few minutes, she recognised the child as her son and went to take him home with her.

Chimney sweeps Christopher Long and Andrew Behan arrived on the scene at that point and took the boy away from his mother, claiming that he was their apprentice and still had five and a half years left to serve.

The court heard that Long had bought the child for half a guinea from William Brennan, who said that he had bought him from another sweep, James Nowlan in Bray, but there was no explanation as to how the child had ended up in Nowlan's hands. Long said that he had only paid half a guinea for the boy because he was in such a poor state of health, and the judge observed that training him as a chimney sweep was no way to improve his well-being. The other master sweep Andrew Behan gave evidence that Long had given the boy to him in part payment of a debt.

O'Donnell was returned to his mother's care and the chimney sweeps were discharged by the court due to lack of evidence.

15 October

Attempted murder in Monaghan

Father Duffy, the parish priest of Tydavnet, County Monaghan was administering the last rites to one of his parishioners on 15 October 1832 when he was attacked by a man wielding a club.

The man, described as a 'the son of a respectable Protestant named Hazlet', then ran to a local yeoman's house where he borrowed a gun with a bayonet attached and returned to look for the priest. Father Duffy saw Hazlet approaching and he ambushed him and tried to take the gun off him. As they wrestled on the ground, Hazlet's brother ran to the aid of the priest and, in the midst of the confusion, the gun went off, blowing part of the attacker's hand off. Duffy then confiscated the gun and brought it to the local magistrate.

An inquiry was held into the incident shortly afterwards, and the priest was asked if he wanted to prosecute Hazlet, but he declined. He did ask that Hazlet be bound over to keep the peace, but the magistrates declined the request.

16 October

Belfast street Arab

Described in the *Northern Whig* as 'one of the street Arabs of Belfast', a thirteen-year-old boy named Patrick Magee appeared at Belfast Police Court on 16 October 1857 on a charge of stealing apples. Magee, who was barefoot and almost naked, was found guilty and sentenced to a month in prison. As soon as he arrived in his cell to begin his sentence, Magee tried to hang himself with a makeshift noose fashioned from a handkerchief, but he was caught and taken back to the magistrate who ordered that he be placed in handcuffs until he settled down. Magee was given a longer sentence for stealing clothes in April 1858. He was sent to Crumlin Road Jail where he succeeded in his second attempt to commit suicide (see entry for 27 April).

17 October

Barber-ous Affair

Extract from *The Warder*, 17 October 1829:
'Limerick City Quarter Sessions. Andrew Lahiff, one of the useful and esteemed tribe of Gentleman Barbers, was tried with a helpmate, for a larceny on the person of Garret

Lane. A poor decrepit countryman, who had unfortunately, "just dropt in" to the chamber of this modern Tonson [Jacob Tonson – a well-known London barber surgeon], in order to be relieved of a surplus age of stubble field from his nether lip and chin. He had scarcely taken the seat of honour, and submitted with proper grace to the magic scythe of Monsieur Tonson, after, as he declared, first posting the luck-penny, when the simple clown felt a pull at his dress. He took alarm at once and exclaimed there was a hand in his pocket. The crafty shaver however, had him as effectually under his magic wand, as if screwed in a vice, for when Lane attempted to turn round and observe the impertinent intruder, Mr. Tonson held him close by the cheek and nasal organ, keeping the razor fast to his throat, and exclaiming ever and anon with the most earnest concern, "don't stir, take care of the razor". The ruse succeeded, and in a few seconds, on being freed from lather, brush and steel, he found, to his utter consternation, he was at the same moment lightened of his beard, and twelve shillings in silver. He swore there was no person there but the barber and his wife, which latter made off immediately after. She had been sitting by him during the operation. Verdict: "both guilty; the wife to be transported for seven years, Lahiff six months hard labour."

18 October

Birched for making noise

On 18 October 1851, several Dublin newspapers carried details of a complaint made by a Captain Nowlan to the magistrates of the Dublin Police Court in relation to the over-zealous disciplinary measures taken against children in the South Dublin Union Workhouse.

Nowlan wanted to have the master of the workhouse arrested for beating ninety-six pauper boys in his care with a birch for shouting. He produced the formidable looking birch in court and invited the magistrates to come forward and try it out. The magistrates declined Nowlan's kind offer, but agreed with him that the master should be summonsed.

19 October

Death of Jonathan Swift

Jonathan Swift, author of *Gulliver's Travels, A Letter to Stella, Drapier's Letters* and other classics died on 19 October 1745. Swift suffered from Meniere's disease, a condition that causes nausea, deafness and vertigo. The disease was untreatable in Swift's, day and he gradually lost the power of speech, leaving him, as he described himself, 'deaf, giddy, helpless and left alone.' In 1742, three years before his death, Swift lapsed into a coma from which he never recovered.

As news of Swift's death spread, large crowds flocked to his house to pay their last respects. According to Thomas Sheridan – Swift's godson – his servants made a small fortune by flogging locks of the great man's hair as souvenirs to the multitudes gathered outside. 'In less than an hour' said Sheridan, 'his venerable head was entirely stripped of all its silver ornaments, so that not a hair remained.'

Swift's remains lie in St. Patrick's Cathedral beneath where, as the Latin inscription beside his tomb reads: fierce indignation can no more lacerate his heart. Go traveller, and imitate, if you can, one who strove with all his strength to champion liberty.'

20 October

Merrion Square streaker

The *Freeman's Journal* of 20 October 1813 reported on a scandalous case heard at the Recorder's Court in Dublin earlier that week. Thomas Meehan – described as a foreman at a highly respectable house in Grafton Street – was accused of 'being a wicked and evil person', who did, 'on the 4th day of September last, in Merrion-square, wickedly, wantonly and maliciously expose his naked person, in the presence of numerous males and females …'.

Meehan told the court that he had never done anything of that nature before and blamed his actions on some medicine he had taken on the morning of the incident. The court, however, didn't believe his story, and Meehan was sentenced to be publicly pilloried for an hour on the following Saturday, followed by a year in prison.

21 October

Death in Drogheda

Extract from the *Hibernian Journal*, 21 October 1782:

'Saturday last, a number of Colonel Talbot's Fencible Regiment, quartered in the barracks of Drogheda, being in pursuit of a deserter, insisted on searching a house in that town where they said he was secreted, and, on their refused admittance, proceeded to force open the door.

A mob immediately assembling and pelting them with stones, they returned to their quarters, procured muskets, sallied out among the people and fired several shots at them. Fortunately, however, no lives were lost at that time, and the Volunteers assembling, fifteen of the Fencibles were secured and lodged in gaol, which it was thought would put an end to the riot; but on the remainder of the party making for the barracks, two of them were wounded in so desperate a manner with stones that they died on Monday.

We are very sorry to hear that this disturbance was renewed on Monday with great animosity on both sides; that another of the Fencibles was killed on the bridge of that town, and that several of the inhabitants were severely wounded. Between five and six o'clock on Monday evening, a strong detachment of the Royal Irish Dragoons set out from this city for Drogheda; and we hear they are to be followed by a party of foot, in order to quell the disagreeable riot existing there.'

22 October

A Crimean Medal

At a meeting on 8 September 1856 in the Round Room of the Mansion House, attended by MPs and the Lord Mayor of Dublin, it was resolved 'to invite to a National entertainment, in the City of Dublin, all the troops now serving in Ireland who are wearers of Crimean medals'.

The 'National Entertainment', which took place on 22 October 1856, was one of the biggest banquets ever held in the city and had a guest list of nearly four thousand – mainly soldiers from Irish garrisons who had seen service in the Crimean War.

A planning committee was quickly put together and a subscription list was circulated among the wealthy and influential members of Dublin society in order to defray the costs of the event. Several venues were considered and rejected before the committee decided to stage the banquet at Mr Scovell's Bonded Warehouse at the Custom House.

Food for the occasion was prepared by the Spadacini and Murphy company, and the meal consisted of 250 hams, 230 legs of mutton, 200 turkeys, 200 geese, 250 joints of beef, 500 meat pies, 100 venison pies, 100 chickens, 6 ox tongues, 100 rice puddings and 260 plum puddings. In addition, there were four thousand pounds of bread and three tonnes of potatoes. All of this was washed down with a quart of porter for each man and a pint of wine or sherry, supplied free of charge by Dublin wine merchant Henry Brennan.

Of the soldiers present at the occasion, 1,500 were from the Dublin garrison, 1,000 from the Curragh and the remainder came from regiments stationed throughout Ireland. Admission to the feast was dependent upon the presentation of a Crimean medal.

Dinner didn't start until the arrival of the Lord Lieutenant at 1.20 p.m., and, despite the huge amounts of food involved, it was all over by 2.05 p.m. when the Lord Mayor said grace after meals. Innumerable speeches, toasts and more speeches followed, and by 4.00 p.m. the last soldier had departed back up the quays and away to their various destinations.

One departing soldier, when asked if he had enjoyed the day, replied: 'If they gave us the same treatment in the Crimea we would never have left it.'

23 October

The world began on 23 October 4004 BC

James Ussher (1581–1656), who served as archbishop of Armagh between 1625 and 1656, was born in Dublin on 4 January 1581. Ussher was a prolific scholar, linguist and theologian, and he entered Trinity College to study Theology at the age of just thirteen.

Ussher's greatest claim to fame was his chronology of creation published in 1650 that has since become known as the Ussher–Lightfoot Calendar. In this work, Ussher came up with a theory that the world actually began on 23 October 4004 BC by counting the number of 'begats' in the Book of Genesis. Later disciples of Ussher's method have even come to the conclusion that the world began at 9.00 a.m. GMT on that date.

24 October

Belfast Police Court

The magistrates were busy at the Belfast Police Court on 24 October 1894. James Greer was sentenced to two months in jail for punching Mrs Jane Finlay in the mouth and hitting her over the head with her umbrella during an unprovoked attack on a Belfast street.

Mary McKenna was charged with causing serious injury to a shopkeeper named Mrs Stewart by throwing weights and a carving knife at her. She was returned for trail at the Recorder's Court. Also up in front of the magistrates that day was Frederick Pollock, a young man charged with attempting to commit suicide by drinking a glass of ammonia while drunk. He was bound over to keep the peace.

25 October

Tragedy at the Bloody Bridge

An all-too-common tragedy took place in Dublin on 25 October 1784 when a woman, with a little girl in her arms, threw herself and the child into the River Liffey near the Bloody Bridge (now Rory O'More Bridge). A passer-by saw what was happening and went to the rescue. He managed to save the woman, but the child was carried away by the current, and was found dead a short time later, stuck under the piles of the bridge.

There was very little sympathy afforded to the child's mother and on 26–28 October the *Freeman's Journal* reported that 'the wretch who committed this rash action appeared to be delirious, and was committed to Bridewell.'

26 October

Westmeath Carders

It was reported in *Saunder's Newsletter* on 26 October 1814 that the group known as the 'Carders' or the 'Threshers', an agrarian secret society, had been active in the Westmeath area and had come up with a new method of torturing their enemies. During the previous week – believing him to be an informer – they had dragged Charles Lennon's cowherd out of his house at Drumrainey and cut off his ears with a pair of shears. A few nights later they cut a woman's ear off at Walderstown.

27 October

A night in the stocks

On 27 October 1770 the *Freeman's Journal* informs us that one Stephen Rix, a Kilkenny bailiff, 'sat in the stocks at the Market Cross from Morning till Night', as punishment for accepting a bribe from a swineherd named Connor.

28 October

Bawds, whores and pimps

A report in George Falkner's *Dublin Journal* on 28 October 1732 illustrates a novel method of dealing with the burgeoning prostitution industry in eighteenth-century Dublin. As part of a crackdown on Dublin's 'community of bawds, whores and pimps', four women and a man were taken into custody on the previous Friday evening at 6.00 p.m. and publicly exhibited in a cage until 11.00 a.m. the next morning. After that the man was incarcerated in Dublin's infamous Black Dog Prison and the women were lodged in the Bridewell.

Among them was the notorious Catty Duffy, who had been captured on a previous occasion but was freed by a mob as she was being escorted from the cage to the Tholsel by the parish watch.

29 October

Eagle

Newry, 29 October 1771, *Hibernian Journal*: Lord Clanwilliam's 'sportsman' or gamekeeper was out hunting in the Mountains of Mourne in County Down when one of his gun dogs raised a hare. The hare shot off, with the spaniel in hot pursuit. However, a large eagle swooped down from the sky, snatched the hare and made off with his prey. The hunter fired at the eagle, winging him and killing the hare. The poor eagle fell to the ground and was attacked by the dogs. The eagle made a 'vigorous defence' but was eventually overcome.

30 October

Needles and pins

Please do not under any circumstances follow this piece of medical advice as given by a 'friend to humanity' in the *Hibernian Journal* on 30 October 1789: 'In the dangerous case of pins swallowed by accident, swallowing one egg undressed, and in the course of one hour after, another, is an infallible remedy for carrying off the pins, if done immediately after they have been swallowed, i.e. before the pins have worked themselves into the coats of the stomach.'

31 October

The Secret Order of the Lock

All Saints' Eve, or Hallowe'en, was the night that Dublin's 'Most Solemn and Most Secret Order of the Lock' held their annual bash in the city. The Order – a Freemason-like organisation – appears to have had a connection with the Lock Hospital in Westmoreland Street, which opened in 1792, as the society's accounts reveal that it received a sum of £150 from the Board of Governors of that hospital in 1794. However, from the few records that survive, it can reasonably be assumed that the Lockmen's main focus was their weekly drinking session.

The all-male organisation seems to have been formed in 1761 and was overseen by a supreme leader known to the members as the 'Pontifex Maximus' or PM. Next in line to the PM was the 'Augur' who was in turn aided by two 'Censors', while the rank and file were simply known as 'Lockmen'. The PM was looked upon as the supreme leader and father of the order and his commands were to be obeyed without hesitation.

During ceremonies, the PM sat on a ceremonial throne while the Augur stood to his right on the second step of the throne, holding the seals of the order in a purse. A large golden key bearing the order's motto was carried by a senior Lockman. It was displayed on a velvet cushion in front of the PM at all meetings and ceremonies.

Investitures of members of the Privy Council or ruling body of the order were carried out partially in private and partially in public in the presence of 'chanting and musical Lockmen'. These members distinguished themselves from the rest of the body by carrying small golden keys which hung from a cord of purple or white lace.

Two members elected every three months had responsibility for the 'usual entertainments' of the Lockmen and were also responsible for the provision of wine at the weekly meetings, which took place in rooms belonging to the order, or any other 'house of public entertainment'. The highlight of the year was the order's annual bash, which took place on the night of 31 October, and every member was expected to attend on this night unless 'he be twenty miles from his circle or hindered by sickness'.

NOVEMBER

1 November

Cork Earthquake

On 1 November 1755, the city of Cork was rocked by a violent earthquake at 9.30 a.m. No injuries were reported. A number of fishing boats at Kinsale were damaged in the tsunami that followed.

2 November

The Devil's Own

'My dearest Mother, I take this opportunity to let you know the dreadful news that I am to be shot on Tuesday morning, the 2nd of November. What harm, it is all for Ireland. I am not afraid to die, but it is thinking of you I am. That is all: if you will be happy on earth I will be happy in Heaven. I am ready to meet my doom.'

These words were written in a last letter to his mother by Private James Daly from Tyrellspass, Westmeath, leader of the Connaught Rangers mutiny in India in 1920.

The Connaught Rangers, nicknamed the 'Devil's Own', had a long record in the service of the British Empire. The regiment was founded in the late eighteenth century by Lord Clanrickarde of Connaught and was originally known as the 88th Regiment of Foot. The regiment was renowned for its prowess on the battlefield and it saw action in the Peninsula Wars, the Crimea and at Gallipoli in the World War I.

When the War of Independence was at its height in Ireland in 1920, the first battalion of the Connaught

Rangers was stationed at Jullundur in the Punjab, India. As news began to filter through to the men of the murderous campaign being waged back in Ireland by the Black and Tans, some of them decided to do something about it.

Toward the end of June 1920 a small group of Connaught Rangers refused to soldier any longer in the service of the King of England while their families and friends at home were being murdered by the Black and Tans. The protest at Jullundur spread quickly and soon over two hundred soldiers were involved in the strike. They refused to go on parade, saying that their action was a 'protest against the state of affairs then existing in Ireland'.

News of the protest soon spread to another unit of the Connaught Rangers based at Solon twenty miles away, and soon a group of seventy soldiers led by James Daly embarked on a similar course of action. After surrendering their weapons, rumours began to sweep the camp at Solon that their comrades at Jullundur had been executed. Daly and the mutineers, armed only with bayonets, attacked the magazine in an attempt to regain their weapons. The soldiers guarding the magazine opened fire, and two of the mutineers – Peter Sears of Mayo and Patrick Smyth of Drogheda – were killed. The mutiny fizzled out after this incident, and Daly and his fellow mutineers surrendered.

The men were tried six weeks later and Daly, who was only twenty-one, was sentenced to death and duly executed at Dagshai by firing squad. Nineteen others were sentenced to death, but eighteen of these sentences were later commuted to penal servitude for life. About sixty others were sentenced to prison terms ranging from two to twenty-one years. One prisoner, Private John Miranda from Liverpool, died while in prison at Dagshai.

James Daly's remains lay in a Dagshai Military Cemetery for fifty years until they were taken back to Ireland in 1970, along with the bodies of Sears and Smyth.

3 November

Alice Kytler's servant burnt at the stake

Although relatively few cases of sorcery in Ireland have been documented, one major exception is the story of Dame Alice Kytler, the fourteeth-century Kilkenny woman who was prosecuted for witchcraft.

Dame Alice was a member of the Kytler family who had settled in Kilkenny sometime after the Norman invasion. She was married on four different occasions, and her first three husbands were said to have died from poisoning. The fourth, John Le Poer, was allegedly driven insane by magical spells cast by Kytler.

In 1324, the Bishop of Ossory Richard Le Drede held an inquisition in Kilkenny and discovered that there was a band of what were described as 'heretical sorcerers' operating in the town led by Kytler. Le Drede accused Kytler and two members of her household, Petronella de Mide and her daughter Basilla, of, amongst other charges, offering live animal sacrifices to demons, and using potions made from chicken's entrails, dead men's fingernails and the remains of unbaptized children, which were all cooked together in the skull of a thief who had been beheaded.

When Kytler's house was raided in connection with the charges, it was said that 'a wafer of sacramental bread, having the devil's name stamped thereon instead of Jesus Christ' was discovered along with 'a pipe of ointment wherewith she greased a staffe, upon which she ambled and galloped through thick and thin'.

What became of Kytler afterwards is unclear. She fled Kilkenny before she could be convicted, and it has been said that she made her way to England, aided by members of the nobility, and spent the remainder of her days there.

In the absence of Kytler, her servant Petronella de Mide bore the brunt of the bishop's anger. She was subjected to repeated floggings until she finally confessed to acting as a medium between Kytler and a demon named as 'Robert, son of Art' who was said to appear in the form of a cat or black dog.

De Mide was found guilty of the charge of sorcery that had been laid against her and she was sentenced to be burned alive at the stake. The sentence was carried out in Kilkenny on 3 November 1324 and is believed to have been the first death sentence carried out in Ireland for the crime of heresy.

Others who had been accused of involvement in the affair were said to have suffered a variety of punishments. According to St John D. Seymour's *Irish Witchcraft and Demonology*, the lucky ones were merely excommunicated and banished from the town, while others were flogged through the streets and marketplace of Kilkenny. Yet others were marked on the back and front with a cross after they had purged their heresy, while a few were publicly burned to death.

4 November

A priest's wedding

Saunders' Newsletter, 4 November 1774: 'A correspondent in the county of Down informs us, that he was a few days ago at a priest's wedding, at which was the following entertainment: Two carcasses of beef, sixteen of mutton, five dozens of fowl, three of ducks, one of geese, and one of turkies[sic.], forty-six puddings, besides fish, bacon, and hams; there were thirty gallons of rum, twenty of whiskey, ten of brandy, and three hogsheads of ale; all conducted with great decency, festivity, and good humour. N.B. What they call a priest's wedding, is when any young man intends going into orders, he gives an entertainment, and every one of the company contributes money to enable him to prepare himself for his church.'

5 November

Edward the picaroon

A well-known Dublin picaroon (pirate or rogue) Edward O'Brien was sentenced to seven years' transportation at a Dublin court on 5 November 1816, for stealing a large quantity of barilla ashes, the property of businessmen Joseph and Joshua Pimm.

The *Freeman's Journal* of 12 November described O'Brien as an 'audacious fellow' who attacked 'Mr. Kelly, the witness on the trial ... and even struck and knocked him down ....The Recorder, in passing sentence on him, said that these fellows considered themselves authorized to prey upon the public, and make forced contributions on the traders and merchants of the City ...'.

6 November

Eight hundred lashes

A soldier received 500 lashes of an 800-lash sentence on 6 November 1784 in Dublin. He was carried almost life-less from the barrack square, where the punishment was administered, and it was feared that he would never recover sufficiently to be given the remaining three hundred lashes. The soldier had been court-martialled for deliberately cutting himself on the Circular Road in order to obtain a disability allowance.

7 November

Murder of a Dublin newspaper seller

Dublin newspaper seller Charles Murray was viciously attacked and beaten by a number of men at his pitch on the Old Bridge over the River Liffey on 7 November 1776. The men – not content with stealing Murray's clothes and his day's takings – threw him over the bridge and left him to die in the Liffey. A number of people, who heard Murray's cries for help, went to his aid and with great difficulty managed to pull him out. However, he had spent too long in the cold water and died a few days later.

8 November

King Billy's birthday bash

The 8 November 1712 edition of the *Dublin Intelligence* newspaper led with a report on the celebrations in Dublin marking the birthday of the deceased King William of Orange, who had died ten years earlier after a fall from his horse. The main event took place at the Tholsel and was attended by the Lord Mayor, sheriffs 'and several eminent citizens'.

However, a sour note was struck when the 'eminent citizens' proceeded to the nearby Theatre Royal to further celebrate King Billy's birthday. There was consternation in the theatre when the actors refused to read out a glowing tribute to the Prince of Orange, but the day was saved when a 'gentleman of goodly, quality and family' – Dudley Moore – leaped on to the stage and read the offending piece himself.

Two or three members of the audience, described by the paper as 'disaffected and obscure' persons, hissed at the stage, but were drowned out by the 'honest gentlemen' in the audience who were well disposed to the 'Great Deliverer'. The day ended with bonfires and fireworks in some quarters of the city.

9 November

Stabbed in Red Lyon Lane

From the *Munster Journal*:

'Whereas Ensign Bickerton, of General Bragg's Regiment about the hour of 12 o'clock in the Night of the 8th of Nov. instant was most inhumanly knocked down, and afterwards stab'd in the Body in Red Lyon Lane in the City of Limerick, when going to his Barrack, by some person or persons unknown, and without any sort of Provocation given or any words exchanged, or seeing the Person who had so barbarously treated him.

'Whoever will within one Month from the date hereof, discover the person or persons who Struck or Stabed the said Bickerton, shall upon such Person or Persons being convicted thereof, receive a Reward of twenty Pounds from the Mayor of the City of Limerick. Dated this 9th day of Nov. 1749.'

10 November

Disorderly vagabonds

Phineas and George Bagnell's *Cork Evening Post* of Thursday, 10 November 1757 reported that the Sheriff Mr Sweeny and his officers had 'seized a great quantity of loots' in Cork on the previous Sunday. The Lord Mayor of Cork had previously issued an order forbidding the profanation of the Sabbath by selling goods on Sunday. The Sheriff also arrested a number of 'disorderly vagabonds' in the city and a number of 'women of bad fame' in Mary's and Stable Lanes.

11 November

The execution of Edmund Budd

On 11 November 1712 the *Dublin Intelligence* carried details of the public execution of soldier Edmund Budd, who had been hanged at St Stephens' Green in front of several thousand spectators some days earlier.

The newspaper also carried details of the dead man's last speech, which was transcribed by the Reverend Dr Finglasse. In the speech Budd denied all knowledge of the killing of Robert Watts, for which he was executed. Budd also took time to repudiate the claims that he had murdered a young woman and thrown her into the Liffey at Usher's Quay and committed 'a vile prank on the body of a young woman in Cook Street...'.

12 November

Cavan court battle

A court report in the *Cavan Observer* on 12 November 1859 provided details of a case which ultimately ended in a bout of fisticuffs between two women at the Cavan Petty Sessions earlier that week.

Margaret Mahon had summonsed Mary Leddy for throwing stones at her, smashing her windows and using abusive language towards her. Mahon told the magistrate that Leddy – who was a regular visitor to the court had held a grudge against her after a previous case in which Leddy had been prosecuted for stealing a shawl from her. Leddy, who had been quiet up to that point, erupted and shouted at her accuser, 'You lie, you old faggot – you gave it to me! Yourself and the sergeant did it nicely between ye!'

With that, she jumped on Mahon with a roar, knocked off her hat and tore her gown and apron to shreds. Leddy wasn't finished, however, and she attacked Mahon's underclothing with great ferocity, damaging – as the court reporter so delicately put it – her 'garment of mystical sublimity'.

It took six policemen to subdue Leddy and, when she had quietened down, the magistrate sentenced her to two months' imprisonment for assaulting Mahon and a further month for her antics in court.

13 November

'Brother of the quill'

It was an unusual occurrence to see an execution take place in the Liberties in Dublin, but that's exactly what happened on 13 November 1734 when 'Liberty Boy' and 'Brother of the quill' [a weaver] John Gibson was hanged at Newmarket in the Coombe for the murder of Cornelius Farrelly. Another man, James Bryan, was forced to stand at the city pillory on the day of the hanging for swearing false evidence during the trial.

14 November

Bodysnatcher snatched

On the night of 14 November 1825, bodysnatcher Thomas Tuite was caught red-handed as he attempted to make off with six corpses that he had just dug up from Bully's Acre Cemetery at Kilmainham in Dublin. Tuite was apprehended by Thomas Evans, a guard at Kilmainham Jail. Bemoaning his ill-luck, Tuite told Evans that he would have had another six corpses dug up by morning if he hadn't been caught. Tuite also said that he received ten shillings for every corpse he delivered, but a good set of teeth would fetch him a pound a pair. He was sentenced afterwards to six months' imprisonment.

15 November

Sympathetic reporting of suicide attempt

'THE ATTEMPT AT SUICIDE IN NEWRY. – The young man Carver who attempted to blow out his brains with a revolver, is still alive, but his death is hourly expected. The deepest sympathy is felt for him, and it is believed he was led to attempt his life under the influence of a bitter disappointment. His father has arrived from Cork' (*Belfast Morning News*, 15 November 1881).

16 November

Rye Bread Mutiny

On 16 November 1848 the *Clare Journal* reported on a mutiny at Nenagh Workhouse in Tipperary, which took place a week earlier when the female inmates were given rye bread for the first time. The women – numbering six or seven hundred – refused to eat the 'black bread' and some of them broke windows in the workhouse in protest. Others were protesting at the prevailing work conditions.

On the morning after the trouble, the governors withheld the women's supply of milk as a punishment, but this only inflamed the situation, and the disturbances kicked off again. The women were particularly aggrieved at the local inspector Mr D'Arcy who had introduced the rye bread to Nenagh after testing it at the Ballyshannon Workhouse.

More windows were broken, and the women refused to eat their stirabout without milk and they again refused to eat the 'black bread'. The police were summoned to the workhouse to quell the disturbances, and a company of soldiers was dispatched to assist them.

However, the soldiers weren't needed and most of the women eventually ate the stirabout without milk, although a good number of them still refused to comply. The protest was largely over by lunchtime, and some of the more militant inmates were locked up in the yards and punishment cells. A small number of women were sent to Nenagh Jail as a result of the protests.

At an inquiry into the disturbances afterwards, some of the workhouse governors agreed with the women, saying that the bread hadn't been baked properly, but the inspector Mr D'Arcy persisted, saying that the rye bread would save £4,000 per annum and would be better for the women in the long run.

17 November

Wicklow tragedy

There was an almost unbelievable family tragedy reported in the *Dublin Courant* on 17 November 1747. The extraordinary chain of events began when a man and his son, from Killincarrick in Wicklow, were out fishing in a boat with two others. The boat was overturned by a sudden squall of wind and all the occupants were drowned. But the tragedy didn't end there. The man's young daughter, who had been playing on the seashore, saw the boat overturning and ran home to tell her mother. As they both ran back to the shore leaving an infant alone in the house behind them, the family cottage caught fire and the baby perished in the flames.

18 November

A stout fool

'On Wednesday night [18 November 1818], about eleven o'clock, an idiot named Dalton, was turned out of the main guard-house in Limerick, where he had been in the habit of sleeping. Shortly after, as he was walking along the causeway, about a mile from the city, he was met by a man named John Kenny, driving a sheep. The fool, who was a stout fellow, bound Kenny's thumbs together with a stout cord, and tying the sheep to him, drove both into the town. On being questioned about the sheep, he said he had bought it in the county of Clare, but it was discovered that he had stolen it off Colonel O'Donnell's lands in that county. The thief is now in jail.' (*Irish Farmers' Journal*, 21 November 1818)

19 November

Marathon man

Extract from a *Freeman's Journal* letter from Armagh, dated 19 November 1773:

'Last Saturday a remarkable race was run on foot from Dungannon to Armagh and back again, without any allowance of stopping, by an old man, a native of Dungannon, who had been famous for exercises of that nature, and an Highland soldier quartered in that town. Their course was just 22 miles; for the first 15 miles of which the contest was doubtful, but finally the Highlander gained the victory over his antagonist, leaving him near two miles behind; and so high was the spirit of gaming carried on, that there were upwards of two thousand guineas depending.'

20 November

Swallowed a knife and fork

It was reported in the *Irish Independent* on 20 November 1908 that an inmate at the Portrane Asylum in North County Dublin complained of stomach pains and, on examination, it was discovered that he had swallowed a knife and fork, a muffler and a quantity of rags. The items were surgically removed and the patient was said to be recovering well.

21 November

Lazarus Lanigan

On 21 November 1781, Dubliner Thomas Lanigan was hanged at the gallows in Baggot Street for the murder of his employer Captain Thomas O'Flaherty at Castlefield in County Kilkenny.

Lanigan had been employed by Captain O'Flaherty and his wife Susannah as a tutor to their sons at their home in Kilkenny in 1776, an arrangement which worked out just fine until Lanigan fell in love with the captain's wife.

The lovers agreed at some point to do away with Captain O'Flaherty and Lanigan decided that the best way to achieve this was by poisoning him. One evening they laced the captain's dinner with a liberal dose of arsenic and just 'to be sure, to be sure' they put another generous helping of the lethal substance into his custard dessert.

Needless to say, the captain went to bed that night in terrible pain and he died in agony some time later. He was buried soon afterwards, and for a while it seemed that Lanigan and Mrs O'Flaherty would get away with their crime.

There was an investigation afterwards when O'Flaherty's son went to the authorities in Kilkenny and voiced his suspicions about his father's death, but there was no evidence to implicate either Lanigan or Mrs O'Flaherty in the crime.

Eventually Mrs O'Flaherty convinced Lanigan to give himself up to the authorities, saying that she would hand herself in once he had done so. Lanigan agreed and gave himself up, but once he was in custody, his lover did a runner, leaving him to face the music alone.

Lanigan's trial took place at the Court of the King's Bench in Dublin on 19 November 1781. He was found guilty of the murder of Captain O'Flaherty and he was sentenced to be 'hanged and quartered' on the gallows at Baggot Street. The sentence was duly carried out two days later on 21 November.

Lanigan's body was left dangling on the scaffold for about twenty minutes before it was cut down. The executioner then administered four cuts to the arms and legs before handing the body over to Lanigan's family for burial.

Unbelievably, Lanigan's friends saw that he was still breathing and they rushed him to a nearby house where they managed to revive him by rubbing his neck and pouring brandy down his throat. Against all the odds, Lanigan slowly came back to the land of the living. He had cheated the hangman.

Later that night his family filled his coffin with stones and carried it to Kilmainham where they proceeded with a mock funeral in the graveyard at Bully's Acre. The deception only worked for a short while, however, and news of Lanigan's amazing escape from death soon became public knowledge.

'Lazarus' Lanigan decided that he didn't want to give the Dublin public a repeat performance on the gallows and fled to London and from there to France, where it was said that he ended his days in a Trappist monastery.

22 November

Stole an infant child

Hue and Cry, 22 November 1854, advertisement from the Dublin Police, A Division:

'Description of a woman, name unknown, who, on the eve of the 11th instant, stole an infant child, about 4 months old, from his brother, Andrew Kenna, who was carrying it in the hall of the house, No. 147, Thomas-street. About 30 years of age, 5 feet, 4 inches high, brown hair and red face; dressed with a black bonnet, and velvet ribbon, a brown dress; decent appearance, and looked like a dealer.'

23 November

Cromwell's first funeral

There would have been very few tears shed by 'the barbarous and blood-thirsty Irish', on 23 November 1658 when the funeral procession of Oliver Cromwell, Ireland's archnemesis and the man who uttered those words, took place in London.

It was a case of the long goodbye for Cromwell. The former Lord Protector had died on 3 September from septicaemia and the funeral ceremonies were planned to begin on 20 September with the removal of his body from

Whitehall to Somerset House in London. However, when the day for the funeral finally arrived, Cromwell's body was not in Whitehall. It had been decided to bury him at Westminster Abbey a fortnight earlier because his corpse was decomposing rapidly by that time.

As might be expected, there was much pomp, pageantry and ceremony on the day of the funeral, but not everything went like clockwork. There had been rumours of malicious damage to Cromwell's effigy that was to be carried at the head of the procession. Someone had apparently pulled off its ears and nose the night before the funeral, forcing the organisers to undertake hasty repairs. The funeral itself was delayed for hours while dignitaries bickered about their place in the procession. When the procession finally reached Westminster after dark, there were no candles in the Westminster Abbey so there were no prayers or speeches.

We'll leave the last word on Cromwell's funeral to the Royalist John Evelyn who actually witnessed it: '[I]t was the most joyful funeral I ever saw, for there were none that cried but dogs, which the soldiers hooted away with a barbarous noise, drinking and taking tobacco in the streets as they went.'

(For Cromwell's second funeral, see the article for 30 January.)

24 November

Clondalkin explosion

The *Dublin Evening Post* of 24 November 1733 reported a large explosion at the gunpowder mills at Clondalkin, County Dublin by which 'several persons received much damage'.

25 November

All-Blacks visit

On 25 November 1905, Irish rugby fans were eagerly awaiting the very first match between Ireland and the New Zealand All-Blacks at Lansdowne Road.

Interviewed in the *Dublin Evening Mail*, former Irish international player E.G. Brunker was of the opinion that no combination of players from Ireland, England, Scotland or Wales could beat the All-Blacks in their current form.

Brunker pointed out that the cunning Kiwis wore silk jerseys, making it harder to tackle them, and warned the Irish players against indulging in what he described as 'pseudo-Welsh passing and weak tackling'.

The game – which the all-conquering New Zealanders won 15-0 – took place at Lansdowne Road in front of a capacity crowd of thirteen thousand. One sports hack was impressed with what he described as the 'savage teeth-grinding pertinacity about the Maori tackling'. Led by their Donegal-born captain Dave Gallagher, the New Zealanders performed their traditional Haka before the game.

Another correspondent gave his impressions of this strange behaviour: 'I have heard Redskins singing a war-whoop, I have heard Zulus giving us a blood-curdling war-cry, but the New Zealanders could lose those coloured gentry at producing an unearthly howl. I do not know the name of this singular canticle. Possibly it is Maori, Maori, quite contraori but in any case it produces a noticeable moral effect.'

26 November

Fishamble Street murder

On the night of 26 November 1768, Catherine Halpenny, who ran a brothel at Marshall's Lane off Fishamble Street in Dublin, was brutally raped and murdered by five men. Some of the men were caught soon afterwards and lodged in Newgate Prison.

27 November

Cork fortune tellers

Hibernian Journal, 27 November 1782, Cork. The people of Cork were warned to be on the lookout for fake fortune tellers following complaints of extortion. In one incident, a pregnant woman nearly died from shock after a fortune teller had shown her a picture of a coffin during a reading:

'Some egregious imposters, assuming to tell fortunes and pretending to be deaf and dumb, at present infest this city, extorting money from all ranks of people. Their terrifying behaviour is frequently attended with fatal consequences; a gentlewoman with child, a few days ago, had like to have lost her life, occasioned by portraying a coffin before her.'

28 November

The little match boy

A fine of five shillings was imposed on Bridget and Joseph Dunbar at the Belfast Summons Court on 28 November 1894 for having custody of a ten-year-old boy named Peter Vallely and making him sell matches on the streets of Belfast.

29 November

Illegal wedding

Being hanged for conducting an illegal wedding might seem like a rather harsh punishment, but that is exactly what happened to the Reverend William Shewell who had served as a curate of St Michan's and Christchurch Cathedral in Dublin. He was taken from Newgate Prison on a horse and cart and paraded through the streets of Dublin on the way to the scaffold at St Stephen's Green in late November 1740. His death was afforded only a brief mention in *Pue's Occurrences* on 29 November 1740 and it refers in passing to the crime for which he was executed:

'On Saturday last, Mr Shewell, a degraded clergyman, was executed at St. Stephen's Green, for a clandestine marriage. He was carried to the place of execution in a coach and behaved in a defeated manner, becoming a person in his unhappy circumstances.'

Shewell had been found guilty of illegally marrying Richard Walker, a wealthy Protestant, and Margaret Talbot, a Catholic, in August of that year. At the end of October, Shewell had been found guilty as charged and, although he had been given a stay of execution on two occasions, he was eventually hanged on 29 November 1740.

30 November

A selection of crimes

Pue's Occurrences, 30 November 1756: At the commission of Oyer and Terminer in Dublin on 30 November, Judges Ward and McCauley presided over a number of cases. Cormick Dolan was transported for stealing tea, Michael Turney for stealing butter and Robert Boswell for robbing a shop in Hell (a narrow laneway beside Christchurch). Two men were sentenced to death: John Dignam for robbing a house and Patrick Bligh for stealing silver from his master, General Bligh. Another man, Walter Bermingham, was sentenced to be whipped from Newgate Prison to Dawson Street and back again for soliciting another man to assist in the robbery at General Bligh's house.

DECEMBER

1 December

Dungarvan ghost

The *Athlone Sentinel* of 1 December 1852 reported on the strange and 'supernatural' events that had bedevilled Dungarvan publican Patrick Christopher and his family for the previous fortnight. They had been living in terror because of the 'strange and unusual' noises coming from their parlour late at night.

On the night of Friday, 26 November, the noises were louder than usual, and Christopher's son John jumped out of his bed to investigate. He went down to the parlour and, peering through the keyhole, he saw a man in black 'of most demonical presence' eating a sandwich and enjoying himself on his father's brandy.

John burst in through the door and discovered to his amazement that the demon was in fact a local chimney sweep. He had apparently concealed himself in the chimney until the family had gone to bed and emerged when they were asleep. He was handed over to the police, who found a sword and three silver teaspoons belonging to Mr Christopher on him.

2 December

Stabbed a horse with a fork

William Kavanagh, a Dublin dray-driver, was convicted in the Dublin courts on 2 December 1894 of brutally and maliciously stabbing a horse with a hay fork.

Kavanagh, who worked for coal merchants Heitons in Dublin, was accused of assaulting the horse on 17

November of that year. Inspector Morrisey of the Dublin Metropolitan Police told the court that he had inspected the horse and had found forty-one stab wounds on the animal's body.

Kavanagh claimed that the horse had been injured in two falls that day, and he also said that the animal had a habit of falling down. In addition, he explained that the horse had fallen while under the care of another driver and that the horse had gotten him sacked.

Kavanagh was found guilty as charged and sentenced to three months' imprisonment with hard labour.

3 December

'Seems to be a lunatic'

Dublin Courant, 3 December 1749, extract from a private letter from a writer in Youghal, County Cork:

'Last Wednesday a most cruel murder was committed at Snugborough, in the County of Waterford, near the Ferry Point of this place, on a poor woman and her son, by one Garret Mernyn of Ardmore, who seems to be a lunatic …'.

Mernyn lured the woman and her son away from the house and cut both of their throats. The woman's body was found in the garden the next morning and her son was found dead in a ditch about half a mile away. The story didn't end there. The two bodies were left unguarded overnight and, according to the letter, Mernyn returned to cut off 'their heads and their limbs, beginning at the ankles, and proceeding by every joint to their hips, which he likewise very dexterously dissected. He also cut out the woman's eyes and heart, and laid open both their faces to the skulls …'.

Mernyn was arrested later at a house in Piltown, County Kilkenny, where it was feared he was about to commit a similar crime.

4 December

Jailed for stealing a prayer book

There was no Christmas cheer in evidence at the Northern Division Court in Dublin on 4 December 1871, where a young Dublin girl, Maryanne Larkin, was sentenced to three weeks' imprisonment and five years in a reformatory for stealing a prayer book.

5 December

Sinkhole in Dundrum

There was a curious incident reported in the *Irish Times* on 5 December 1823 concerning a sinkhole in Dundrum, County Dublin. It was reported that Mr Dugan's servant, Francis Dempsey, was attending to a horse and cart in Dugan's backyard when Dempsey, along with the horse and cart, disappeared into the bowels of the earth. The ground had given way beneath them to reveal an old well that was forty feet deep.

Police and neighbours managed to rescue Dempsey, who escaped the incident without a scratch. A man named Joe Duffy climbed down the well and tied a rope around the horse so he too could be hauled back to the surface.

6 December

'His better half, Bridget'

Eighty-year-old John Hetherton of Cakestown, County Meath described in the *Meath Herald* as 'a decrepid old man', gave evidence at Kells Court of Petty Sessions on 6 December 1858 that his − 45-year-old wife Bridget, described as 'his better half', 'had hit him with a shovel, threatened to kill him with a hatchet and then burn his body'.

The case was adjourned until 20 December and when it resumed, Hetherton told the court that on 23 November, Bridget, who was always threatening to 'do him in', had beaten him with a shovel while he was in bed, severely injuring him. He also said that she was going to cut him into little pieces and 'burn his bonce', so that no one would know what had happened to him.

In her defence, Bridget told the court that she had accidentally dropped the shovel on her husband's leg because she was feeling ill, but she didn't explain why she felt the need to have a shovel in the bedroom in the first place!

Bridget was found guilty of assaulting her husband and was bound over to keep the peace for six months.

7 December

Devastating floods in Dublin

In December 1954 some of the worst flooding ever seen in Ireland devastated many parts of Dublin. The north inner city was particularly badly affected. The days of 7 and 8 December 1954 were described in the *Irish Press* as 'the worst day following the worst night in memory'.

On the night of 7 December Ireland was battered by gale-force winds, blizzards, heavy rain and sleet, which brought much of the country to a standstill. Dublin's road and rail network ground to a complete halt and air traffic at Dublin Airport was grounded by 60 mph winds.

The North Strand was particularly badly affected, and the *Dublin Evening Mail* described it as being 'more like Venice than Dublin'. The Strand Cinema was flooded out while Cusack's Bar nearby was under six feet of water.

The most serious incident in the area occurred at East Wall Road where the metal railway bridge collapsed and fell into the Tolka River. Army engineers dynamited the mouth of the river in a bid to clear it of debris from the fallen bridge.

Hundreds of evacuees were given temporary accommodation in a shelter run by St John's Ambulance at North Strand. Others rendered homeless by the floods were given food and shelter at the Sisters of Charity convent in North William Street.

Lord Mayor of Dublin Alfie Byrne initiated a flood relief fund for the victims of the disaster, and Brendan Behan urged his fellow countrymen to give generously to the fund in an amusing article written in the *Irish Press* on 13 December under the heading: 'The Northside can take it but now it has need of all it can get.'

Behan urged his country cousins to forget any 'little jackeen sneers' that they may have associated with the north inner city and to put their hands in their pockets for the victims of the flood. Behan was also fulsome in his praise for the actions of the emergency services and – unusually for him – he even had a good word for the police, warning any of his readers that might have a weak heart that he, 'Brendan Behan, aged thirty-one, described as a journalist, is about to talk well about the Garda Síochána.'

8 December

Melancholy news

There wasn't too much news of a positive nature in the *Cork Evening Post* on 8 December 1757. First, there was tragic news concerning the schooner *Betsy* that had left Cork the previous Saturday. Twenty people on board perished when the ship struck Miner's Head off Dungarvan in County Waterford.

There was further bad news from Dublin, where a man and a small boy were killed in a stampede at St Mary's Church. The church was packed to the rafters and the stampede occurred when the congregation became alarmed by some shouting at the back of the church. Many others were seriously injured.

9 December

The pernicious effects of dissipation

In the puritanical Belfast of the nineteenth century, imbibing alcohol on the Sabbath day was a serious misdemeanour in the eyes of the law. To that end, the Town Clerk and Sergeants of Belfast set to check on some of the city's publicans on Sunday, 9 December 1814.

They found that many of the pubs they visited were in breach of the strict licensing laws and some were reported in the *Belfast Newsletter* as being 'so disorderly as to incur the penalty prescribed by law'. The writer went on to moralise about the evils of drink, saying that there was no worse vice 'than that of spending the Sabbath day in dissipation'. He went on to give the example of a young man named Underwood who had been hanged for a murder near Randalstown. The 'unfortunate youth,' said the writer, 'declared, with his last breath, that cock-fighting and the misspending of the Sabbath day, were the means of bringing him to an untimely end.'

10 December

Dundalk flogging

An editorial written in the *Dundalk Express* on Saturday, 10 December 1864 expressed outrage at the flogging of a soldier at Dundalk Barracks earlier that week. The soldier, Private Mervin of the 4th Hussars, was given a prison sentence and fifty lashes for assaulting his sergeant major. The writer argued that the two-year sentence and dismissal from the army would have been enough punishment for Private Mervin without what he called 'the barbarous system of corporal punishment by flogging'.

'This brutal flogging system is an outrage on humanity,' he said. 'Especially when it is suffered for a hasty blow, given by one soldier to another, and we trust the day is at hand when the British soldier, no matter how irregular he may be, will be safe from this greatest of degradations, and no man should enlist so long as it is a part of the army regulations.'

11 December

With pistol and with sword

Two soldiers fought a duel near Thurles in County Tipperary on 11 December 1773. The men, named Creagh and McCormack, who were privates with the 2nd Horse Regiment, unloaded a case of pistols at each other before going at each other with broad swords for forty minutes. The duel ended when Creagh, who was exhausted from loss of blood, surrendered. He had been cut twelve times, while McCormack had eight wounds.

The dispute between the men was reported to have been as a result of Creagh bringing a Methodist piper into McCormack's room. However, it's not clear as to why this would have become an issue between them.

12 December

Chimney cleaning

Dublin woman Anne McCormick came up with a novel solution to fix her neighbour's smoky chimney at Great Brunswick Street. According to a report in the *Freeman's Journal* on 12 December 1839, McCormick, who worked in the house next door as a servant, climbed onto the roof with a companion and emptied two large buckets of water down the smoky chimney, which had been annoying local residents for some time.

Unfortunately for them, the doctor who lived in the house was warming himself at the fireside when the water descended into his living room 'to the great astonishment and annoyance of the gentleman'.

McCormick was arrested and appeared before the City Magistrate's Court in College Street. The magistrate told her that her actions were unjustifiable and ordered for her to be held in prison until someone could come up with enough bail to ensure that she would behave herself in the future.

13 December

Carlow Escape

Three prisoners made a daring escape from Carlow Jail on the night of 13 December 1790. They first poisoned a vicious dog who was allowed to roam the prison to intimidate the inmates. Then the trio made good their escape using skeleton keys and a rope ladder to scale the walls. The prisoners were Michael Moore, who was under sentence of death for sheep stealing, Mary Kinsella, on remand for robbing a comedian, and Margaret Murray, who had been accused of poisoning her husband.

14 December

Stormy night in Dublin

At least two people were killed during a violent storm in Dublin on the night of 14 December 1790. An old house in Tucker's Row was blown down by the wind, killing a poor woman who lived there. Another house was blown down in Smithfield, while a wall fell down at Drumcondra, killing a woman who was passing by. The wind was strong enough to dislodge slates from the roofs of many houses, and a woman walking through Stoneybatter had her skull fractured by a falling slate.

15 December

A sight for sore eyes

Who wouldn't want to use a product that could cure the eyes after smallpox, give healing after late-night drinking or allow the user to dispense with glasses?

The following medical advertisement appeared in *Pue's Occurrences* on 15 December 1739:

'Just arrived from London. A large quantity of the famed Royal Eye-Water, which is sold nowhere in the City of Dublin but at Dick's Coffee-House in Skinner-Row, at a British six pence per bottle, with directions how to use the same; at which place it has been sold these 26 years past, with great success, and nowhere else in the said city; greatly esteemed by all that have used it, having cured many thousands of persons, both old and young in this kingdom, & never was known to fail in curing any red, swelled or sore eyes; it strengthens weak or watery eyes, adds vigour and briskness to the sight, takes away the scum and bloodshed from the eyes, keeping them in constant good temper. The said water is known to be infallible in curing and strengthening the eyes after the smallpox, sitting up late hard drinking, or a cold in the head; it cools and gives ease to the eyes in 2 or 3 minutes after using. Several persons, by using a bottle or two of the said water, have found such benefit thereby that they have thrown away their spectacles.'

16 December

The local county jail

Seven prisoners escaped from Waterford County Jail on the evening of 16 December 1809. They made their getaway by removing the bars from their lower cell window and climbing the outer walls of the prison using a rope ladder that had been thrown over by accomplices who were waiting outside on Thomas Hill in Waterford. Another prisoner, who had just been on the verge of escaping, was apprehended by the jail keeper when the ladder broke under his weight.

Five of the escapees had been transferred from Waterford City Jail to the County Jail a few weeks earlier because the authorities were afraid that they would escape from there. Some of them had made several attempts to escape. The other three were already incarcerated in the County Jail.

17 December

Rotten eggs and snowballs

A man described as 'the notorious Edgworth' was pilloried at the Tholsel in Dublin on 17 December 1788. Robert Edgworth was found guilty on 11 December of inducing a woman named Ann Molineux to give false evidence in a case against three other people. He was sentenced to a year in prison and to stand in the pillory for one hour in December and another hour in July of the following year.

On the morning of his first stint in the pillory, at the junction of Nicholas Street and High Street in Dublin, Edgworth was escorted to his punishment by a party of musketeers. A huge crowd looked on as Edgworth – who seemed to be unaffected by the whole event – was tied to the pillory. A poster highlighting his crime was hung from his neck with the words 'Subornation of Perjury' written on it. The baying crowd threw snowballs and rotten eggs at him. After an hour, Edgworth was untied and taken off to Newgate Prison to begin his jail sentence.

18 December

Oldest Dub?

Could this possibly have been our oldest living Dubliner? It doesn't seem feasible but it was recorded in the *Treble Almanack* that a man named Collins, who lived in the Liberties area of Dublin, died on 18 December 1749 at the ripe old age of 137 years.

19 December

Tipperary drunk tank

The revelation that more than half the prisoners in a Tipperary Bridewell in 1860 were there for drunkenness is surprising, even to the journalists of the era. The following report appeared in the *King's County Chronicle*, 19 December 1860:

'Thursday last the Rev. James Morton, Little Island, Local Inspector of the gaol and bridewells of the South Riding of the county of Tipperary, visited the Tipperary bridewell, and made the report which was submitted to the magistrates presiding at petty sessions on that day: *The neat and orderly appearance of this important bridewell is very creditable to the keeper. Two males in custody, and 182 prisoners in the quarter, of whom 101 were drunkards. signed J. Morton.* This is a terribly large proportion of this class of offenders, and when we remember that the quarter specified will not terminate until the 31st instant, that the crime of drunkenness generally increases as Christmas approaches, and that a number of cases are disposed of summarily – the fines being paid, no committal taking place – we are pained to think that the large number of 101 will fail to represent the real number of inebriety in Tipperary. It is, however, but justice to that town to observe, that a large quota of the arrests have been of persons belonging to Limerick and elsewhere, who come into Tipperary to transact business.'

20 December

Anyone own this head?

This item in the *Freeman's Journal* of 20 December 1768 wins my vote for the most bizarre lost-and-found column ever. About three weeks earlier some fishermen were out on the river at Arklow in County Wicklow and they found a man's head near the bridge there. The head, with curly black hair and a neat beard, appeared to have been that of a young man and had not been in the water for very long. The fishermen couldn't establish his identity so they came up with the bright idea of sticking the head on a pole and leaving it on the beach at Arklow for a few days to see if anyone knew who he was. When that didn't work, the fishermen advertised the find in the local and national newspapers. It is not known if the man was ever identified.

21 December

Wexford Floods

December 1771 was a cold month in Ireland. The River Slaney in Wexford was swollen by melting snow and on 21 December it was reported that a severe east wind blew directly into the mouth of Wexford Harbour, causing 'the most extraordinary inundation known in the memory of man'.

The *Hibernian Journal's* Carlow correspondent related that 'The water rose in many places ten feet above what was ever known by the oldest man living here. People, coaches, carts and animals were swept away by the floods and many were forced to take refuge on the roofs of their houses. Several dead bodies were washed up on the shore.'

22 December

'Armed mummers'

According to the *Freeman's Journal* on 22 December 1759, the Lord Mayor of Dublin issued a proclamation to the police, ordering them to crack down on cockfighting, gambling and other unlawful pursuits over the period of the 'Christmas Holydays'.

He also commanded the police to pay particular attention to what he called 'a set of idle and vagrant persons, styling themselves Mummers, who at this season of the year stroll through different parts of the city armed, to the great disturbance and terror of the inhabitants, and to bring them before his Lordship that they may be dealt with according to law'.

23 December

Mountrath abduction

The *Freeman's Journal* of 23 December 1767 reported the death of 'one Patrick Keenan, a noted Hurler', who died during an abduction in Mountrath in Queen's County (now Laois). Keenan was shot dead while he and his companion were in the act of kidnapping a young girl from a house in Raheen.

24 December

Christmas eviction

A resident magistrate, backed up by forty policemen, descended on Curlough in County Cavan on a cold, wet and miserable Christmas Eve in 1886 to evict three families from the estate of David Finlay J.P. The families had been evicted nine months earlier and were living on the estate as caretakers. The evictions were carried out under the watchful eye of Finlay himself, who had turned up to witness the event in person. One of the tenants, a widow named Dolan, paid two years' rent to Finlay and was allowed to stay, and another promised to pay on the following Monday. A man named Hugh Prior and his family of six were evicted. The police sergeant started a whip round for the evicted man and raised two pounds on his behalf.

25 December

Christmas Day disaster

In an ideal world, Christmas Day would be a day of joy, peace, happiness and goodwill to all, but there was no joy in evidence at St Nicholas's Church in Galway city on Christmas Day 1842.

The day began well enough as people gathered in the dark for the early morning Christmas mass at 6.00 a.m. Father Roche, the parish priest of St Nicholas's, had just started to say the opening prayers when someone shouted that the upstairs gallery of the church was collapsing. It wasn't, but terror-stricken mass goers thought it was, and fell over each other as they scrambled to flee from the church. Others jumped from the upstairs windows in an effort to escape the carnage.

When order was eventually restored, it emerged that thirty-seven men, women and children had died in the tragedy and many more were injured. The majority of those who died were crushed in their efforts to escape from the church.

26 December

'Hacked to death with a sword'

On St Stephen's Day 1787 a large group of Dublin butchers travelled out to Finglas in County Dublin to go bull-baiting with their dogs. Unable to find a bull, the butchers spent the day drinking instead.

While returning to the city later in the day, they became violent and attacked some local people at Finglas Bridge. During the riot that followed, two people were killed and many others badly injured. The butchers attacked the home of James McLane and, during the ensuing struggle, McLane was stabbed with a bayonet by a butcher named David Bobbit.

Bobbit himself was killed during the altercation by a man wielding a slash hook. The butchers were chased out of the house, and a violent melee broke out on the bridge during which a man by the name of Tom Legget was hacked to death with a sword.

27 December

Poacher turned gamekeeper

The Maynooth-born thief George Barrington – 'the prince of pickpockets' – was one of the most notorious thieves of eighteenth century Dublin and London. Barrington was born George Waldron in Maynooth, County Kildare in 1755, the son of a local silversmith. He was educated in Dublin, but his schooling was cut short when he stabbed one of his classmates with a penknife. Barrington fled Dublin and joined a travelling theatre company owned by a convicted London fraudster, John Price.

When the theatre company folded, Barrington ditched his acting career to become a gentleman thief in London. He initially preyed on members of London's high society. No pocket was safe from 'the prince'. He was once said to have gatecrashed a royal birthday party dressed as a parson, where he managed to pick several pockets without being detected.

Following several stints in prison, Barrington decided that London was getting too hot for him and resolved to try his hand back at home. The *Freeman's Journal* announced Barrington's return to Dublin in February of 1788 in much the same fashion as it would a visit from a famous actor or other performer:

'By various accounts, the noted and famous Barrington is lately arrived in this city: doubtless he intends honouring some of our crowded churches, the law courts, Promenade, Theatre, and other public places, to keep in practice his unrivalled sleight of hand.'

Despite the widespread reporting of Barrington's alleged Dublin crimes, he was never actually caught in the act. However, during his extended crime spree in London he was arrested and imprisoned on at least seventeen separate occasions.

Barrington's life of crime finally came to an end when he was sentenced to seven years' transportation for stealing a gold watch at Enfield racecourse in England in 1790. He allegedly tried to escape from Newgate Prison dressed in his wife's clothes, but he was caught and sent to

Sydney, Australia on board the convict ship *Active* in 1791. On arrival at Botany Bay, he was rewarded for his good behaviour on the voyage with the post of Superintendent of Convicts at Parramatta in Sydney's western suburbs. In November 1792 he was given a pardon and, in a classic 'poacher to gamekeeper' scenario, he became chief constable of Parramatta in Sydney's western suburbs in 1796.

He thrived for a time in Sydney and owned a substantial farm on the Hawkesbury River. He resigned from his position of chief constable in 1800 due to mental illness, and he died on 27 December 1804.

28 December

Cork kidnap

Cork man Patrick Fitzgerald was arrested by the Reverend John Lawless and lodged in Cork County Jail on 28 December 1787. Fitzgerald was accused of breaking into the house of another Cork man, Michael Lander. Fitzgerald stripped him naked, tied him to a horse and placed furze bushes and blackthorn bushes between his thighs before 'obliging said Lander to take an unlawful oath'. The report in the *Hibernian Journal* doesn't explain what oath Mr Lander was forced to take, but it was, in all probability, linked to Whiteboy activity in the Cork area.

29 December

Killer Cravats

The *Irish Times* has been a familiar fixture of Irish life since it was first published in 1859, but there was a newspaper with the same title that made a brief appearance on Irish news stands between the years 1823 and 1824.

There wasn't an awful lot to distinguish the earlier *Irish Times* from other contemporary publications, but it was a great newspaper for the scare stories. On 29 December 1823, the *Irish Times* had a story about the dangers of wearing neckties or cravats under the heading: 'Tendency of cravats to promote apoplexy.' The writer claimed that wearers of cravats were dicing with death, especially while imbibing alcohol and wearing a tie at the same time. Urging his readers to dispense with the cravat altogether – 'like Lord Byron, Milton and Shakespeare' – he declared that cravat wearing led to apoplexy, high blood pressure, flushing, choking, headaches, fits, mental illness and early death.

There was an even better medical scare story a few weeks earlier, on 5 December, in an article entitled 'Nervous and other diseases caused by novel reading.' Claiming that tea, music and drugs were bad for the nerves, the writer singled out 'visiting the library' as the main cause of nervous disorders. Urging his readers to give up reading novels for 'sober history', the writer argued that reading 'interesting novels and fascinating tales' was liable to trigger 'a ghastly train of nervous diseases, accompanied with disorders of the liver and the stomach'.

30 December

No milk for the paupers

It was definitely a case of the Ebenezer Scrooges at the Christmas meeting of the Athlone Board of Guardians on 30 December 1850. It was discovered at the meeting that someone had given the paupers in the workhouse milk with their dinner on Christmas Day. Chairman Lord Castlemaine was not happy and he strongly criticised the decision to give them milk against the express wishes of the board.

At the same meeting Lord Castlemaine and the board made the seemingly bizarre decision that no tobacco was to be given to inmates unless it was ordered by the medical officer for medicinal purposes.

The board approved further cost-cutting measures by recommending that, in future, bread was to be baked using two-thirds oatmeal and one-third wheaten meal. There were 1,547 people in the workhouse at that time.

31 December

Ducking

Throughout the course of this book we've come across many types of punishment – both corporal and capital. From public hangings to flogging to pillorying, half-hanging, burning, imprisonment and transportation, we've seen it all. Or have we? It just wouldn't be right to finish off on a cheerful note, so let's end with another type of punishment dreamed up by our ingenious ancestors in their efforts to rid the streets of Dublin of crime.

The *Dublin Courant* of 31 December 1748 informs us that a woman, who was caught picking pockets at the chapel in Liffey Street, was carried to the river 'where for the seventh time she underwent the wholesome Discipline of Ducking'. The practice of ducking may seem a relatively benign one when compared with other punishments, but we have to remember that it was the end of December and the Liffey – which was an open sewer at the time – would also have been freezing cold at that time of the year.

Acknowledgments

Finding interesting stories for a history book is a fascinating, but solitary business. Weeks and months spent in the National Library of Ireland in Dublin's Kildare Street digging through old newspapers to unearth new insights, were illuminating and deeply fulfilling.

I am indebted to the staff there – too numerous to mention – for their help and unfailing courtesy. I would particularly like to give a shout out to two jewels, Gerard Kavanagh and Francis Carroll of the NLI for sustaining me with their wit and humour when the going got rough.

Thanks are due also to the staff of New Island for their support and encouragement and to Eoin Purcell in particular for the coffees, the insights and the banter.

On a personal level, I am very grateful to my family for putting up with me while I buried myself in research. Thanks to my wife Nóirín Hegarty for the editing, the moral support and keeping the show on the road. Thanks to my son Jack for sub-letting me his man-cave when I needed a quiet place to work. Thanks to my daughters Róisín and Ella for their no-nonsense constructive critiques.

Finally, I'd just like to say a special thank you to my good friends Larry Kelly, John Hedges and Bob White for the conversations, the craic and the pints that so often helped to maintain my sanity on this and many other journeys down through the years.

This book is dedicated to the memory of Sean MacConnell, my friend for twenty five years and the best man I ever knew.

Select Bibliography

Books

Abbott, Richard. *Police Casualties in Ireland, 1919-1922.*(Mercier Press, Cork, 2000)

Barrington, J., *Personal Sketches of his Own Times* (London, 1830-2)

Dean, Joan Fitzpatrick. *Riot and Great Anger: Stage Censorship in Twentieth-century Ireland.* (University of Wisconsin Press, Madison, 2004)

Dixon, D., *Arctic Ireland - the extraordinary story of the Great Frost and forgotten famine of 1740-41* (White Row Press Ltd., Belfast, 1997)

Egan, Pierce, and George Cruikshank. *Boxiana, Or, Sketches of Antient and Modern Pugilism ... Dedicated to Captain Barclay.* (Printed for Sherwood, Neeley, and Jones, London, 1818-1824)

Fitzgibbons, J., *Cromwell's Head* (National Archive, Kew, 2008)

Holinshed, Raphael, Richard Stanyhurst, Liam Miller, and Eileen Power. *Holinshed's Irish Chronicle: The Historie of Irelande From the First Inhabitation Thereof, Unto the Yeare 1509.* (Atlantic Highlands, N.J. Humanities Press, 1979)

Hayes, Richard Francis., and Hilaire Belloc. *Ireland and Irishmen in the French Revolution.* (Phoenix Pub. Co., Dublin, 1932)

Henry, B., *Dublin Hanged - Crime, law enforcement and punishment in late eighteenth-century Dublin* (Irish Academic Press, Dublin, 1994)

Hopkins, Frank. *Hidden Dublin: Deadbeats, Dossers and Decent Skins.* (Mercier Press, Cork, 2007)

Hopkins, Frank. *Rare Old Dublin: Heroes, Hawkers & Hoors.* (Marino Press, Dublin, 2002)

Igoe, V., *Dublin Burial Grounds and Graveyards* (Wolfhound Press, Dublin, 2001)

Joyce, Weston St. John, *The Neighbourhood of Dublin* (Dublin, 1921)

Kelly, F., *A History of Kilmainham Gaol* (Mercier Press, Cork, 1988)

Kelly, J., *Gallows Speeches from Eighteenth-Century Ireland* (Four Courts Press, Dublin, 2001)

Knapp and Baldwin, (eds.), *Newgate Calendar* (3 vols., London, 1824)

Lambert, R.S., *The Prince of Pickpockets: A Study of George Barrington Who Left His Country for His Country's Good* (Faber & Faber, London, 1930)

MacDonagh, Michael. *Irish Graves in England: A Series of Articles.* (Dublin: Evening Telegraph Office, 1888)

MacThomais, Shane. *Dead Interesting: Stories from the Graveyards of Dublin* (Mercier Press, Cork, 2012)

Pollock, Sam. *Mutiny for the Cause: The Story of the Revolt of Ireland's "Devil's Own" [the Connaught Rangers] in British India.* London: Leo Cooper Ltd, 1969)

Porter, F.T., *Twenty years' recollections of an Irish police magistrate* (Hodges, Foster and Figgis, Dublin, 1880)

Reece, Bob. *The Origins of Irish Convict Transportation to New South Wales: Mixture of Breeds.* (Macmillan, Basingstoke, 2000)

Sheridan, Philip Henry. *Personal Memoirs of P.H. Sheridan, General, U.S. Army: In Two Volumes.* (Chatto & Windus, London, 1888)

Tuckey, Francis H., and Jaspar Robert Joly. *The County and City of Cork Remembranced: Or, Annals of the County and City of Cork.* (O. Savage and son, Cork, 1837)

Zimmermann, G. D. *Songs of Irish rebellion: Political street ballads and rebel songs, 1780-1900.* (Four Court Press, Dublin, 2002)

Newspapers

Arklow Reporter
Armagh Guardian
Athlone Independent
Athlone Sentinel
Ballina Chronicle
Ballyshannon Herald
Belfast Morning News
Belfast Newsletter
Belfast Telegraph
Bray Herald
Carlow Post
Cavan Observer
Christian Herald
Chute's Western Herald
Clare Journal
Clare Weekly News
Comet
Connaught Telegraph
Connaught Watchman
Cork Advertiser
Cork Evening Post
Corke Evening Post

Cork Examiner
Cork Journal
Cork Observer
Daily Express
Derry Journal
Drogheda Conservative Journal
Drogheda Journal
Dublin Chronicle
Dublin Courant
Dublin Evening Herald
Dublin Evening Mail
Dublin Evening Post
Dublin Intelligence
Dublin Journal
Dublin Weekly Journal
Dublin Newsletter
Dublin Sunday Observer
Dundalk Express
Enniskillen Chronicle
Evening Freeman
Evening Herald
Evening Telegraph
Faulkner's Dublin Journal
Fermanagh Reporter
Fermanagh Times
Finn's Leinster Journal
Freeman's Journal
Galway Express
Galway Vindicator
General News-letter
Hibernian Chronicle
Hibernian Journal
Hue and Cry
Irish Ecclesiastical Record

Irish Farmers' Journal
Irish Independent
Irish News
Irish Press
Irish Times (1823-25)
Irish Times (1859-)
Kerry Sentinel
Kilkenny Journal
King's County Chronicle
Leinster Journal
Leitrim Gazette
Limerick and Clare Examiner
Limerick Echo
Limerick Journal
London Observer
Longford Journal
Mayo Examiner
Meath Herald
Munster Journal
Munster News
Nation
Newry Examiner
Newry Express
Northern Whig
Penny Despatch
People
Pue's Occurrences
The Register, Adelaide, South Australia
Roscommon and Leitrim Gazette
Saunders' Newsletter
Sligo Independent
Southern Reporter
Telegraph
Times (London)

Time Magazine
Tyrawly Herald
Walker's Hibernian Magazine
The Warder
Waterford News
Wexford Herald
Wicklow Newsletter

Public Records

Ireland. Court of Justiciar., and Ireland. Public Record Office. *Calendar of the Justiciary Rolls, Or, Proceedings in the Court of the Justiciar of Ireland (1295-1314)*. Dublin: Printed for H. M. Stationery Office, 1952

Great Britain. Public Record Office., and Jaspar Robert Joly. *Calendar of State Papers Relating to Ireland ... A. D. 1509-*. London: H. M. Stationery Office, 1860